Who Can Speak?

Who Can Speak?

Authority and Critical Identity

Edited by
Judith Roof and Robyn Wiegman

University of Illinois Press   *Urbana and Chicago*

© 1995 by the Board of Trustees of the University of Illinois
Manufactured in the United States of America
1 2 3 4 5 C P 5 4 3 2 1

This book is printed on acid-free paper.

Library of Congress Cataloging-in-Publication Data

Who can speak? : authority and critical identity / edited by Judith
   Roof and Robyn Wiegman.
       p.   cm.
     Includes bibliographical references and index.
     ISBN 0-252-02191-6 (acid-free paper). — ISBN 0-252-06487-9 (pbk. :
   acid-free paper)
     1. Authority. 2. Discrimination. 3. Identity (Psychology).
   4. Communication. I. Roof, Judith, 1951–   . II. Wiegman, Robyn.
   HM271.W48   1995
   303.3'6—dc20   95-4115
                                                                      CIP

Contents

Acknowledgments

We would like to thank the contributors to this volume, who graciously participated in the numerous readings and revisions required for the collection's conversations, and Ann Lowry, who patiently supported the project from its inception. In addition, we thank Frank Smigiel and Eric John Martin for their editorial assistance and A. and E. for more than sound.

Introduction:
Negotiating the Question

Conversation begins in response, not in a speaker's singular assertion. But professionalism has its demands and we are bound to its disciplinary performance. Or are we? What determines the form of academic speech? What defines speech as "academic"? And how have we
sought legitimation through form, through the particularities that define and circumscribe academic speech? These questions are both pre-
amble and postscript to this volume's various discussions.

Contemporary conversations about knowledge and the institution
often focus on the way that academic discourse legitimates itself by disavowing the historical, cultural, and corporeal specificities of its speaking. By exposing the way that objective and neutral methodologies repress the precise locations from which the speaker comes, academic
discourses have begun to interrogate themselves from within, calling
scholars to account, so to speak, for their own inescapable epistemic
contingencies. It is no accident, in the United States at least, that these
challenges to the unquestioned authority of academic discourses are
tied to broadly based and often highly organized civil rights and feminist political struggles outside of the academy. These movements have
been powerful vehicles for contesting not only the inequalities of social
power arrangements but also the implicit authority and privilege that
have historically accrued to certain social subjects.

This anthology contributes in a variety of ways to the conversation
concerning the authorization of academic speech. Rather than re-
hearsing the history of the institutional emergence of these issues, we
pay particular attention to their contemporary consequences. For the
project of making the subjectivities of the "margins" visible as repre-
sentational and/or political presences has proven to be not only difficult but at times politically suspect. Too often, the minoritized subject

who has sought to speak from the specificity of its cultural position has been recontained through a new, deafening "authenticity," one that disturbingly reduces the complexity of social subjectivity. While such authenticity and its concomitant authority can carry high rewards for the chosen few, speech authorized by the mere fact of cultural specificity is rarely about equality or the massive reorganization of social power. For example, we only need to think of Clarence Thomas. Indeed, speech founded on its representativity as "minority speech" is more often an authorized guarantee for continued, albeit newly visible, social subordination.

The complexities around issues of visibility, marginality, and authorized speech underlie current reassessments of identity-based politics in as well as out of the academy. These debates have been especially charged because of the simultaneous success and failure of twentieth-century social struggles. Although we have witnessed a number of rather remarkable social transformations—the dissolution of institutional segregation, for instance—the cultural hegemony of white masculinity certainly has not ceased. In fact, it has become far more nuanced in its languages and practices of legitimation, thereby stalling in a variety of ways the discourses of protest that have in the past three decades so decisively threatened it. That a representative visibility of the marginalized is now a precondition to the continued hegemony of those both white and male is itself one of the more pressing political realities of the late twentieth century. While some may find this a situation simply to be lamented, political struggle is never a transhistorical practice whose total success can be wagered from the outset. For this reason, we understand, as others have sought to impress, that conversations about the contours of contemporary politics constitute cultural struggle itself.

Essays in this collection contribute to this conversation from a variety of perspectives, moving across critical discourses we might identify as feminist, postcolonial, queer, ethnic, and racial. Feminism most often links these essays, thereby establishing an overarching formulation of issues of identity and critical authority that have emerged from the political practices and institutional questions raised within contemporary feminist thought. After all, it has been feminists who have forged, often with a great deal of hesitation, challenges to the white, middle-class, heterosexual ethos of authority that governs institutional speech. In paying attention to the conjunction of multiple kinds of differences on the construction of the social subject, feminism has become centrally concerned with what qualifies a critic to speak from and about a particular position. By interrogating the categories, critical analogies, and paradigms by which differences are comprehended, these essays focus in particular on the relations of race, gender, class, sexual "orientation," nationality, ethnicity, and academic positioning that both enable and complicate our critical analyses.

At the same time, we transform the format through which these issues have traditionally been investigated by eschewing the discrete serialization typical of academic anthologies in favor of an analytical, dialogical, and heterogeneous form. Using a combination of essays, responses, and editorial interventions, this anthology juxtaposes multiple positions in order to define the problems and capture the contradictions and tensions inherent in the urgent and unsettling question: Who can speak?

Part One

Manners of Speaking

1

Identification and Difference: Structures of Privilege in Cultural Criticism

I attended recently a meeting of a postcolonial reading group, and that evening the reading was comprised of Gayatri Chakravorty Spivak's "Can the Subaltern Speak?" and Gilles Deleuze and Felix Guattari's *Franz Kafka: Towards a Minor Literature*. It became clear in the discussion that Kafka was not wanted for a feminist critique of literature and culture, despite his minor status for Deleuze and Guattari, because his work is major literature for the academy. How many times is *The Metamorphosis* read in college classes (forget the structures of critique of bourgeois culture that Kafka undertakes)? And why is he read? Because the academy finds value in him. In other words, Kafka's position within the literary academy means that he is already and always preceded by the Kafkaesque; his works are advertisements for his canonical image. On a recent trip to Prague I visited Kafka's grave. It has a beefy hunk of clean white marble at its head, a plot of clean white gravel covered with fleshy flowers. The Kafka "garret" is newly painted in the Hradcany district just behind St. Vitus cathedral, one of the quaint stops on the tourist's itinerary.

I want to connect this double bind—a writer who is marginalized in his culture and writes a powerful critique of that culture but who later becomes championed as a major cultural voice by the academy—to the question of my own authority to speak. In the following discussion I address this question in specific ways: Hannah Arendt speaking for African Americans in the controversial exchange over the events in Little Rock, Arkansas, in 1957; James Agee and Walker Evans speaking of the poor white southern sharecroppers in the 1930s; and Zora Neale Hurston ventriloquating the voices of African

American folk. None of these speaking situations are simple; all of them, in some way, make risky incursions on the uncommon grounds of groups that have not been accorded the authority to speak for themselves and on whose behalf these writers have chosen to speak. Yet all of these instances speak to my own authority to speak—as a teacher, a conference participant, a writer of criticism.

I write under the imperative of thinking about this complex and unresolved situation. On the one hand, I entered this profession—academic literary studies—precisely because I found most interesting the literature that questioned both the cultural and political authority of American life. On the other hand, I have undergone a process of testing and evaluation (school) that has made me an authority of my culture. I write this essay with an intent to think through how attention in the academy to minor literatures and cultures—to postcolonial texts, African American texts, literature by lesbians and homosexuals, by Asian and Latino Americans, American Indian texts, and, in short, the broadly alternative literary traditions—increasingly transforms a minority report on major American culture into the canonical. Moreover, I want to think about my own subject position in these debates; as a white, male, heterosexual Jewish academic who has worked in nearly all-white public institutions of higher learning, I am without question a part of the dominant culture.

So, who has the authority to speak? How far does that authority extend—to what classes of addressees? What does it mean to speak from authority? To be authorized sufficiently that we might pass unmolested through the significant passageways of our culture, to come, as Kafka himself has written, before the law, to speak from within the institutional forms of ventriloquism, citing the authorities—the precedential law—on a particular subject: What is it that gives passage to authority? To put the question most baldly, is it good to have authority? If we no longer chant, Down with authority, perhaps that is only because we have discovered that negotiating the question of authority is unavoidable, that we are necessarily implicated in multiple articulations of authority.

I speak finally from within the question of authority in another sense: I am not an authority on the issue of my own authority. Hence the question for this essay must be: How will my own authority[1] shape itself in the process of coming to terms with other articulations of the question? Part of what I want to acknowledge is the central recognition of my own role as a critic in the construction of reality. Raised in California's public school system from age five to age twenty-nine by white teachers (with one exception as an undergraduate), by mostly male teachers (here the exceptions are more numerous, particularly in my earliest education and in my most recent), and becoming a teacher at a public institution in the Midwest (which has a decided homogeneity in both the student body and the faculty—I mean mostly white, mostly upper-middle class), it is not particularly a stretch to say that I have routinely existed within the dominant power structure in the United States. Given these affiliations and experiences, I have to face the reality that I am, despite the small difference of being Jewish,[2] a part of the ruling establishment—or could be if I chose to. Or let this formula be more precise: I am a part of the dominant order, the elite (I have no choice but to be that); I can choose to accept or reject my part in the dominant order. This is not, therefore, a question of either/or: I am the product of my experiences and affiliations, my knowledge and my identifications, *and* I am capable of accepting and rejecting all or part of that.[3] The "and" here may seem infelicitous to neat formula making, in part because it announces that we are and I am in the vicinity of contradiction, and I think that is right: part of the difficulty of articulating my own stake in these questions of authority is that I must fail to create as reality something that emerges as a desire.

Finally, in my essay I want to look at what is perhaps the most significant historical context for this question of authority, without which it surely would not be a question: in the modern period, traditional forms of authority suffered from a reorganization of social modes so that, in Michel Foucault's schema, as the monarchy and the church gave way to a variety of institutions—medicine, law, prisons, psychiatry, the modern army and police force, the university—authority (and power) became diffused and disseminated over a wide range of sites. Without buying into a certain Foucauldian paranoia about the reach of these institutions, I want to suggest that the writers considered here respond to this situation of modern authority by attempting both a resistance to and subversion of that authority. In each example, I believe I have discovered a writer who, like myself, is encountering a culture—and attempting to represent it—from the position of an authority that is radically different from that culture. That position might best be described as "literate," though that is not the whole of it.

I am looking at writers who are encountering and trying to represent social others, like James Agee who writes of the rural poor of the South. Insofar as he too is from the South, we might say that Agee comes out of the same social position as his subjects, but his class belies that regional identification, and he is at pains throughout his text to deal with that difference. Zora Neale Hurston, insofar as she is a southern African American, writes about people she might have known growing up, but she removes herself, crosses over into both literacy and the white world of the establishment academy. Going back to the folk in her narratives means revisiting a people she, in some intellectual and experiential way, left behind.

I begin with Hannah Arendt, a European Jewish intellectual who crosses many borders to assert her authority on the question of segregation in the United States. She speaks most dramatically to my situation: an individual who is sympathetic to the disadvantages of others but who is necessarily blinded in some fundamental way by her or his own authority to write through to the object. Is it possible to enter benignly into the law, to speak from within these very pages—as professor, academic, white male—to the situation of those in the realm of hard facts that these fictions and structures of thought seek to understand, represent, and perhaps ameliorate? The paradox seems to be that, while these texts in their own way seek imaginative routes to social change, the structures of authority through which they are channeled and distributed are the very structures against which such social change would have to compete. Such authority to speak itself, according to this hypothesis, would have to be dismantled for the social order to achieve the kind of equalitarian state Arendt, Agee, and Hurston imagine and seem to desire with some real intensity.

The Appearances That "Appear"

My reflections on authority stem in large measure from a desire to respond to Gayatri Chakravorty Spivak's analysis of the problem of speaking to the subaltern (or speaking to the issue of class consciousness) in literary criticism. Her first published version of "Can the Subaltern Speak?" stressed the necessity of foregrounding the critic's own positionality and interest in any investigation. A more recent version of this essay begins with skepticism toward that principle of self-critical reflection: "Although I will attempt to foreground the precariousness of my position throughout, I know such gestures can never suffice" ("Subaltern" 1988, 271).[4] In an interview with Harold Veeser, she elaborated on her relation to the subaltern:

> I don't think that I declare myself to be allied to the subaltern. The subaltern is all that is not elite, but the trouble with those kinds of names is that if you have any kind of political interest you name it in the hope that the name will disappear. That's what class consciousness is in the interest of: the class disappearing. What politi-

cally we want to see is that the name would not be possible. So what I'm interested in is seeing ourselves as namers of the subaltern. If the subaltern can speak then, thank God, the subaltern is not a subaltern any more. (Veeser 158)

Spivak is trying to negotiate the very complicated positionality of the postcolonial critic who, on the one hand, declares herself to be on the side of social justice—the hope that a name, and the thing it names, will disappear—but who, on the other hand, speaks from a position of the elite, the class against which the subaltern is defined. We cannot have it both ways, Spivak seems to recognize; to declare allegiance to a class that is not one's own involves a large degree of bad faith. At the same time, it should be clear from Spivak's comments that without a kind of faith in naming as almost magical—certainly powerful— such hope must have a status not too far from the declaration of alliance that Spivak puts aside as naive and false, dangerously utopian.

I am interested in the moment when the elite recognizes its own positionality vis-à-vis the oppressed, as well as what that recognition accomplishes, what sorts of strategies it calls forth. Hannah Arendt's "Reflections on Little Rock" presents a series of speculations that seem to have been sparked by a photograph published in the newspapers a few years after the U.S. Supreme Court outlawed segregation in the nation's schools. The photograph shows an African American girl in Charlotte, North Carolina, being escorted by a white man to school, with a mob of angry, taunting white children in the background.[5]

Arendt's essay is controversial partly because she challenges conventional liberal ideology of the time by arguing for the relative insignificance of education as a priority when laws preventing basic civil rights remained on the books in many southern states. She singles out antimiscegenation laws as the most fundamental civil rights abuse, an argument that infuriated many white male intellectuals, including Sidney Hook, David Spitz, and Melvin Tumin, who held that African Americans were uninterested in these laws, a fact supported by the National Association for the Advancement of Colored People (NAACP), which did not have these laws high on their list of priorities for social change in the late 1950s.[6] Just as infuriating to some of the respondents was Arendt's self-confessed positionality in relation to "all oppressed or underprivileged peoples" (46). Werner Sollors registers this complex ambivalence in subject position that marks Arendt's address: on the one hand, she writes as an elite European (albeit exiled) and member of a privileged class, one who does not share the North American history of racial discrimination and thus is foreign to its character and etiology. On the other hand, she writes with what Ralph Ellison called an "Olympian authority," making a judgment about civil rights and the priorities for social change that seems to come down from on high.[7]

The passage that most infuriated commentators is Arendt's apparent dismissal out of hand of the voices of the oppressed. Arendt replies here, in her introduction, to Sidney Hook's claim that African Americans are uninterested in the antimiscegenation laws:

> I have my doubts about this, especially with respect to the educated strata in the Negro population, but it is of course perfectly true that Negro public opinion and the policies of the NAACP are almost exclusively concerned with discrimination in employment, housing and education. This is understandable; oppressed minorities were never the best judges on the order of priorities in such matters and there are many instances when they preferred to fight for social opportunity rather than for basic human or political rights. ("Reflections" 46)

This passage raises a fascinating question, particularly in relation to Spivak's analysis of the subaltern. If the very ontology of being subaltern is silence, illiteracy, lack of voice and agency, and thus lack of those elements of personhood that we take for granted as constituting the grounds for individual social and political rights, then Arendt, by naming the oppressed as silent, thereby silences the oppressed.[8] Her statement that oppressed minorities do not know what is best for them because they want "social opportunity" (which a poor person might understand as food and shelter) rather than "rights" (which that same person might not understand at all since it has no immediate referent) marks her as elite and qualifies what she says later in her introduction:

> I should like to remind the reader that I am writing as an outsider. I have never lived in the South and have even avoided occasional trips to Southern states because they would have brought me into a situation that I personally would find unbearable. Like most people of European origin I have difficulty in understanding, let alone sharing, the common prejudices of Americans in this area. Since what I wrote may shock good people and be misused by bad ones, I should like to make it clear that as a Jew I take my sympathy for the cause of the Negroes as for all oppressed or underprivileged peoples for granted and should appreciate it if the reader did likewise. ("Reflections" 46)

As Spivak has made the case in her work, it is precisely sympathy or empathy that cannot be taken for granted; the mere desire to be on the side of the underprivileged is not enough, never enough. For what

sympathy or empathy must always cover or neglect is the very relationship between the elite and the subaltern that constitutes the oppressive situation Arendt would like to address with her good will.

Placing Arendt and Spivak side by side details the problem. On the
one hand, Arendt writes that African Americans are not in a position to
judge what is best for themselves. This statement, along with Spivak's
announcement that the subaltern cannot speak, indicates that we cannot merely drop our common prejudices, take our sympathies for granted, and permit the underclass to speak; that they are an underclass is
precisely what constitutes their silence. It is a function of the elite—and
what makes them elite—to indicate and instantiate this silence. On the
other hand, Arendt identifies with these particular underprivileged people, for in her experience as a European Jew she understands especially well that the visible marks of racial difference function to permit a
society to discriminate against the others in its midst. The impasse or
difficulty that Arendt faces is that she both identifies with and distances
herself from the oppressed. As a Jew, she carries with her in her flesh
the marks of difference that during the war would have helped the
Germans to separate her out for killing, but as an intellectual she sees
herself as in a better position to judge what is best for society as a whole.
Arendt does not, of course, see this contradiction as a difficulty; indeed,
she does not see it as a contradiction.

In writing about the role that skin color plays in this situation of
discrimination, Arendt contrasts the experience of new immigrants,
who must drop the language of their home country to learn English,
with those for whom the mark of their difference is written on their
skin. She underscores the importance of this difference: "In the public
realm, where nothing counts that cannot make itself seen and heard,
visibility and audibility are of prime importance. To argue that they
are merely exterior appearances is to beg the question. For it is precisely appearances that 'appear' in public, and inner qualities, gifts of
heart or mind, are political only to the extent that their owner wishes
to expose them in public, to place them in the limelight of the market
place" (47). With the phrase "appearances that 'appear,'" Arendt is
suggesting that blackness is more important as a sign than as the determining mark of racial difference. Arendt thus indicates that blackness is only real as a sign of African Americans' underclass status, a
sign produced within that marketplace of signs called politics. This is
another way of remarking upon the constructedness or fictionality of
race as a sign sufficient to create a social hierarchy, but it is also a way
of confronting the space or location of where that creation takes place:
within ruling class ideology. That Arendt sees this issue of the origins

of discrimination as a matter of ruling class ideology has everything
to do with why she addresses antimiscegenation laws as key to social
change; as an elite, she would reform society from the top, making
broad constitutional changes that would reform society without having to do it on the backs of children.

Yet the issue of identification does not stop there. Arendt prefaced
her hotly debated (even before its publication) essay with her identification of herself as a European Jew and her declaration of sympathy
for African Americans; but in the body of her essay, written more than
a year before the preface, she articulates another identification that
complicates these initial (but later) gestures of empathy: what really
motivates her essay is sympathy for the young high school student
who must endure the harassment of the other children in their expression of hatred for her:

> The girl, obviously, was asked to be a hero—that is, something nei-
> ther her absent father nor the equally absent representatives of the
> NAACP felt called upon to be. It will be hard for the white young-
> sters, or at least those among them who outgrow their present bru-
> tality, to live down this photograph which exposes so mercilessly
> their juvenile delinquency. The picture looked to me like a fantastic
> caricature of progressive education which, by abolishing the author-
> ity of adults, implicitly denies their responsibility for the world into
> which they have borne their children and refuses the duty of guid-
> ing them into it. Have we now come to the point where it is the
> children who are being asked to change or improve the world? And
> do we intend to have our political battles fought out in the school
> yards? ("Reflections" 50)

Buried in this description of the famous photograph is a critique
Arendt developed in another essay of education in America, which
she found followed too insistently a Rousseauian ideal that refused to
take responsibility for educating the young ("Crisis in Education"). It
is necessary, as well, to point out that this child's parents—and uncles
and aunts and cousins and grandparents—did in fact make public their
opposition to white oppression, or would in the coming years of the
civil rights movement. Still, having said this, what I want to focus on
is the identification submerged here of Arendt as woman.

As Arendt became more and more embattled by critics of her position, she responded by a more and more specific reference to her own
subject position. In her description of the photograph, the point of
view from which she writes is almost indiscernible, and we can understand how it was possible for Ralph Ellison to say that she writes
from an "Olympian" position. In this passage, however, she writes

from the point of view of an adult chiding other adults for abdicating their responsibilities and authority over children. In other words, her point of view is Olympian vis-à-vis children because she understands that relationship to be based on a strict hierarchy of master and tutor. In the preface to the essay, however, she identifies herself more specifically as European and Jewish, an identification that is meant to establish her credentials and authority as someone sympathetic and connected to African Americans. Anyone familiar with Nazi propaganda from the 1930s would understand the implications of this identification; anti-Semites in the United States made and make frequent use of this connection in their propaganda. Finally, in her "Reply to Critics," as if introducing her trump card, she identifies herself explicitly as a mother and aligns herself with the black mothers of these children, an identification about which I will say more later. This ultimate identification is implicit from the outset, since the initial essay seems so powerfully motivated by the experience of seeing these African American children—both female—harassed by white students and barred from entering schools by white policemen.

In any event, in her description of the photograph she makes the implicit claim that as a woman she has an authority to reprimand the adults for failing in their responsibility to this child. This is perhaps her most powerful gesture in the essay, one that she does not own up to (to use her language of ownership) until her "Reply," but one that is congruent with her decision to address the antimiscegenation laws as a more important issue than discrimination in education. In the male literature from Frederick Douglass to Richard Wright, the important moment signifying freedom for the African American male comes when the individual acquires literacy. By contrast, Arendt seemingly stresses the importance of a legal and political structure that does not set up barriers for human relations; for Arendt, the most significant aspect of freedom is not the knowledge/power equation so bound up in education and equal opportunity in employment and housing but rather that laws not be made that determine in advance what sorts of associations we can have, what relationships might develop. Arendt's critique has authority, then, only if we grant the validity of her identification as a woman writing in sympathy and solidarity with African American female children, identifying with the needs and concerns of children.

Seyla Benhabib has written recently that for her the main problem in Arendt's form of critique is what she calls a "phenomenological essentialism" in which the public space is carefully delimited so that certain human activities such as work and education are relegated to the private sphere, leaving to public space such matters as civil rights. For Benhabib, Arendt's problem is that she views schooling as a more or less private matter of social preference rather than of public justice (73–98).[9] Given the European experience that Arendt knew well, it is understandable that she should want to keep these spheres separate.

Since I have invoked this sort of identification, I need at this point to return to Spivak, who calls for us to use extreme caution. It is not enough, she would say, merely to identify our positionality as a subject, though it is necessary to do that as a first step. By naming the specular moment, when Arendt looks at the photograph and produces a powerful "reading" of the social situation based upon emotional responses that come out of her experience as a woman—as constitutive of authority—we also have to recognize that it comes with its own limitations. For it is not enough to recognize here that Arendt's identifications are limited precisely by the very boundaries of experience that her imaginative bridging cannot overcome. We must go further. While appeal to our own subject position can generate rhetorical authority, it cannot in itself address another important issue: that the very structure of authority that allows us to identify and empathize inserts us back into the structure of inequality the identification would dismantle. In other words, because I am an elite I have the luxury of feeling empathy for the oppressed. The very authority I have permits such identification, which undoubtedly threatens and maintains that authority at the same time.

Ralph Ellison is the figure who most significantly indicates the problems with identification of this sort. In an interview by Robert Penn Warren, Ellison explains the importance for African American children of going to school with whites, even when those whites do not want them there:

> Hannah Arendt's failure to grasp the importance of this ideal [of sacrifice] among Southern Negroes caused her to fly way off into left field in her "Reflections on Little Rock," in which she charged Negro parents with exploiting their children during the struggle to integrate the schools. But she has absolutely no conception of what goes on in the minds of Negro parents when they send their kids through those lines of hostile people. Yet they are aware of the overtones of a rite of initiation which such events actually constitute for the child, a confrontation of the terrors of social life with all the mysteries stripped away. And in the outlook of many of these parents (who wish that the problem didn't exist), the child is expected to face the terror and contain his [sic] fear and anger *precisely* because he is a Negro American. Thus he's required to master the in-

ner tensions created by his racial situation, and if he gets hurt—then his is one more sacrifice. It is a harsh requirement, but if he fails this basic test, his life will be even harsher. (Warren 344)

What is interesting, here, is that Ellison speaks of a kind of identification, of a coming face to face with white racism and hostility, an identification of the self through this confrontation with the harassing other. In her "Reply," Arendt writes that her "first question was: what would I do if I were a Negro mother?" (179); in making this identification she was thinking from within the context of the persecution of Jews in Europe just a few years before: it was clear during the campaign against Jews in Germany and other countries that assimilation was a losing cause.

In both cases, the writers put themselves in the place of the other: Arendt identifies with the African American mother, Ellison identifies with the sacrificing black parents sending their "sheep" to be slaughtered or to survive. While Arendt eventually acquiesced to Ellison[10] and acknowledged that she had made a mistake, perhaps we can say that the mistake is compounded by another one: she foregoes her authority in relation to an individual who has a still greater claim to authority, since Ellison is an African American who has the primary experience to support his claim. Should Ellison have the last word on this controversy? In what sense, according to what scale of values, is Ellison's experience a better authority than Arendt's? Ellison refers to himself as an African American from the South; he knows how black parents feel about this issue because he's been there, yet why should that experience take precedence over Arendt's identification with the mothers? The history of virtually all cultures tells us why the masculine has taken precedence over the feminine, but this situation is still further complicated by another category: race. Does Ellison's identification with Abraham, the one who would sacrifice his child to appease his God, the Old Testament patriarch, come before Arendt's identification with the New Testament matriarch, Mary, who mourns her sacrificed child?

De-authorizing the Postmodern Subject

The previous section concludes with an unanswered question. In this section I address the same question in another site: James Agee and Walker Evans's remarkable text *Let Us Now Praise Famous Men*. In this book, Agee writes of and Evans photographs a visit to the South during the Great Depression to research a documentary on sharecroppers for *Fortune* magazine (they received the assignment in June 1936). The magazine never published the piece; in fact, Agee worked five years on the book before it saw publication. Unlike either Arendt or Ellison, Agee in the text portion of *Praise* is exceedingly uncomfortable with the responsibility his authority has bestowed upon him. Agee often talks about himself as a voyeur and is deeply conscious that his observations have something improper about them. He calls himself a "reverent and cold-laboring spy" (134), writes scathing criticism of the very institution (journalism) that asked him to undertake the project in the first place, and seems to make virtually no effort to tell the story or stories of these sharecropping families in the course of more than four hundred pages, as if to say his encounter with them is the significant story, not their lives (despite the title). Agee certainly describes each member of the family and, with maniacal detail, aspects of their lives including the house, farming, economics, education, and so on. There is virtually no dialogue and little in the way of family anecdotes, but there is ample discussion of Agee's own position as writer and interloper.

Indeed, about halfway through the text, Agee even writes that his words should not be called a book. In this comment, he raises the central issue for this analysis: What is my role, as writer, in coming to terms with and representing a life of people whose very existence is at once related to my own (as species, as southerners, as white) but as remote as possible in social and economic terms: "George Gudger is a man, et cetera. But obviously, in the effort to tell of him (by example) as truthfully as I can, I am limited. I know him only so far as I know him, and only in those terms in which I know him; and all of that depends as fully on who I am as on who he is" (239). I know of no modern American writer with a more withering self-critical stance than Agee, and this stance in itself I feel explains the strange form of his text: multiple fragments, nonnarrative, quotation, obsessive detail interspersed with passages of philosophical speculation and political harangue, almost everything except a writer writing the story of these families. This self-critical stance leads Agee to say,

> You should so far as possible forget that this is a book. That you should know, in other words, that it has no part in that realm where disbelief is habitually suspended. It is much simpler than that. It is simply an effort to use words in such a way that they will tell as much as I want to and can make them tell of a thing which happened and which, of course, you have no other way of knowing. It is in some degree worth your knowing what you can of it not be-

cause you have any interest in me but simply as the small part it is of human experience in general. (246)

Agee is hypersensitive that readers will come to his book with expectations about what is inside, based on what they know from their experience of reading books. No doubt for this reason he chose to place Walker Evans's photographs as the first sixty pages of the text before the title page, without headings or titles of any kind. It is an attempt, to borrow on the authority of experience, as if to say "here they are, these people, these towns in the south; just as we found them you may know them herein." Unlike the photographs, however, the written record, it would seem, requires a number of titles and headings, and more of the same to undo what went before, the text functioning like a kind of postmodern narrative with no center, no continuous plot line, but rather a series of exfoliations around multiple modules, each one commenting upon the other, each one building and unbuilding the textual reality at the same time.[11]

Toward the end of the book, just as Agee is describing an intense and wordless encounter between himself and Louise, the oldest Gudger child who has just completed the third grade (the family members are not described until about page 300), an encounter that borders on the pedophilic, he admits, "I must give this up, and must speak in some other way" (403). Part of what seems to have stopped him at this moment is his recognition that "I am from Mars" (405), that he is so completely alien from these people that he has "no real right, much as I want it, and could never earn it, and should I write of it, must defend it against my kind" (410). On the one hand, Agee admits that in order to get at these sharecroppers, to tell the truth of their lives in both their utter poverty and in what love and joy they manage to live like the rest of us, he must turn his camera eye back on himself as a representative of his "kind." On the other hand, he must defend his right to articulate this representation of poor white southern culture *against* his own authority to make that representation, an authority bestowed upon him, as he writes, by his participation in and affiliation with the dominant power structure of modern American society. He must defend his right against the presumption of his authority. Or to put it another way, he has no right except where that right has been de-authorized, disaffiliated from the very authority that in fact gives him the right in the first place—to watch, to observe, to write, to publish.

I can think of no way to extricate Agee from this double bind of being, on the one hand, affiliated with a society that produced this utter poverty and, on the other, disaffiliated in both the form and content of his representation. It is not a question of Agee trying to have it both ways; he has no choice. He is who he is. If Arendt's limitation is that she was unable to see the race question in either its theory or practice because she privileged for the moment of her analysis her position as woman, then Agee's limitation is that he has tried to address the question of class differences through a rhetoric of Christian love, although this love is completely mundane. He describes the "trembling" (368) he gets when he is in the same room with ten-year-old Louise, that he is "probably going to be in love with" (369) her, as if this were an answer to the alienation and division created by the capitalist mode of production. He is not apologetic about his own desire: he wants "a piece of tail" (376), he writes soon after this encounter with Louise, as if to suggest that anonymous sex with a prostitute might help him to overcome the intense feelings he has for these families. Without ever articulating this thinking, he seems to be banking on his own authentic feeling of good will toward these people as enough, or as something that might help, as if what these people needed were a savior to rescue them from their circumstances: a marriage, say, that old plot of capitalist upward mobility. But neither the marriage plot, nor any other sexual plot, is consummated in this text; perhaps the most we can say is that a kind of liberal desire is activated by the text and by the author's deep need to appear genuine (he says throughout the book he hopes they will neither fear nor hate him).

The subaltern does not speak in Agee's text—in this, the book recognizes what is surely of utmost importance: Agee has unlearned his privilege, to use Spivak's formula, a privilege that demands he speak for them and through them. He refuses to speak for them. The book is foremost a book about Agee, about an encounter of the elite with the underprivileged. In this, Agee repeats in a different key the gesture by Arendt, who also speaks for herself and in doing so recognizes the silence and silencing of the other. In fact, Agee seems particularly sensitive about his own subject position as a writer because he is writing for an institution—*Fortune* magazine—that represents an entire panoply of interests and concerns which simply does not include within its horizons the southern tenant farmer. He is not writing *for* the farmers. To use Edward Said's phrase, Agee does not give himself "permission to narrate" the story of the Gudgers, Woods, and Ricketts—as a conventional journalist would—because he wants to preserve in his text the full scope of his relationship to them.

With Zora Neale Hurston, the final example of this essay, we enter the problematic of engaging the situation of the oppressed without, however, pretending to speak for them. Yet what is interesting to me as a literary critic working through my own question of authority—my own bodily distance from, say, the feminine, yet at the same time with a connection to feminist thought—is that by their examples these writers name their own authority and the role it plays in structuring their approach to the other. If we are—or I am—to find a productive way to address otherness in critical analysis, it must be first by a self-reflexive glance at the very optical machine that gives access to the other in the first place, that actually constructs the other as other.

Their Eyes Were Watching Others

For me, some of the most powerful moments in Zora Neale Hurston's writings occur when a figure in the narrative is represented as watching events unfold, when such acts of looking become constitutive of the entire question of identity. In *Their Eyes Were Watching God,* this question is crucial and is foregrounded by a group photograph of Janie Crawford with her white "family," the family her grandmother works for and among whom Janie spends her early developmental years. Until Janie had seen that photograph she did not know she was black. Indeed, her skin is light, a mark of her family genetics: her slave grandmother, Nanny, gave birth to Leafy, the child of her white master; Leafy, in turn, was sexually assaulted by a white man making Janie one quarter black. However, Janie did not recognize this until she saw the picture and could not identify the little brown-skinned girl in it, who looked so different from the others in the white family. In addition to this mark of her identity, Janie also has a linguistic mark that functions to disrupt her identity: she comes to be called Alphabet precisely because she has so many different names, depending on who is talking with her. This is not, I feel, merely a question of optics, hallucinations, or linguistic accident; in part, it must be the result of Janie's indoctrination by Nanny, who has always taught her granddaughter that the proper model for her should come from the middle-class white family for whom she works. Nanny felt that marrying Logan Killicks, a potato farmer with sixty acres and a mule, would make that possible for Janie; when Janie leaves Logan for Jody Starks, she does not deviate that far from Nanny's goal: Jody wanted to be a mayor and a big voice in an all-black town, and he has learned capitalist style exploitation from the white businessmen in Georgia where he did his apprenticeship work, in a manner of speaking.

By the time Janie marries Tea Cake, her last husband, she is, by the standards of her community, comfortable and financially secure. She has sold her store but continues to collect rent on property she owns in Eatonville. She has a bank account with nine hundred dollars. Her life with Tea Cake is a love game, she says, and she has the leisure to do whatever she wants, even if it is to go down to the muck and pick beans with the rest of Tea Cake's cronies and the migrant workers from Barbados. Even the muck, which so many readers have taken to symbolize the site where Janie learns to tell stories, play cards, and shoot a gun, where she finally learns to come into her own as a human being, is also the place where that earliest photograph comes to assert itself in all its peculiar power, as in the roles that Mrs. Turner and her brother play at the end of the novel. They are both light-skinned blacks who feel very strongly that their skin color makes them superior. Turner, in fact, is the figure who occasions Tea Cake's insane jealousy during his illness, leading him to keep a loaded pistol under his pillow.

Tea Cake may have been of a lower class than Janie's other husbands, which made him a more casual and fun-loving partner, but like the others he maintains the culturally inscribed ideology of wife as possession, indeed, wife as slave. He beats Janie, so the novel puts it, in order to reassert and reassure himself "in possession" of her. And no wonder: under conditions of slavery the black man could not be guaranteed the right to marry. Mrs. Turner suggests to Janie in effect that the white blood in her family gives her brother a higher claim to the right to marry Janie than Tea Cake, a very dark African American. Mrs. Turner, in fact, articulates a wish for genocide pure and simple as a way to solve the color problem. She believes her white blood will protect her.

Janie's response to all of this is not particularly heroic. As Jennifer Jordan has written, Janie seems to merely laugh it all off; she only becomes indignant when Mrs. Turner speaks out against Tea Cake, the man she deeply loves.[12] Janie seems to have nothing whatever to say about the racial issues raised by the Turners. If Janie is the African American feminist hero who returns to Eatonville with an achieved voice as a sign of her new freedom and agency as so many critics have written,[13] why does she seem so uninterested in taking her place on the porch with the other members of her community to establish herself and her story as the focus of community life? Jordan's reading of the novel represents perhaps the harshest assessment of this aspect of Hurston's vision of the folk: "In the long run her story makes light of the fate of the majority of black women in the thirties by turning migrant labor into fun and games and wife beating into a prelude to sexual ecstasy" (112). Hazel Carby's reading offers a similar assessment:

"Hurston could not entirely escape the intellectual practice that she so despised, a practice that reintroduced and redefined a folk consciousness in its own elitist terms" ("Politics" 76). These two essays, along with Richard Wright's early and scathing attack on the novel, represent a serious and convincing statement of the limitations of Hurston's work for our time.

Looking at herself in the photograph from her childhood, Janie sees an unfamiliar picture: it is herself, but she doesn't immediately recognize it. The darkness of the skin, in relation to the whiteness of the rest of the figures, does not signify for her. Hurston's novel is an attempt to recover the meaning of blackness, of her childhood and her roots in a small all-black town in Florida after having left home, left her people, and become educated in a white university, the second African American woman to receive a doctorate at Barnard College. Carby raises this point in her essay: Hurston has left her folk, and to return to them she must do so mediated by the white forms she has adopted as an anthropologist. Carby says Hurston looks through anthropologist's eyes, which is not an objective, truthful gaze but one constructed by the academy and by professors like Franz Boas, one of Hurston's mentors. That is what Carby means by elitist terms: Hurston must look at the folk from the point of view of the elite. Carby suggests that the elite viewpoint is ahistorical and cannot challenge the realities of the present because those realities—the devastation of the Great Depression, the migration of blacks to the industrial North, the horrible conditions of sharecropping that Agee and Evans attempt to confront in their book—are simply too troubling.

For Hurston, to return to the folk means to give herself over to a nostalgic pleasure in contemplating the simpler life and times of a simpler people, who do not suffer overtly from the economic deprivations of their condition. Indeed, elements of the African American experience, such as the sexual assault of women by white men, are represented as something having taken place in the distant past—Janie's mother, Leafy, long gone from her life, and Nanny both experienced such violence. The intrusion of white racism comes only after the hurricane, a brief moment in the narrative when Tea Cake is forced to help with the process of putting the dead to rest—whites in pine boxes, blacks in mass burial pits.

In reading and teaching *Their Eyes* to nearly all-white groups of students year after year, do I in fact perpetuate a view of American culture and society that refuses to take responsibility for either its past—the record of oppression that characterizes the culture out of which I come—or its present (a culture ready to explode again as the cities exploded in the sixties in racial violence)? The events in Los Angeles in April 1992 seem to confirm my own and my culture's insistence on remaining blind to these conditions, for it is precisely as a text that introduces difference into the middle-class white classroom that Hurston's novel has been incorporated into the canon.[14] Among the many possible motives, perhaps I read this book, in this particular context, in order to demonstrate that I have thought about racism and am happy to confirm my liberal desire for equality and justice; it allows me, if not my students, to think about an aspect of culture—both aesthetic and social culture—that would otherwise torture me as it does James Agee. But is that it? Does recreating the storytelling culture of the African American folk of the South always and only mean bad faith and nostalgia? For me, the answer to this question is located in the photograph of the little girl, Alphabet, later Janie Mae Crawford, Killicks, Starks, Woods.

If *Their Eyes* is a novel that nostalgically, and with unhappy consciousness, returns readers to an idealized folk origin for Hurston and for an uneasy academy wishing to assert social change as achieved before it is earned and accomplished, then we should specify exactly what that origin is. In this novel, the origin is not the singular thing we might expect: African American folk culture. Instead, it is the hybrid, the amalgamation, that Janie as white person comes to embrace blackness, after finally recognizing it as her own, or as a black person who learns of her blackness only by looking at the child in the photograph and failing to see a white girl. Indeed, Janie consistently rejects the model of middle-class white domesticity by rejecting Logan Killicks and later, after many years of marriage, Jody Starks, yet all of these models are black versions of white domesticity. She does not exactly reject whiteness (the aspect of Janie that irritates Jennifer Jordan), as we can see in the passages with Mrs. Turner.

In fact, the very sequence of events that includes Tea Cake's maniacal jealousy of Janie and fear that the whiter Turner will take her away from him leads to Tea Cake giving Janie a beating and ends with Janie shooting Tea Cake. This event has been read as tragic accident, unfortunate act of self-defense, and unconscious act of a woman asserting her independence over an oppressive male, but it has not been read in the context of the color valance. To be sure, Janie emphatically does not, after the death, trial, and funeral, link up with the Turners; she goes home to Eatonville alone. And that return, as Jordan has argued, is not a celebratory return of the wandering storyteller to her community to take up the task of informing and unifying that community as its new leader. Instead, there is something tentative and somber about her return, some regret that the community does not in fact welcome her into its arms: "'If they wants to see and know, why they don't come kiss and be kissed? Ah could then sit down and tell 'em things'" (6). With all of the talk about *Their Eyes Were Watching God* as a great novel of storytelling and community building, it remains difficult to reconcile that claim with the fact that Hurston's fiction does not include Janie getting up on the porch with the rest of the town and telling her tale.

In her autobiography, *Dust Tracks on a Road,* Hurston addresses the race question in a chapter entitled "My People! My People!" She tells us she faced an insuperable dilemma growing up trying to reconcile what for her was a contradiction in the African American community. On the one hand, the "racialists" were blacks who preached the superiority of the black race and that "race consciousness" is something designed to keep African Americans thinking about their origins and what good devolves from those origins. Yet, on the other hand, her experience told her that lighter-skinned blacks were treated with greater respect in the black community, black people who misspoke would be chided for being black, and, in perhaps the most amusing passage of that chapter, black people took no end of pleasure in telling self-deprecatory folk tales about the proverbial monkey who always loses in the end. Hurston's solution to this problem is the one that has troubled critics of her work for a long time: she appeals to a kind of bourgeois individualism, rejecting any need to think about the group. While others, both black and white of course, are busy trying to "Tar Brush" up their genealogies by finding Jefferson or Pocahontas in their background, Hurston finally maintains that "the Negro" does not exist. She calls herself an in-betweener and writes that "it took more than a community of skin color to make your love come down on you" (235).

Thus, I return to that photograph of Alphabet, the recognition of which brings a cry of "'Aw, aw! Ah'm colored!'" (9). It is by no means obvious how we might understand this brief response, but in the context of the narrative it is merely the occasion for the white folks to "laugh real hard" (9). The child may have experienced it as traumatic, but in retelling the story Janie does not register it that way. My point, however, is that in part Janie's reason for returning to Eatonville, like Hurston's own reason for returning to her home village, is to tell that story, a story about the ambiguity of an individual's sense of social and racial identity poised right at the very origins of her emerging self-consciousness. She comes to know who she is at the very moment when she recognizes that she had been mistaken or ignorant. To return home is not to recover an origin or reconnect with some long lost moment of fullness and presence where life and love are whole.

Nellie McKay's recent reading of the novel seems to suggest precisely this story, in configuring the narrative as a movement from being "male-identified" in the beginning to being "female-identified" at the end, as if the narrative moved in a perfect circle from that (implied) idyllic period when mother and daughter make a charmed circle of intimacy, to that period in the middle of inauthenticity when women are forced to identify with men ("compulsory heterosexuality" to use Adrienne Rich's phrase), and finally a return in the end to her beginning, her kissing friend Phoebe standing in for that earlier, brighter figure of the mother. While I can see the great attraction of this representation of the narrative, it does not fit with Hurston's novel: Janie's mother Leafy is hardly a figure for Janie of lost primal love; she comes to hate her grandmother, the one who raises her, for having burdened her with inappropriate and harmful expectations; and Phoebe, certainly an important friend crucial for the narrative structure, is only a faint beginning of female homosocial community.

Hurston's *Moses* is a text that enacts a similar gesture, making it impossible to say exactly where Moses the great man gets his power and implying strongly that he does not get it from his biological or racial origins but rather in Miriam's storytelling and in his own ability to "cross over" into the speech of others. That he can cross over never means that his position as political leader of a unified community is secure; there is dissension and insurrection, and at one point things go so badly that he must use violence against the very community he wishes to restore. Hurston was no sentimentalist about slave mentality. She holds in abeyance the quest for pristine origins, for that elusive community of the folk where everything must have been better.

Carby criticizes Hurston's final figure in the novel *Their Eyes Were Watching God*—of Janie pulling a fishnet horizon around her like a cloak with all of her life experiences caught in it—as suggestive of a "discourse that exists only for the pleasure of the self" which then "displaces the folk as community utterly and irrevocably" ("Politics" 87). Embedded in this criticism is the same ideology that motivates McKay's wholly laudatory evaluation of the novel: that African American fiction ought to be in the service of this ideal community, that it build community in itself. The problem with this as either criticism or praise is that a simple definition of the community is never available to us; the displacement is always and already an aspect of community. Moreover, this is particularly true if our starting point in community building is racial identity.

Coda

Three years ago I attended Passover services in the old synagogue in Prague, a place of worship dating back to the late thirteenth century, which functions as the spiritual center for the tiny Jewish community that remains in that city. It is impossible to describe precisely the sense of displacement—"utterly and irrevocably"—I felt in this space. Upon entering the building one must walk through the women's gallery to get to the inner temple, a feature of synagogues foreign to me. I was immediately taken for a tourist, and a gatekeeper, a Czech Jew, exploded in anger and only reluctantly allowed me to enter after a woman who took notice of the commotion interceded on my behalf, repeating over and over, "He's a Jew, He's a Jew," in a language I did, but did not, understand. I found a seat and a yarmulke and waited for the service to begin, thirty minutes late. While I was clearly not the only "visitor" from outside the Prague Jewish community, it struck me as a significant part of the proceedings that the small group of male worshippers who knew one another gathered themselves together into a community almost in opposition to the other Jews who had found themselves traveling over the high holidays. It reminded me of synagogue years before, a reform congregation in Fresno made up of transplants from the East trying hard to hold on to a religious identity. Circles within circles guarded suspiciously.

When the cantor began to sing, I knew I had lost any connection I might have had to the proceedings and was suddenly, surreally, in a place I had never been before. His song was strange, conjuring for me the hot, dusty streets of the Middle East—where I have never been—in an idiom that could have been Arabic for all I knew. It was during one of these songs that I received a sudden shock: Perhaps this was what my mother had to face in her conversion, for she came from a white-bread Protestant family from Milwaukee and Pittsburgh and was asked to comprehend a strange new religion and social milieu. She had died only two months before, so I would not be able to ask her this question. A woman sitting next to me (against all the rules, of course—she should have been in the outer circle behind thick walls) chatted to her female friend throughout the entire service, making the central circle of Czech male Jews exercise their eyebrows in constant exasperation. After the service she introduced herself to me as the French Ambassador to the Czech and Slovak Republic, inviting me to the Seder—a simple gesture: join this group for this evening. I couldn't. Community was as far from me at that moment as a southern village where people play the dozens on each other, tell stories of signifying monkeys, sing work songs, put on the dog.

The price that Hurston's novel must pay for becoming a part of the canon is that it will be a little, or a lot, harder to see. Hurston's book is an event with an impact that is daunting—a best-seller for the publisher, an industry for academic critics, the object of symposia, workshops, classrooms, research projects funded by both the government and private organizations. For now, it is central, no longer sitting on the margins, and that status is sufficient I should think for us to consider just what is happening in American academic culture. If we happen to be one of the "women" of this new orthodoxy, we will either have to be satisfied with the view through the tiny, narrowing slits of the outer gallery walls or, if we bring with us the sufficient authority and chutzpa of an ambassador, we can storm the inner circle.

For me, Hurston's novel is an allegory of what happens when we try to return to origins and what we find there—not something upon which to build a stable, unifying, sense of identity. We have taken this novel into the canon as a lost masterpiece, a bit of marginalia that the male academic establishment could never see as authentic in its representation of a woman's quest. Now that it is central to many American literature survey courses, American studies courses, not to mention African American studies, women's studies, and others, it is harder to see that in fact the book was written from the point of view of an elite returning to find a home for herself and having to face the difficulty of seeing it. As part of the reconstruction of Hurston as culture hero, we can now make the pilgrimage to central Florida to find her grave; Alice Walker writes that it has a big hunk of marble standing upright in a barren place with an impressive inscription: "Genius of the South." It is in a St. Lucie county cemetery, just south on the Florida turnpike from Walt Disney World and Epcot Center and the assembly lines of nostalgia.

Andrew Lakritz

Notes

1. While it is clear that I *have* the authority to speak as teacher and writer, to call this "my own authority" suggests quite wrongly that it is possible to possess singly what amounts to a social and political *relation*. When I say "she speaks/writes with great authority," what I am indicating is a metaphor that has come to be hypostatized in practical usage. It can mean several things: that the critic speaks from an experience that, lacking it myself, I must admire or respect because she makes available to me ideas and knowledge hidden from me; that the critic speaks from a knowledge of a subject that has

come from long and careful study or research; or that she speaks with a care that demonstrates a powerful or brilliant juxtapositioning of elements. To say any of these things is to make an intrinsic judgment of the authority of the speaker, that she has authority because she "owns" authority.

Yet, there is always more at stake and more at work in authority. Take the authority of experience, for instance, which gives her access to information and to a lived, bodily relation to her subject which I do not have. This may already be at work before I even am aware of it: because my experience and my body are constituted differently, I lend my credulity and perhaps even awe to this speaker who offers knowledge that I otherwise cannot have. She has authority over her subject—and over me—because I do not and cannot speak as she speaks. Another way of putting this is to say that because I cannot speak for her, in relation to her she has authority over me and over anyone else who stands in something of the same relation to her regarding a given subject.

2. This difference is complicated in many ways. First, though I was raised a Jew and certainly identify myself culturally as a Jew, I have always had to deal with the fact that my mother converted to Judaism as a young woman— only two years before I was born—and that culturally I also descend from her background of upper-middle-class Wisconsin WASP. Second, it is part of the very heritage of being a Jew to struggle with these questions of assimilation and autonomy, and in this postholocaust world with so many Jews returning to Orthodoxy, these questions have become more and more urgent, as the stakes seem more and more elevated. Jacques Derrida has recently written about Hermann Cohen's philosophical position vis-à-vis assimilation, the position that claims that German Jews are as much German as they are Jews and that the philosophical tradition of German idealism is as much a Jewish phenomenon as it is a German one. After the holocaust it is much easier to see assimilation and amalgamation as a mistake *for those who lived in Europe between the wars*, yet even with this well of profound experience behind us— for those who went through the war and for those others of us who look back on it—it is impossible to come to any conclusions about the future. Experience may be powerful as something that informs knowledge and authority, but it is never absolute.

3. This gesture of rejection has a tendency to make those who feel they have no choice in the matter indignant or incredulous. Terry Eagleton writes of his suspicions about the upper-class radicals he knew in college. In "Can the Subaltern Speak?" Gayatri Chakravorty Spivak writes of the first worlders who have the luxury of throwing off their privilege as if it were just another one of their privileges. Elaine Showalter writes of male critical cross-dressers, Tootsie academics. I feel these suspicions come from a deep-seated belief that biology and experience are enough (and necessary) to earn authenticity for an individual and that biology and experience are mutually informing and, in any case, prior to all other forms of identification and identity making. While I agree that these aspects of identity are powerful, if I thought they were prior and primary and ultimate, as a limit to the kinds of coalitions that might

be built, then I could not write this essay. To echo Hazel Carby's *Reconstructing Womanhood*, to rely too heavily on experience is to make ahistorical and essentialist theoretical claims (16).

4. The earlier version of Spivak's essay, under the same title, was published in *Wedge*. See "Can the Subaltern Speak? Speculations on Widow-Sacrifice."

5. Although Arendt never identifies the photograph precisely, she appears to be describing the one of Dorothy Counts being escorted to school by Dr. Edwin Tompkins, a white friend of her father's who was his colleague at a local seminary. The photograph was printed just below a similar one with Elizabeth Eckford being barred from entering Central High School in Little Rock, both under the headline "Soldiers and Jeering Whites Greet Negro Students" (*New York Times*, Sept. 5, 1957).

6. Werner Sollors demonstrates, however, that while African Americans did not in large numbers agitate for the right to marry whites, there is a long history of discussion of and argument against laws that prohibit interracial marriage (189n. 18). For the David Spitz and Melvin Tumin comments, see the same issue of *Dissent* that published Arendt's initial essay.

7. See Sollors (176). Ellison's remark is addressed principally to the antagonist of his essay "The World and the Jug," Irving Howe, who is said to write "with something of the Olympian authority that characterized Hannah Arendt's 'Reflections on Little Rock'" (108). Ellison was moved to write his rebuttal to Howe's essay "Black Boys and Native Sons" because Howe made the judgment there that younger black writers, including Ellison, had failed to live up to the promise of Richard Wright, whose work was properly political. Ellison resented Howe's notion that to be an African American writer one had to write protest novels first and foremost and that black experience was nothing but hell in America because that was how Wright represented it.

8. One objection to Spivak's nomenclature is that it simply cuts too broad a path, that while it is true that the oppressed have very serious difficulties trying to be heard, they do speak and speak for themselves, if those of us among the elite would only listen. Structures of oppression are never monolithic, just as power itself brings with it precisely those fissures that threaten to topple it at any moment, without which the police would be unnecessary. To say that the subaltern cannot speak, then, may be another way of making an undialectical hypostatized identification of the other as absolute and the dominant order as utterly dominant and separate.

9. I want to thank Lauren Berlant for directing me to this essay.

10. In her biography of Arendt, Elizabeth Young-Bruehl quotes a brief passage of a letter from Arendt to Ellison which indicates that she acknowledged her misunderstanding to him: "It is precisely this idea of sacrifice which I didn't understand" (316).

11. See the essay by T. V. Reed on the book as an example of postmodern writing.

12. For Jordan, Janie "turns away Mrs. Turner's condemnation of . . . loud ways, laughter, and songs [of the black people in the muck] with a statement that puts an aesthetic distance between her and poor blacks. 'They don't wor-

ry me atall, Mis' Turner. Fact about de thing is, they tickles me wid they talk'" (113). Among all of the laudatory writing on *Their Eyes,* Jordan's essay represents a new trend in critical work. Along with Michael Awkward's critical view of Tea Cake ("Introduction") and Chidi Ikonne's criticism of Hurston for her alleged contempt for African Americans, Jordan's essay suggests that this text represents not achieved status as canonical—if any text could ever do that—but rather a contested and uncommon ground of ideological battle. It is that battle that most interests me.

13. For this line of thinking, see Mary Helen Washington's foreward to *Their Eyes;* Wendy McCredie, "Authority and Authorization"; Mary Jane Lupton, "Zora Neale Hurston"; and most recently, Nellie McKay's profoundly teleological reading of Janie's narrative, "'Crayon Enlargements of Life.'" McKay writes that "her conscious journey is of major importance for her psychological development from a male-identified woman to a self firmly grounded in a positive sense of independent black woman-hood" (58). This formula makes for neat critical presentation but that neatness comes at the cost of excluding some of the more interesting complexities involved in Janie's identifications: with nature, for instance, in the form of the bee and the pear tree, with herself in the photograph, and with her grandmother's dream of economic independence; finally, the idea of "independent black womanhood" sounds itself suspiciously modeled after a bourgeois (and "male") paradigm for selfhood.

14. One sure sign that *Their Eyes* has become such an important text by a novelist with such a small output (not counting the folklore, roughly that of Nathanael West) is that Harold Bloom, that master of canon building, has not only included Hurston in his series "Modern Critical Views" but has written a glowing introduction placing *Their Eyes Were Watching God* in the tradition of D. H. Lawrence, Henry David Thoreau, and Theodore Dreiser. Although feminists may have no reason to celebrate Bloom's inclusion of Hurston in the canon *on his terms,* at the very least we can begin to see how this book has taken on multiple new lives in contemporary literary culture.

Works Cited

Agee, James, and Walker Evans. *Let Us Now Praise Famous Men.* 1941. Boston: Houghton Mifflin, 1988.

Arendt, Hannah. "The Crisis in Education." Pp. 173–96 in *Between Past and Future.* New York: Viking, 1961.

———. "Reflections on Little Rock." *Dissent* 6, no. 1 (1959): 45–56.

———. "Reply to Critics." *Dissent* 6, no. 2 (1959): 179–81.

Awkward, Michael. *Inspiriting Influences: Tradition, Revision, and Afro-American Women's Novels.* New York: Columbia University Press, 1989.

———, ed. *New Essays on* Their Eyes Were Watching God. New York: Cambridge University Press, 1990.

Benhabib, Seyla. "Models of Public Space: Hannah Arendt, the Liberal Tradition, and Jürgen Habermas." Pp. 73–98 in *Habermas and the Public Sphere,* ed. Craig Calhoun. Cambridge: MIT Press, 1992.

Bloom, Harold. "Introduction." Pp. 1–4 in *Modern Critical Views: Zora Neale Hurston*, ed. Harold Bloom. New York: Chelsea House, 1986.

Carby, Hazel. "The Politics of Fiction, Anthropology, and the Folk: Zora Neale Hurston." Pp. 71–93 in *New Essays*, ed. Awkward.

————. *Reconstructing Womanhood: The Emergence of the Afro-American Woman Novelist.* New York: Oxford University Press, 1987.

Deleuze, Gilles, and Felix Guattari. *Franz Kafka: Towards a Minor Literature.* Trans. Dana Polan. Minneapolis: University of Minnesota Press, 1986.

Derrida, Jacques. "Interpretations at War: Kant, the Jew, the German." *New Literary History* 22, no. 1 (1991): 39–95.

Eagleton, Terry. "Response." Pp. 133–35 in *Men in Feminism*, ed. Alice Jardine and Paul Smith. New York: Methuen, 1987.

Ellison, Ralph. *Shadow and Act.* New York: Random House, 1964.

————. "The World and the Jug." In *Shadow and Act.*

Gates, Henry Louis, Jr. *The Signifying Monkey: A Theory of Afro-American Literary Criticism.* New York: Oxford University Press, 1988.

Howe, Irving. "Black Boys and Native Sons." *Dissent* 10, no. 4 (1963): 353–68.

Hurston, Zora Neale. *Dust Tracks on a Road: An Autobiography.* Philadelphia, Pa.: J. D. Lippincott, 1942.

————. *Moses, Man of the Mountain.* 1939. New York: HarperCollins, 1991.

————. *Their Eyes Were Watching God.* 1937. New York: Harper and Row, 1990.

Ikonne, Chidi. *From Du Bois to Van Vechten: The Early New Negro Literature, 1903–1926.* Westport, Conn.: Greenwood Press, 1981.

Jordan, Jennifer. "Feminist Fantasies: Zora Neale Hurston's *Their Eyes Were Watching God.*" *Tulsa Studies in Women's Literature* 7, no. 1 (1988): 105–17.

Lakritz, Andrew. "The Equalizer and the Essentializers, Or Man-Handling Feminism on the Academic Literary Left." *Arizona Quarterly* 46, no. 1 (1990): 77–103.

Lupton, Mary Jane. "Zora Neale Hurston and the Survival of the Female." *Southern Literary Journal* 15 (1982): 45–52.

McCredie, Wendy. "Authority and Authorization in *Their Eyes Were Watching God.*" *Black American Literature Forum* 16, no. 1 (1982): 25–28.

McKay, Nellie. "'Crayon Enlargements of Life': Zora Neal Hurston's *Their Eyes Were Watching God* as Autobiography." Pp. 51–70 in *New Essays*, ed. Awkward.

Reed, T. V. "Unimagined Existence and the Fiction of the Real: Postmodernist Realism in *Let Us Now Praise Famous Men.*" *Representations* 24 (1988): 156–76.

Said, Edward. "Permission to Narrate." *London Review of Books*, Feb. 16, 1984, 13–17.

Showalter, Elaine. "Critical Cross-Dressing: Male Feminists and the Woman of the Year." Pp. 116–32 in *Men in Feminism*, ed. Alice Jardine and Paul Smith. New York: Methuen, 1987.

Sollors, Werner. "Of Mules and Mares in a Land of Difference: Or, Quadrupeds All?" *American Quarterly* 42, no. 2 (1990): 167–90.

Spitz, David. "Politics and the Realms of Being." *Dissent* 6, no. 1 (1959): 56–65.

Spivak, Gayatri Chakravorty. "Can the Subaltern Speak?" Pp. 271–313 in *Marxism and the Interpretation of Culture,* ed. Cary Nelson and Lawrence Grossberg. Urbana: University of Illinois Press, 1988.

———. "Can the Subaltern Speak? Speculations on Widow-Sacrifice." *Wedge* no. 7/8 (1985): 120–30.

———. *In Other Worlds: Essays In Cultural Politics.* New York: Routledge, 1988.

———. *The Post-Colonial Critic: Interviews, Strategies and Dialogues,* ed. Sarah Harasyn. New York: Routledge, 1990.

Stepto, Robert B. *From Behind the Veil: A Study of Afro-American Narrative.* Urbana: University of Illinois Press, 1979.

Tumin, Melvin. "Pie in the Sky . . ." *Dissent* 6, no. 1 (1959): 65–71.

Walker, Alice. "In Search of Our Mothers' Gardens: Honoring the Creativity of the Black Woman." *Jackson State Review* 6, no. 1 (1974): 44–53.

Warren, Robert Penn. *Who Speaks for the Negro?* New York: Random House, 1965.

Washington, Mary Helen. "Forward." Pp. vii–xiv in *Their Eyes Were Watching God,* by Zora Neale Hurston. New York: Harper and Row, 1990.

Young-Bruehl, Elizabeth. *Hannah Arendt: For the Love of the World.* New Haven: Yale University Press, 1982.

2

"For Every Gesture of Loyalty, There Doesn't Have to Be a Betrayal": Asian American Criticism and the Politics of Locality

At the end of Amy Tan's *The Joy Luck Club,* Jing-Mei, the alienated daughter whose conflicts with her mother frame the narrative, neatly resolves her ethnic angst. "And now I also see what part of me is Chinese," she concludes, "It is so obvious. It is my family. It is in our blood" (331). In mystifying ethnicity as a matter of genetic inheritance, Jing-Mei's comment seems to play to dominant representations of Asian inscrutability within a culture still willing to accept as norm a certain opacity about Asian Americans. While this racial insiderism may go unchallenged in other areas as well ("It's a black thing, you wouldn't understand"), it is easy to see why a simple substitution would provoke feminist outcry: "And now I also see what part of me is female. . . . It is in our blood."

Given the current context of suspicion that an appeal to essence invokes, it is interesting that while the critical debate focused on "woman" has produced a significant body of work, the question is not often as rigorously investigated when it comes to race. Yet both "minority discourse" and feminist theory have attempted to articulate theoretical positions that seek, in Gayatri Chakravorty Spivak's words, "to question the authority of the investigating subject without paralysing him" (201). In the process, as bell hooks notes, "to be a feminist" is no longer the question; rather, one advocates feminism (182). Henry Louis Gates, Jr., reveals race as "a trope of ultimate, irreducible difference," a dangerous and arbitrary classification that pretends to scientific truth (5). As theorists begin to foreground culture over biology and ideology over identity, the conversation turns from questions of race to ethnicity. In order to allow for the subject's intervention in socially constructed categories, for example, the anthropologist Michael Fischer posits ethnicity as dynamic, as "something reinvented and reinterpreted in each generation by each individual . . . not something that is simply passed on from generation to generation" (195). Yet, however much these new modes of theorizing difference allow for the subject's mediation in potentially determining categories of race and gender, they can also imply that identity formation takes place in a value free space; more attention is devoted to furthering the concept that we *can* "shuttle between identities" than how we go about it or what it means to make that attempt. In the theoretical emphasis on employing without avowing difference, discussions about how the subject negotiates between often contradictory positionings become elided.

In looking at one forum in which these issues are foregrounded, Asian American women's writing, it becomes clear that racial and gender identifications are often experienced as oppositions. As tensions between American and ethnic home cultures are played out over issues of gender (particularly in regard to feminism and sexuality), cultural nationalism and feminism appear as mutually exclusive. In this context, discussions of the "strategic assertion of identity" as a means of dealing with multiple categories of identity across lines of race, class, gender, and sexuality can fail to acknowledge the contentious framework in which Asian American women and other women of color are forced to negotiate identity. If feminism is positioned as a betrayal of ethnic culture, the question of alliance becomes not one of strategy, but of loyalty.

In examining the ways in which the opposition between cultural nationalism and feminism is constructed, I realize that as an Asian American feminist literary critic I am likewise implicated in this trope of betrayal. Am I an Asian Americanist or a feminist? How I position myself within theories of ethnicity and race, Asian American studies, cultural studies, U.S. third world feminism, or Euroamerican feminism indicates my priorities and critical allegiances. To what extent does an alliance with one cast suspicion on my placement within another, and how does this dynamic indicate the limitations of the concept of free and "shifting" positionalities?

I have structured this essay partly in response to this question, not only as it applies to the role of the critic in overlapping and competing schools of thought and engages current debates within standpoint theory, but also as it reflects my own location as an Asian American academic woman. The issue of authority within the discipline of Asian American studies arises at a time in which the coherence of "Asian American" as a subject position is becoming increasingly contested. The question of identity politics is particularly overdetermined for writers and critics because of the recent commodification of Asian American literary texts and the response it has precipitated in the form of gender debates within the academic and writers' communities. While these debates have been analyzed elsewhere, the way that authority circulates within them points to a crisis of representation reflective of current scrutiny over the implications of identity politics in general.[1] In drawing an analogy from what Valerie Smith has called the "third stage" of black feminist work, I discuss "the effect of race, class, and gender on the *practice* of literary criticism" in a self-reflective narrative (47). In other words, what difference does difference make in the critic's relationship with language and literature? Underlying my inquiries are questions about the current theoretical emphasis on multiple positionalities, an emphasis that can obscure both the divisions within and the consequences of "shifting" between specific positionings. The title of my essay echoes lines from Bharati Mukherjee's novel *Jasmine,* whose protagonist's Americanization causes her to shed her past selves and, in the process, the communities she embraced. I take Mukherjee's question as my own: Is critical positioning necessarily a question of loyalty, and if so, does every gesture of loyalty also indicate a betrayal?[2]

* * *

The term "Asian American" does not describe what Cherríe Moraga would call "a natural affinity group" ("Refugees" iii). Like the term "woman of color," Asian American is not necessarily culturally coherent but specifies a coalition based on a similarity of treatment within the United States.[3] As Lisa Lowe notes, it is a term used for political expediency: "Taking seriously the heterogeneities among Asian Americans in California, we must conclude that the grouping 'Asian American' is not a natural or static category; it is a socially constructed unity, a situationally specific position that we assume for political reasons" (41). Yet the diversity encompassed by the grouping threatens its coherence.[4] Not surprisingly, issues of authenticity and representation have become points of contention within the Asian American academic and literary communities precisely at a time in which the heterogeneity implicit in Asian American group identity would seem to contest its political viability.

The debate between Maxine Hong Kingston and Frank Chin,

dubbed the "parents" of Asian American literature, is a well-publicized case in point. Chin's accusation that Kingston has sold out her Chinese heritage by falsifying Chinese myths and pandering to a white feminist readership sets up a division between feminist and nationalist loyalties. While the debate takes on gendered overtones in ways that reflect those occurring in African American literature, it is at heart about Asian American representation, what constitutes an "authentic" Asian American voice, and who is in the position to define it.

In 1974, Frank Chin, Jeffrey Paul Chan, Shawn Wong, and Lawson Fusao Inada broke new ground by editing and publishing one of the first anthologies of Asian American writing, entitled *Aiiieeeee!: An Anthology of Asian-American Writers.*[5] After initially being discouraged by publishers who mistook the volume for Asian writing in translation, the editors submitted the volume to Howard University Press which accepted it. During the same year, Random House sent the manuscript of Maxine Hong Kingston's *The Woman Warrior* (1975) to Chin for review. His subsequent response to her work is neatly summarized by his statement, "Her conception of Fa Mu Lan is racist. Her portrayal of the Chinese—racist! Every assertion she makes about Chinese culture is wrong."[6] Chin charges that Kingston confirms white expectations of "the Christian fantasy of the Chinese as a Shangri-La people" ("Come All Ye" xii).[7] Chin reveals a taxonomy for "real" Chinese American writing based on his evaluation of how much a work seems to capitulate to stereotypes of Chinese male emasculation or endorse a self-hatred based on the myth of dual personality. This evaluation applies to any Chinese American who writes autobiography, a form condemned through its association with Christian conversion, as well as to writers such as David Henry Hwang and Amy Tan who are, not coincidentally, also the most commercially successful.

Feminism, Chin asserts, becomes one means of courting American publishers who "went crazy for Chinese women dumping on Chinese men" (27). In reference to Jade Snow Wong's autobiography, *Fifth Chinese Daughter,* he notes, "Misogyny is the only unifying moral imperative in this Christian vision of Chinese civilization. All women are victims. America and Christianity represent freedom from Chinese civilization. In the Christian yin/yang of the dual personality/identity crisis, Chinese evil and perversity is male. And the Americanized honorary white Chinese American is female" (26). A matter of "bashing" men, feminism is seen as complicitous in the Christian conspiracy to undermine Chinese culture through its representation of patriarchy as another Chinese evil to be eradicated. Chin's portrayal of feminism as a betrayal of cultural nationalism echoes debates over feminist content in literature by African American women. In "Reading Family Matters," Deborah McDowell writes that what "female readers see as an implicit affirmation of black women," men see as "a programmatic assault on black men" (76). The "rupture in the unified community" and the black family appears as "the white woman offering the fruit of feminist knowledge" (78). Within this scenario, the allure of white feminism lies in its tie to the publishing industry. McDowell notes that Ishmael Reed's novel, *Reckless Eyeballing*, "allegorizes Reed's now well-known and predictable perception that the work of talented black men is being eclipsed by the power bloc of black women writers mid-wifed and promoted by white feminists" (95).

Within the framework articulated by Reed and Chin, commercial success is associated with co-optation, an association that may reveal less about men of color and feminism than what Valerie Smith refers to as "anxiety about institutionalization" (42). Because Chin's condemnation of certain writers coincides with their mainstream distribution, his argument has been dismissed as "sour grapes." While his connection between ethnic marketability and political content is significant, his argument takes an absolutist stance: "Those who were to be published," he writes, "simply blanked out all experience that didn't gibe with the stereotype."[8] McDowell notes that the debate over black women's portrayal of black men is ultimately not the issue, rather "what lies behind this smoke screen is an unacknowledged jostling for space in the literary marketplace" ("Reading" 83). But underlying even this issue, what this space represents beyond financial remuneration (though this in itself is not insignificant) is the authority to define and, in the process, to speak for an ethnic community whose voice in that marketplace has been so selectively restricted, muted, or absent.

Questions about authority derived from visibility apply not only to literature but to literary criticism as well, where, with some exceptions, positions within controversies over representation seem to be aligned according to gender. Yet in a reversal of the cultural nationalism/feminism opposition, women of color question high profile men of color who may betray, in Barbara Christian's words, "our needs and orientation" as "black, women, and third world critics" (335).

While the debate between Joyce A. Joyce, Henry Louis Gates, Jr., and Houston Baker, Jr., over the applicability of poststructuralist theory to interpreting African American texts appeared in *New Literary History*, less widely publicized was the controversy surrounding the promotion of the historian Ronald Takaki's *Strangers from a Different Shore: A History of Asian Americans* in *Amerasia Journal*.[9] Although critically acclaimed and characterized as the most "definitive, authoritative, and comprehensive" history of Asian Americans, Takaki's book provoked some interesting responses from other Asian Americanists. While some responses concern issues of originality and accuracy—elisions, the reliability of sources, inferences—others reflect the issues surrounding authority and representativeness underlying the debates among creative writers. Several of the concerns about the book have centered around the question of voice—how the voices of the historical subjects are represented, how the voices of other researchers are acknowledged, and, within criticisms about the paucity of primary research, the extent to which the voices of those interviewed are representative.

In addressing what she sees as Takaki's subordination of both individual and communal histories to a narrative totality, the feminist literary critic Elaine Kim raises the point that his methods are in contradiction to his aims: "Although Takaki contends that he will establish the self and subjecthood of Asian Americans by retrieving their voices . . . his strategy in fact takes away the voices of those Asian Americans who spoke, disempowering their constructions while giving voice only to himself as master storyteller" (105). For Kim, Takaki's methodology and style carry political significance, particularly in regard to his treatment of gender; by portraying Asian American women only in relation to men, his rendering conforms to patriarchal norms in its failure to represent women as subjects of history.

Kim's comments on the inclusion of Asian American women as mere addendum reflect a concern echoed by other respondents about the limitations of a single authorial voice to represent a communal history.[10] Taking Takaki to task for his failure to credit his sources more precisely, the historian Sucheng Chan writes that "by failing to acknowledge adequately his debt to other researchers and writers, [Takaki] has taken our communal history and commodified it, while garnering all the credit for himself" (98). What stands out among the various critiques is the connection between marketability and ideology. Both Chan and Kim note that the work's triumphalism ends up substantiating American pluralism. "The ultimate effect of the oral history quotes," Chan writes, "is to affirm the belief that, in America, even the downtrodden have a chance to demonstrate the triumphant tenacity of the human spirit" (97).[11]

Echoing the Kingston/Chin debate, these critiques draw a significant link between ethnic textual commodification and political content, between marketplace privilege and ideological conformity. Without reducing the complexity of positions taken within each debate, I also want to suggest that this framework arises, to some extent, out of an anxiety about representation and contestations over who can speak. At one level, what is being evaluated in both controversies is authenticity as it is tied to oppositional politics. Feminism's status as an oppositional stance functions differently in each debate: among writers, feminism is aligned with co-optation; among critics, feminist reading challenges status quo historical paradigms. While it is clear that feminism can function both in accordance with and in opposition to Asian American cultural nationalism, here I merely want to highlight the way in which feminism becomes a standard by which ethnic loyalties are measured. One issue being contested in both controversies, then, is the ideological position feminism holds in regard to the dominant culture and to cultural nationalism.

In addition, if authenticity and authority are issues, who will be in a position to evaluate them? Chin's criticism of other writers no doubt arises from his perception that Asian American literary worth is evaluated by whites and measured in terms of marketability. This reflects one of the most salient concerns expressed in Ling-Chi Wang's response to Takaki's book, that because its reviewers came from outside the field, Asian Americanists seemed to be excluded from the process of defining their own standards of scholarship: "If we cannot define our own field," Wang asks, "what would be the point of advancing the interests and maintaining the integrity of our profession?" (75).

This question points to the context in which these "family matters" occur, the limited forum in which ethnic voices can be heard, and it highlights the paucity of Asian American representation in humanistic fields of inquiry. Is the literary debate fostered by meaningful political or artistic differences or by competition over a perceived scarcity of resources? While African American literature has been said to reflect an "anxiety of institutionalization," the anxiety expressed here seems to arise from *impediments* to institutionalization as Asian American texts continue to be marginalized in spite of the current perception of Asian American literature as "hot property."[12] Kingston and Takaki are characterized as media-created Asian American spokespersons. The controversies respond to this construction and evaluate how representative, authentic, or capable they are to speak for Asian American letters. In this regard, anxiety about representation is also an anxiety about *lack* of representation.

Characterizing these debates as simple infighting obscures their source, namely, the power that the white media wields in seeming to valorize one Asian American voice at a time. Yet speaking about the debates highlights the difficulty of establishing a space that is outside their terms—to speak at all may constitute a violation of "family" codes. This violation represents a kind of betrayal, paralleling dynamics that arise in the literature when Asian American women are forced to choose between familial and sexual alliances or between gender collectivity and Asian cultural identity. The controversies within the academic and creative communities represent another manifestation of that same dynamic; here, as sides are drawn along lines of gender, friendship, discipline, methodology, ideology, or levels of institutionalization, the concept of "shifting" or shuttling between positionalities even within one field becomes compromised. In the Takaki controversy, it is easy to imagine how a critic could be positioned, if not for or against Takaki himself, then for or against his representation of a communal history. The Kingston/Chin debate suggests a binarism into which bodies can easily be read: to do any kind of feminist work is to be an assimilationist. For a critic, then, is being *for* something necessarily to be *against* something else?

To some extent these oppositions are literally manifested in the form of academic divisions between Asian American studies, cultural studies, ethnic studies, women's studies, and American studies. The material necessity of choosing between them automatically places them in a competitive relationship in ways that go to the heart of these debates. Given this, it is easy to forget the experience/knowledge equation that underlies these disciplines, some more than others. While identity politics has been open to critique in regard to Asian American cultural production,[13] the origins of my academic alliances as a critic are clear: I study Asian American literature because I am Asian American. Yet I hesitate to state this obvious connection if only because marking a personal investment this way often seems to open one to charges of obsessive self-interest. But there is always a body behind the text, one that remains unacknowledged for the sake of critical objectivity. In the next section, I want to reflect upon what difference this body makes by discussing one way in which my identity as an Asian American woman affects my role as critic.

*   *   *

Over my mask
is your mask
of me
an Asian woman
grateful
gentle
in the pupils of your eyes
as I gesture with each
new play of
light

and shadow
this mask be
comes you.

—Mitsuye Yamada,
"Masks of Women"

There is an image in Maxine Hong Kingston's *China Men* that stays
with me: the girl-narrator hunched over in the darkened basement
entertaining herself with stories of her own invention. "I talked to the
people whom I knew were not really there," she writes, "I became
different, complete, an orphan. . . . I named this activity Talking Men"
(180). For me, reading fulfilled this need for a performative act of creation—through literature I talked to people who were not there, and
for that moment, while inhabiting a fictional universe, I too was "different, complete, an orphan." In reading I could experience the centrality of my subjectivity through the act of creation—all characters
and beings became *relative to me*.

But this feeling of completeness, of wholeness, is momentary and
illusory. Coming up from the basement returns Kingston's narrator to
what she is in the social world, a working-class Chinese girl in Stock-
ton, California, and a problem for urban renewal. Kingston's portrait
of the artist attempting to transcend the limiting implications of her
social positioning through creativity reveals an epiphany resulting not
in a perfectly aesthetic moment but a moment in which she becomes
autonomous and complete, her authority absolute. This relationship
between subjectivity and writing, speaking, and reading lies at the
heart of this collection where the question "Who can speak?" acknowledges that the condition of oppression limits the agency of the
subject. Speech signifies nothing less than the movement from object
to subject, a movement accompanied by a heightened awareness of
one's social status.[14] My own authority as a critic, reader, and writer is
intimately related to my history with language, speech, and literacy
as an Asian American woman. The categories "Asian" and "woman"
have affected how I was positioned and ultimately how I position and
represent myself. While in academic work our literacy sometimes allows us to forget "that we are natives too," my own ambivalent relationship to speech and literature is a constant reminder that difference
makes a difference.

While English is my first and only language and I should have been
comfortable using it, I never spoke in school; I was the little Chinese
girl who didn't talk, who did what she was told, got A's, and was otherwise benignly insignificant and harmless. I did not play—I read

books at recess and established as advanced a literacy as the local public library could offer. My past benefits me now as a critic; not speaking, I became an observer. In the process of experiencing myself by watching myself, I experienced my subjectivity as objectivity and at that time did not have the language to ascribe the process to anything other than the inevitability of fate.

In Charlotte Brontë's *Villette,* there is a passage in which Lucy Snowe descends a staircase and catches a glimpse of herself in the mirror. There is nothing unusual about it—the mirror is merely part of the decor—but at this moment, the full force of her image hits her. Viewing herself from outside, she sees herself for what she is—a plain woman, no longer young, in respectable, undistinguished clothing—nothing more, nothing less. For Lucy, the event shatters the complacency built around believing in the primacy of her own sense of self. She experiences the recognition of her class and gender position as a loss.

This self-doubling would not be so unsettling, so disruptive, but for this fear—to see yourself as others see you and be diminished in your own eyes. Kingston discusses this in the documentary, *Maxine Hong Kingston Talking Story.* As a child reading Louisa May Alcott's *Eight Cousins,* she comes across this passage: "But Fun See was delightfully Chinese from his junk-like shoes to the button on his pagoda hat; for he had got himself up in style, and was a mass of silk jackets and slouchy trousers. He was short and fat, and waddled comically; his eyes were very 'slanting,' as Rose said; his queue was long, so were his nails; his yellow face was plump and shiny, and he was altogether a highly satisfactory Chinaman" (74). Seduced into identifying with the subjects of the book, Rose and her Uncle Alec on a jaunt to "chin-chin with the Celestials," Kingston is filled with the reminder of her own difference; as a Chinese person she recognizes that she would be designated as the object of this characterization, not the subject of its creation. "Don't ask me to speak to them, uncle," Rose warns, "I shall be sure to laugh at the odd names and the pig-tails and the slanting eyes." For Kingston, the very process of reading is disrupted—she can't laugh, she is there to be laughed at. "Up to that time," she notes in an interview with William Satake Blauvelt, "I had identified with all those little women, then I saw this guy and I thought, 'My God, that's who I'm supposed to be—this little "chinaman" guy.' It ejected me out of literature" (8). This recognition constitutes a fall from grace, a betrayal attending the awareness of one's status in the social world. If the simple fact of racial oppression were not enough, to be conscious of it is worse. As Maya Angelou writes, "If growing up is painful for the

Southern Black girl, being aware of her displacement is the rust on the razor that threatens the throat. It is an unnecessary insult" (3).

For the most part, literary depiction of Asians always seemed so hyperexoticized and dehumanized that it bore no relation to me. As a reader, I was complicitous in participating in the racial spectacle, as Jane Miller notes about gender disidentification, "seduced" into an alliance with the source of defining power (22). Yet I experienced a similar shift while reading what is ironically considered a bible of the counterculture, Jack Kerouac's *On the Road*. The journey of Sal and Dean had a certain glamour that had appeal even for me, such is the power of identifying with those who are in control, who direct the action, who drive the car. While reading Kerouac's novel, I participated in their activities. I *was* a Merry Prankster until I read, "The parties were enormous; there were at least a hundred people at a basement apartment in the West Nineties. People overflowed into the cellar compartments near the furnace. Something was going on in every corner, on every bed and couch—not an orgy but just a New Year's party with frantic screaming and wild radio music. There was even a Chinese girl" (126).

"There was even a Chinese girl." Sometimes you are so convinced of your own humanity, the existence of your own personhood (or as Nel says in Toni Morrison's *Sula,* your Me-ness), that you forget that this is not how the world sees you—it doesn't see a subject. That recognition—a sort of desubjectification—spells the moment in which you begin participating in your doubleness. As in Frantz Fanon's discussion of the "epidermalization" of racial inferiority, consciousness of alterity is not so much realizing who you are, but what you represent (11).

In considering W. E. B. Du Bois's 1903 concept of "double-consciousness," "the sense of always looking at one's self through the eyes of others" (3), Richard Wright notes that the "gift of second-sight" provides the potential for radical social critique: "Now imagine a man inclined to think, to probe, to ask questions. Why, he'd be in a wonderful position to do so, would he not, if he were black and lived in America? A dreadful objectivity would be forced upon him" (2). The objectivity he is forced to experience is contradictory, at once "dreadful" and productive. Yet what Wright does not acknowledge is that the very condition of that forced objectivity inhibits the possibility that the results of an individual's thinking, probing, and asking questions can be heard. The irony of the relationship between language and race is that while the position of being both inside and outside American culture grants the capacity to see with clarity socially constructed modes of power, that positioning denies one the authority to act as a cultural critic. I note this in regard to my own location as an Asian American academic. While my class status enabled a college educa-tion, my race and gender suggested I was not to do anything signifi-cant with it. As my mother noted before I graduated, "Better brush up on your typing." Like Richard Rodriguez's "scholarship boy," I had mastered the moves for success and could synthesize the views of oth-ers without ever thinking that my own were significant or valid.[15] And even if I had thought so privately, I would not have known how to express my ideas with anything approaching eloquence.

I realize that there are more significant ways in which access to lit-eracy on one level and access to the word on another are denied. Yet gender and race do "make a difference" in terms of how I position myself in relation to language, a medium by which I am supposed to earn my keep. While current literary theorists have had to convince academics of the illusory nature of discursive mastery, they only reit-erate what to me is obvious. I echo Kit Quan who writes, "My various activities now help to remind me that my relationship with language is more complex than just speaking enough English to get by. In cre-ative activity and in anything that requires words, I'm still eight years old" (220). The same history that enabled me to develop a privileged relationship to the written word left me stumped and stupid in any kind of social interaction that necessitated speaking up. Fulfilling the stereotypes of my race, I was an Asian female nerd without a pocket protector. Without suggesting the typicality of this experience, when I think about my own identity as an Asian American what first comes to mind is this relegation to social impotence. Almost accepting this as inevitable, I was, for a significant part of my life, a highly satisfactory Chinaman.

* * *

You know Benita Parry recently has accused Homi Bhabha and Abdul JanMohamed and me of being so enamored of decon-struction that we're not able to let the native speak. She has for-gotten that we are natives too, eh?
    —Gayatri Chakravorty Spivak[16]

Given my awareness of the ways in which my racial and gender difference from the mythical norm serve to diminish my social pres-ence, it is interesting to me that in the present academic context my body now authenticates my "knowledge claims," if only about Asian Americans, Asian women, and, to a lesser extent, women of color. The recency of this change makes me acutely aware that we can be positioned not only according to our own agenda, but to that of others. Fanon's comment, "I was responsible at the same time for my body, for my race, for my ancestors" (112), is a reminder that we do not have the privilege to renounce the baggage that attends our cultural representation. Yet putting ourselves in the frame of academic writing by speaking personally is still a risk. While claiming a basis of authority in identity would seem to secure what Fredric Jameson wearily calls "a badge of group membership for the intellectual" (24), at worst it can be seen as a prescriptive and politically correct game ("As a white male, I . . . ") and dismissed as exclusion, separatism, "biological insiderism," or "cultural apartheid."[17]

Yet bell hooks's statement about the importance of the identity of the critic is straightforward and compelling: "Even if perceived 'authorities' writing about a group to which they do not belong and/or over which they wield power, are progressive, caring, and right-on in every way, as long as their authority is constituted by either the absence of the voices of the individuals whose experiences they seek to address, or the dismissal of those voices as unimportant, the subject-object dichotomy is maintained and domination is reinforced" (43). Still, *presence* may be a necessary but insufficient condition to ensure that the subject-object dichotomy will be dislodged and domination challenged.

Deborah McDowell's attempt to define the parameters of black feminist criticism reveals the difficulty of assuming a correlation between identity and political positioning: "I use the term here simply to refer to black female critics who analyze the works of Black female writers from a feminist or political perspective. But the term can also apply to any criticism written by a Black woman regardless of her subject or perspective—a book written by a male from a feminist or political perspective, a book written by a Black woman or about Black women authors in general, or any writings by women" ("New Directions" 191). The statement's all-inclusiveness provoked Hazel Carby to comment, "The semantic confusion of the statement gives cause to wonder at the possibility that an antifeminist celebration of a racist tract could be called black feminist as long as it was written by a black woman!" (13). If, as Carby notes, "black feminist theory is emptied of its feminist content if the perspective of the critic doesn't matter," then which perspective is the one that matters?

If I attempt to assign a perspective to Asian American literary criticism, the most conservative answer would probably be the most accurate—that critics are motivated by the desire to understand the ways in which Asians in the United States both mark and have been marked as a social group. This motivation is inherently political if to understand the nature of difference is to critique the power inequities that result from hierarchizing differences. But as the debates reveal, the question is how this agenda should be evaluated and by whom? As an Asian American critic, I am so conscious of the sometime conflation of critical identity with critical perpective that I second-guess my own literary readings—for some I am overly radical and for others not radical enough. While in some texts I describe the emergence of Asian American women's collective consciousness, one that enables them to critique self-consciously their racial and sexual inscription, in others I point out the ideological conformance to a liberal individualism characteristic of the American national mythos. Yet it seems risky to suggest that some Asian American texts contain ethnic dissent by conforming to American beliefs in equality, autonomy, mobility, and individuality. Challenging the idea that marginalized literature is resistance literature is particularly overdetermined in regard to Asian American texts because such a positioning supports a widespread belief in, and dismissal of, Asian Americans as the model minority. Who better to extol the virtues of an American ideology than a group perceived to have benefited by it? To return to the dominant trope of this essay, in this context a refusal to privilege resistance over capitulation in interpretation represents another aspect of a critical betrayal.

Exposing the pervasiveness of ideology by naming the ways in which hegemony functions is as crucial and politicized an endeavor as championing the ways in which people of color subvert potentially determining categories of race, class, gender, and sexuality. I would echo Chandra Talpade Mohanty who writes, "I do challenge the notion 'I am therefore I resist!' That is, I challenge the idea that simply being a woman, or being poor or black or Latino, is sufficient ground to assume a politicized oppositional identity. In other words, while questions of identity are crucially important, they can never be reduced to automatic self-referential, individualist ideas of the political (or feminist) subject" (33). Assuming the existence of that "politicized oppositional identity" in writing by people of color can ignore the overarching framework that signals the need for the development of such an identity. This tension between naming the ideological enclosure and asserting its disruption is reflected in Elizabeth Grosz's question about the process of theorizing group identity: "Is the concept of sexual difference a breakthrough term in contesting patriarchal conceptions of women and femininity? Or is it a reassertion of the patriarchal containment of women?" (87).

For U.S. third world critics, methods of judging levels of politicism occur not only in terms of content but also in terms of form. Centering on the contradiction between critical methods and critical aims, debates over whether or not the master's tools can dismantle the master's house focus on the inaccessibility of academic theoretical language and the possibility that critical theory can end up replicating differences in social power that theorists hope to expose. In regard to black, woman, and third world academics, Barbara Christian points out that "some of our most daring and potentially radical critics . . . have been influenced, even co-opted into speaking a language . . . alien to and opposed to our needs and orientation" (68). Henry Louis Gates, Jr., certainly implicated as one of the potentially radical, now co-opted critics, addresses the question somewhat less definitively, merely stating that "the concern of the Third World critic should properly be to understand the ideological subtext which any critical theory reflects and embodies, and the relation which this subtext bears to the production of meaning" (15). Here, I am trying to understand not "the ideological subtext" of any critical theory in particular but the ideological context in which the critic is placed. The shift reveals that these debates add another criterion for authenticity—not only about critical orientation as it is derived from identity but also as it is extrapolated from methodology.[18]

If, as Michael Awkward has suggested, race and gender are "merely tropes for political orientation," then what orientation does the Asian body signify? (12). As an Asian American critic, I occupy a position that provokes ambivalence in others—I am either held in suspicion for "making an issue" of my race, assigned honorary whiteness for being the "good" kind of minority, or subject to racial erasure for being "overrepresented." My critical, intellectual, and personal authority are very much tied to this representation so that regardless of how I position myself critically, a certain amount of that positioning is done for me. Among white feminists, I can be a "woman of color," a designation that was bestowed upon me before I had, if not the consciousness, then the articulation to ascribe it to myself. I learned fairly quickly that the designation carries certain expectations. First, I am expected to speak personally and this is how what I say will be most valued, but only in a relative sense. If the accusation of "doing" identity politics, a charge that places us on the lowest rung for critics in Dante's inferno, is often leveled against feminists, it is even more so toward feminists of color. I am to get the sense that theorizing "Woman" is somehow off-limits; to take it further, too often women of color are only visible within feminist conferences when they critique some aspect of white feminism. The role that garners most attention and validation is that of a watchdog who keeps white feminists honest about their own theories.

While I feel comfortable enough to claim a position among women of color without questioning that alliance in every instance, I know there is a hierarchy of authenticity within it. "The danger lies in ranking the oppressions," Cherríe Moraga notes (*Loving* 52), yet this occurs most consistently around contentious issues like race. Asian American women's authority to speak as, if not for, women of color is subtly and sometimes not so subtly contested. I attribute this to the continual resurfacing of the "model minority" discursive framework in which Asian Americans must operate—and questioning our inclusion or authority in this coalition represents a failure to transcend it. It seems that Asians are sometimes relegated to a secondary category of racial "otherness," somehow less absolute, less meaningful than the black/white binary that dominates racial discourse in the United States.

While the current emphasis on "multiculturalism" might seem to dislodge such a binarism, it is interesting that multiculturalism is held under such suspicion by the white academic left, the "progressive, caring, and right-on in every way" academics of hooks's commentary. For instance, Amy Kaplan makes the significant point that multiculturalism, which "analyzes American society and culture in terms of internal difference and conflicts, structured around the relations of race, class, and gender," also runs the risk of being "bound by the old paradigm of unity if it concentrates its gaze only narrowly on the internal lineaments of American culture and leaves national borders intact instead of interrogating their formation" (15). This caution, which seems to target ethnic studies as a manifestation of American studies, is based on a fairly narrow definition of multiculturalism, one that positions its practitioners as singularly obsessed with the politics of *inclusion*. It is odd that what might more accurately be called "liberal multiculturalism"—which supports the vision of American pluralism—ends up subsuming the variety of approaches within ethnic studies. Because Asian American studies has always been concerned with an Asian diaspora and therefore Western imperialism, I question the supposedly new examinations of alterity that are granted a certain symbolic capital via a supposedly new focus on empire and nationalism, examinations that purport to provide comprehensive critiques of axes of domination ignored in other work concerned with similar issues.[19]

The shift from a focus on Asian immigration to Asian postcoloniality, from questions of Americanization to questions of transnationalism, raises significant issues about critical location and critical authority. What does it mean for Asian theorists like Trinh T. Minh-hà and Gayatri Chakravorty Spivak to identify as third world cultural critics rather than as Asian Americanists? What is the effect of disavowing American national affiliation? I wonder about the politics inherent in leaving unmarked one's identification with the United States as a first world power, while at the same time benefiting from its resources. It is a seductive positioning—at once to claim an outsider's position to lend credibility to one's first world critique, *and* to mark one's distance from U.S. "colonized minorities" because of the traditional association between race and class in this country. Looking at this process of critical naming leads me to question where "postcolonial" spaces exist and how the position of exile affects the authority of the cultural critic.

While I grapple with these questions of identification and alliance within feminism, U.S. third world feminism, and Asian American studies, I am also very much aware of the larger context in which they occur. To some academics they are nonissues; the debates and controversies inspired by the questions become homogenized and reduced under the overarching umbrella term "political correctness." It seems strange then to engage in some of the issues I do—as if they indicate that I have lost sight of the bigger picture. In discussing the current media backlash against political correctness in the academy, Gerald Graff notes that the "academic left" has not helped its cause by "preaching to the converted" without reiterating in clear language the justification for their work. "If those of us who identify with the dissenting wing of the academy do not get better at engaging with those who disagree with us," he writes, "we will only lose ground to those who defame us as politically correct authoritarians" (17). It is a wonder to me that he does not confront "those who disagree" with him on a daily basis. Too often I am left without a position from which to speak about my work other than defensiveness. When I think of Graff's call for educating "those who disagree," I think of the anecdote that Amy Ling recounts about a departmental chair who demanded, "Give me one good reason why I should read your [Chinese American women] writers, other than guilt" (158). In the face of these challenges that seek to invalidate the basis of our scholarship, it would seem that questioning the place Asian American women hold in the sisterhood of women of color or marking the discontinuity between U.S. third world and third world women matters very little. Yet if we spent most of our time answering to the reductive view of "identity politics," we would never get to these self-reflective critiques.

More interesting investigations of what it means to attribute characteristics and ways of knowing to socially constructed groups come
from inside the "dissenting wing of the academy." Toril Moi's point
that "to define 'woman' is necessarily to essentialize her" prompts
Elizabeth Grosz to ask, "If women cannot be characterized in any
general way . . . how can feminism be taken seriously? If we are not
justified in taking women as category, what political grounding does
feminism have?" (98). As a case in point, I was recently chastized
for asking what I considered a very general question about conditions for women in the Middle East. "I have a problem with that
question," my European acquaintance replied. "People in the West
always assume that it's much more sexist there because of their own
positioning." At the time, I was sufficiently chastened—in posing the
question, I had judged the culture according to my own standards of
feminism fostered by an upbringing in the post–women's movement
United States. But is it not fair to assume that their situation is more
oppressive than my own? While I do have Western biases, I also
have common sense.

My frustration with the incident calls to mind Tzvetan Todorov's
pointed, if disingenuous, response to the concept of orientalism: "It is
true that 'the Orient' is far too broad a category, including as it does
both Syria and Japan; it is also true that the very existence of such a
category teaches us a great deal about the obsessions of scholars and
world travelers. But does this mean that there is no such thing as a
Japanese culture or Near Eastern traditions—or that this culture and
these traditions are impossible to describe?" (37). His response characterizes the way in which standpoint theory can become reduced by
those who consider it a threat to an objective and knowable truth.
Still, my impatience with being reminded of my own positioning
when stating what I considered to be a generally accepted tenet reminds me that we need to develop theories even at the risk of fixing
cultural identity.

For example, in discussing the reasons for Asian American wom-
en's lack of participation in the feminist movement, Esther Ngan-Ling
Chow writes,

> Adherence to Asiatic values of obedience, familial interest, fatalism,
> and self-control may foster submissiveness, passivity, pessimism, tim-
> idness, inhibition, and adaptiveness, rather than rebelliousness or po-
> litical activism. Acceptance of the American values of independence,
> individualism, mastery of one's environment through change, and
> self-expression may generate self-interest, aggressiveness, initiative,
> and expressive spontaneity that tend to encourage political activism;

but these are, to a large extent, incompatible with the upbringing of Asian American women. (368)

On the surface, it would seem that in its negative coding of Asian cultural attributes, the list conforms to every Western stereotype about Asians in circulation today. Yet I would defend Chow's attempt to name these distinctions in the interest of defining group identity. In Asian American studies there is a disorienting outward movement toward theorizing a Pacific Rim, characterized by Rob Wilson and Arif Dirlik as a "hyper-capitalist . . . *terra incognita* of staggering complexity, discrepant hybridity, and nomadic flux" (1–2)—ironically at the same time that uncertainty arises on a more local level as to whether a designation such as "Asian American women" resists categorization on the basis of ethnic and class diversity.

While poststructuralism and standpoint theory have enabled a decentering of epistemological authority that acknowledges the legitimacy of people of color to create their own theories about themselves, as the essays in this volume explore, they can also be employed to undermine the very concept of group identity. The feminist theorist Nancy Hartsock notes that suspicion about creating totalizing narratives comes at a historically significant moment. In regard to the position of the marginalized critic in postmodernity, she asks, "(Why is it . . .) just when we are forming our own theories about the world, uncertainty emerges about whether the world can be adequately theorized? Just when we are talking about the changes we want, ideas of progress and the possibility of 'meaningfully' organizing human society become suspect?" (196). There is no simple answer to this postmodern contradiction, but I agree with Donna Haraway that "it is not enough to show radical historical contingency and modes of construction for everything" (579). Her call for a feminist objectivity "about limited location and situated knowledges" (583) is instructive and useful in negotiating the power/knowledge equation. Haraway's argument for embodying the nature of vision in defiance of the "conquering gaze from nowhere" (581), for "a view from a body . . . versus the view from above" (589), reauthorizes historical specificity as a basis for speaking and theorizing.

So even while I investigate the meaning and agenda behind critical naming, I do not hesitate to "speak as." I am still exploring ways of speaking personally in academic contexts that do not appear as grandstanding or self-indulgence but instead will mark my self-interest and stakes, as well as signal an accountability to the knowledges and experiences beyond my own positioning. The challenge is in the constitution of a critical authority based in an awareness of the-self-in-the-world that does not undermine or forego an ability to see the societal structures that exceed that self. In the interest of furthering Hartsock's call for progress and the "possibility of meaningfully organizing human society," I echo Cherríe Moraga when she writes, "If it takes head-on collisions, let's do it. This polite timidity is killing us" (*Loving* 59).

Leslie Bow

Notes

1. For an overview of the debates in the literary community provoked by Maxine Hong Kingston's *The Woman Warrior* and its implications for other Asian American writers, see Sara Solovitch, "Finding a Voice." In an academic context, the debates are most notably addressed in King-Kok Cheung, "The Woman Warrior versus the Chinaman Pacific"; Elaine Kim, "'Such Opposite Creatures'"; and Sau-ling Cynthia Wong, "Autobiography as Guided Chinatown Tour?"

2. The question takes on political overtones in the novel's portrayal of Jasmine's movement from old world immigrant to "adventurous" American as "genetic," not "hyphenated." In other words, the novel supports an ethnic assimilationist agenda in its suggestion that retaining ethnic ties in American culture represents a backward movement, a refusal to transform and grow. The overriding "betrayal" here is not necessarily of ethnic community per se (Jasmine has none) but of the most American of promises, that of self-transformation (Mukherjee 201).

3. In particular, Asians in the United States share a history around issues of naturalization and immigration policies, labor patterns, and bilingualism, as well as a specifically American "orientalism," racist discursive structures that elide and reduce the historical specificity of each Asian ethnic group.

4. There are limits to which "Asian American" can continue to present itself as a viable, unified subject position given the diversity of experience and history that it suggests. "Asian American" most often refers to Americans of Japanese, Chinese, Korean, Vietnamese, Thai, Hmong, Indonesian, Burmese, Kampuchean, South Asian, Filipino, and sometimes Pacific Islander origin. While "Asia" would imply a geographic connection to the continent, Japan, the Philippines, and other Pacific Islands (such as Hawaii and Guam) bear no such contiguity. In addition, the sovereignty movements and colonial history of Pacific Islanders more closely align them with American Indians than with Asian Americans. Geography is a somewhat arbitrary criterion for inclusion; immigrants from the Middle East are not considered Asian American, yet Edward Said's *orientalism* conflates the Middle East with the Far East and locates their inhabitants within the same discursive framework vis-à-vis the West. Moreover, nationalist antagonisms often transplanted to ethnic communities

in the United States also uncover the forced nature of the coalition; inherited or maintained ethnic nationalisms between Asian groups add to a list of obvious differences based on "home" culture, language, region, immigration history, generation, and class background. While no culture is monolithic or singular, the very diversity encompassed by the term "Asian American" indicates the difficulty in defining a cohesive group identity, highlighting the insupportability of any claim to "speak for" Asian America.

5. Another anthology, *Asian-American Authors,* edited by Kai-yu Hsu and Helen Palubinskas (Boston: Houghton Mifflin), was published in 1972.

6. Frank Chin quotation from Solovitch, "Finding a Voice" (20).

7. While the original volume included literature by Chinese, Japanese, and Filipino Americans, the subsequent anthology, *The Big Aiiieeeee!,* includes only Japanese and Chinese American writing, thereby excluding all other Asian ethnic groups. This absence is notably unremarked in the introduction. Interestingly, the editors' emphasis on authenticity may have undermined their own authority as Chinese and Japanese Americans to represent other Asian Americans in the second volume.

8. This connection certainly bears sustained scrutiny. Frank Chin's writing could serve as a viable warning about the nature of ideological consent and the ways in which alterity—in this case, gender difference—may serve to confirm the beliefs of the dominant culture. Unfortunately, his argument rests on two simple equivalencies, that feminism equals co-optation and that co-optation is necessary for commercial success. These equivalencies are so absolute that they lack complexity. While Chin's oppositional stance is part of the lifeblood of Asian American literature, it is ultimately directed toward the wrong target (Chin 8).

9. The debate in *New Literary History* (18, no. 2 [1987]) includes Joyce A. Joyce, "The Black Canon: Reconstructing Black American Literary Criticism," with responses by Houston A. Baker, Jr., "In Dubious Battle"; Henry Louis Gates, Jr., "What's Love Got to Do With It? Critical Theory, Integrity, and the Black Idiom"; and Joyce's response, "Who the Cap Fit: Unconsciousness and Unconscionableness in the Criticism of Houston A. Baker, Jr., and Henry Louis Gates, Jr."

Tey Diana Rebolledo raises similar questions for Chicano literary criticism in "The Politics of Poetics."

Commentaries by L. Ling-Chi Wang, Sucheng Chan, and Elaine H. Kim were initially delivered at the Association of Asian American Studies conference in 1990 and reprinted in *Amerasia Journal* (16, no. 2 [1990]), which also included a commentary by Russell C. Leong, viewpoints by Paul Wong, Frank Chin, and Karen Leonard, and two responses by Ronald Takaki.

10. The feeling that the voices of other researchers were subordinated to Takaki's narrative totality was reflected in criticisms about his handling of secondary sources. The responses of the Asian Americanists Ling-Chi Wang, Sucheng Chan, and Karen Leonard criticize Takaki for his failure to credit his sources clearly. With a more explicit accounting of the origins of his sources, Chan notes, "readers would more readily realize that the book could not pos-

sibly have been written without the combined efforts of hundreds of individuals over the last several decades" (84). For Chan, this would not be so significant if Takaki had not portrayed his position in the book as that of a "listener," a stance that counters what she finds to be a limited amount of "listening" done by way of original interviews.

11. The point that the text conforms to an American ideology is also reflected in E. San Juan, Jr., "Beyond Identity Politics." He writes, "Despite its encyclopedic scope and archival competence, Takaki's somewhat premature synthesis is a learned endeavor to deploy a strategy of containment. His rhetoric activates a mode of comic emplotment where all problems are finally resolved through hard work and individual effort, inspired by past memories of clan solidarity and intuitive faith in a gradually improving future. What is this if not a refurbished version of the liberal ideology of a market-centered, pluralist society where all disparities in values and beliefs—nay, even the sharpest contradictions implicating race, class, and gender—can be harmonized within the prevailing structure of power relations?" (546). Points such as these form what I see as the most significant critique of Takaki's book and why, despite the personal overtones in some of the responses printed in *Amerasia*, the dialogue contributes positively to Asian American studies.

12. Here I am referring to mainstream media representation. See, for example, Edward Iwata, "Hot Properties." The effect of this perception and of the high visibility of a writer like Amy Tan on an emerging canon remains to be seen.

13. Even as these controversies unfold, E. San Juan, Jr., questions the concept of Asian American cultural production as an oppositional strategy in its adherence to "the assumptions of identity politics, which functions as the controlling paradigm in mainstream comparative cultural studies." Such attention to identity politics, he writes, provides only the semblance of radicalism to the exclusion of developing alternative strategies "that can challenge the logic of liberal, possessive individualism and the seductive lure of consumerism" (549).

14. In autobiographical works by ethnic American writers, for example, issues of voice and literacy are linked to class, race, or gender consciousness, and writing functions as a catalyst for a fall from "wholeness" as the writer recognizes her/his alterity and the possibility of recovering a complete sense of self. Richard Wright connects a literal hunger born of poverty to hunger for the emotional sustenance provided by books; Richard Rodriguez links English literacy with the pain of familial loss; Maya Angelou recovers her voice through reading after a period of silence caused by childhood sexual abuse. In each case, writing is connected to an awareness of difference and the realization that the centrality of self we take for granted is not assumed by others.

15. Rodriguez borrows the phrase from Richard Hoggart's *Uses of Literacy* to describe the process of his academic success, the apparent cause of his increasing alienation from his working-class family. Because conservatives have used Rodriguez's personal narratives as proof of the inadequacies of bilingual

education and affirmative action, Rodriguez is held in suspicion by what he calls the "ethnic left." I am inclined to read his autobiography more sympathetically because it refuses to be glib about the intersection between race and class, making the unpopular move of ranking oppressions and suggesting that class position matters *more* than race in the United States. Rodriguez is certainly an example of an ethnic spokesperson unable to control or direct his own representation.

16. Spivak, "In a Word," interview by Ellen Rooney (*differences* 1 [Summer 1989]: 141).

17. The term "biological insiderism" is employed by Werner Sollors, and Tzvetan Todorov uses the term "cultural apartheid."

18. This jostling for critical hegemony is more interesting to me than the question about the adequacy of specific modes of theorizing to understand group experience. I like Norma Alarcon's metaphor of the "marriage" between theory and Chicana texts: "Look on them as an unhappy couple that has occasionally a nice dinner out" ("Chicana Literary Theory," lecture at the University of California, Santa Cruz, 1988).

19. I do not want to suggest that analyses of forms of racial domination falling under the rubric of cultural studies appropriates previous scholarly work or fails to take that work further. However, I question the suddenness with which this area of academic inquiry achieved scholarly legitimacy given that a generation of scholars in ethnic studies had been marginalized for precisely those interests. In discussing the "traffic jam . . . that black feminist studies has become," Ann duCille raises a similar concern. She notes that the explosion of interest in black women's literature and history has ironically had the effect of marginalizing "both the black women critics and scholars who excavated the fields in question and their black feminist 'daughters' who would further develop those fields" (596).

Works Cited

Alcott, Louisa May. *Eight Cousins*. Boston: Little, Brown, 1925.

Angelou, Maya. *I Know Why the Caged Bird Sings*. New York: Random House, 1970.

Anzaldúa, Gloria, ed. *Making Face, Making Soul/Haciendo Caras: Creative and Critical Perspectives by Women of Color*. San Francisco: Aunt Lute, 1990.

Awkward, Michael. "Race, Gender, and the Politics of Reading." *Black American Literature Forum* 22, no. 1 (1988): 5–27.

Blauvelt, William Satake. "Talking with 'The Woman Warrior.'" *Pacific Reader: International Examiner Literary Supplement*, July 19, 1989, 8.

Brontë, Charlotte. *Villette*. 1853. New York: Oxford University Press, 1990.

Carby, Hazel. *Reconstructing Womanhood: The Emergence of the Afro-American Woman Novelist*. New York: Oxford University Press, 1987.

Chan, Sucheng. *"Strangers from a Different Shore as History and Historiography."* *Amerasia Journal* 16, no. 2 (1990): 81–100.

Cheung, King-Kok. "The Woman Warrior versus the Chinaman Pacific: Must a Chinese American Critic Choose between Feminism and Heroism?" Pp. 234–51 in *Conflicts in Feminism*, ed. Marianne Hirsch and Evelyn Fox Keller. New York: Routledge, 1990.

Chin, Frank. "Come All Ye Asian American Writers of the Real and Fake." Pp. 1–92 in *The Big Aiiieeeee!*, ed. Chin et al.

Chin, Frank, Jeffrey Paul Chan, Lawson Fusao Inada, and Shawn Wong, eds. *Aiiieeeee!: An Anthology of Asian-American Writers*. Garden City, N.Y.: Anchor Press/Doubleday by arrangement with Howard University Press, 1974.

———, eds. *The Big Aiiieeeee!: An Anthology of Chinese American and Japanese American Literature*. New York: Penguin, 1991.

Chow, Esther Ngan-Ling. "The Feminist Movement: Where Are All the Asian American Women?" Pp. 362–77 in *Making Waves: An Anthology of Writings by and about Asian American Women*, ed. Asian Women United of California. Boston: Beacon Press, 1989.

Christian, Barbara. "The Race for Theory." *Feminist Studies* 14 (1988): 67–79.

Du Bois, W. E. B. "The Souls of Black Folk." Pp. 207–390 in *Three Negro Classics*. Introduction by John Hope Franklin. New York: Avon, 1965.

duCille, Ann. "The Occult of True Black Womanhood: Critical Demeanor and Black Feminist Studies." *Signs: Journal of Women in Culture and Society* 19 (1994): 591–629.

Fanon, Frantz. *Black Skin, White Masks*. 1952. Trans. Charles Lam Markmann. New York: Grove Weidenfeld, 1991.

Fischer, Michael M. J. "Ethnicity and the Post-Modern Arts of Memory." Pp. 194–223 in *Writing Culture: The Poetics and Politics of Ethnography*, ed. James Clifford and George E. Marcus. Berkeley: University of California Press, 1986.

Gates, Henry Louis, Jr. "Writing 'Race' and the Difference It Makes." Pp. 1–20 in *"Race," Writing, and Difference*, ed. Henry Louis Gates, Jr. Chicago: University of Chicago Press, 1985.

Graff, Gerald. "Academic Writing and the Uses of Bad Publicity." *South Atlantic Quarterly* 91, no. 1 (1992): 5–17.

Grosz, Elizabeth. "Sexual Difference and the Problem of Essentialism." *Inscriptions* 5 (1989): 86–101.

Haraway, Donna. "Situated Knowledges: The Science Question in Feminism and the Privilege of Partial Perspective." *Feminist Studies* 14 (1988): 575–99.

Hartsock, Nancy. "Rethinking Modernism: Minority vs. Majority Theories." *Cultural Critique* 7 (fall 1987): 187–206.

Hoggart, Richard. *Uses of Literacy: Aspects of Working-Class Life, with Special Reference to Publications and Entertainments*. London: Chatto and Windus, 1957.

hooks, bell. *Talking Back*. Boston: South End Press, 1989.

Iwata, Edward. "Hot Properties, More Asian Americans Suddenly Are Winning Mainstream Literary Acclaim." *Los Angeles Times*, Sept. 11, 1989.

Jameson, Fredric. "On 'Cultural Studies.'" *Social Text* 34 (1993): 17–52.

Kaplan, Amy. "'Left Alone with America': The Absence of Empire in the Study of American Culture." Pp. 3–21 in *Cultures of United States Imperialism*, ed.

Amy Kaplan and Donald E. Pease. Durham, N.C.: Duke University Press, 1993.

Kerouac, Jack. *On the Road*. 1955. New York: Penguin, 1976.

Kim, Elaine. "A Critique of *Strangers from a Different Shore*." *Amerasia Journal* 16, no. 2 (1990): 101–11.

———. "'Such Opposite Creatures': Men and Women in Asian American Literature." *Michigan Quarterly Review* 29, no. 1 (1990): 68–93.

Kingston, Maxine Hong. *China Men*. 1977. New York: Ballantine, 1980.

———. *Maxine Hong Kingston Talking Story*. Produced by Joan Suffa and Steve Talbot. Directed by Joan Saffa. CrossCurrent Media National Asian American Telecommunications Association (NAATA), 1991. Videocassette.

———. *The Woman Warrior: Memoirs of a Girlhood among Ghosts*. New York: Random House, 1975.

Ling, Amy. "I'm Here: An Asian American Woman's Response." *New Literary History* 19, no. 1 (1987): 151–60.

Lowe, Lisa. "Heterogeneity, Hybridity, Multiplicity: Marking Asian American Differences." *Diaspora* 1, no. 1 (1991): 24–44.

McDowell, Deborah. "New Directions for Black Feminist Criticism." Pp. 186–99 in *The New Feminist Criticism: Essays on Women, Literature, and Theory*, ed. Elaine Showalter. New York: Pantheon Books, 1985.

———. "Reading Family Matters." Pp. 75–97 in *Changing Our Own Words*, ed. Wall.

Miller, Jane. *Seductions*. Cambridge, Mass.: Harvard University Press, 1991.

Mohanty, Chandra Talpade. "Cartographies of Struggle: Third World Women and the Politics of Feminism." Pp. 1–47 in *Third World Women and the Politics of Feminism*, ed. Chandra Talpade Mohanty, Ann Russo, and Lourdes Torres. Bloomington: Indiana University Press, 1991.

Moi, Toril. *Sexual/Textual Politics: Feminist Literary Theory*. London: Methuen, 1985.

Moraga, Cherríe. *Loving in the War Years*. Boston: South End Press, 1983.

———. "Refugees of a World on Fire." Pp. i–iv in *This Bridge Called My Back*, ed. Cherríe Moraga and Gloria Anzaldúa. Latham, N.Y.: Kitchen Table: Women of Color Press, 1983.

Mukherjee, Bharati. *Jasmine*. New York: Ballantine, 1989.

Quan, Kit Yuen. "The Girl Who Wouldn't Sing." Pp. 212–20 in *Making Face, Making Soul/Haciendo Caras*, ed. Anzaldúa.

Rebolledo, Tey Diana. "The Politics of Poetics: Or, What Am I, A Critic, Doing in This Text Anyhow?" Pp. 346–55 in *Making Face, Making Soul/Haciendo Caras*, ed. Anzaldúa.

Reed, Ishmael. *Reckless Eyeballing*. New York: St. Martin's, 1986.

Rodriguez, Richard. *Hunger of Memory: The Education of Richard Rodriguez*. New York: Bantam, 1982.

San Juan, E., Jr. "Beyond Identity Politics: The Predicament of the Asian American Writer in Late Capitalism." *American Literary History* 3 (1991): 542–65.

Smith, Valerie. "Black Feminist Theory and the Representation of the 'Other.'" Pp. 38–57 in *Changing Our Own Words*, ed. Wall.

Sollors, Werner. *Beyond Ethnicity: Consent and Descent in American Culture.* New York: Oxford University Press, 1986.

Solovitch, Sara. "Finding a Voice." *San Jose Mercury News,* June 30, 1991, 18–22.

Spivak, Gayatri Chakravorty. *In Other Worlds: Essays in Cultural Politics.* New York: Routledge, 1988.

Tan, Amy. *The Joy Luck Club.* New York: Ballantine, 1989.

Todorov, Tzvetan. "'Race,' Writing, and Culture." Pp. 370–80 in *"Race," Writing, and Difference,* ed. Henry Louis Gates, Jr. Chicago: University of Chicago Press, 1985.

Wall, Cheryl A. *Changing Our Own Words: Essays on Criticism, Theory, and Writing by Black Women.* New Brunswick, N.J.: Rutgers University Press, 1989.

Wang, Ling-Chi. "A Critique of *Strangers from a Different Shore.*" *Amerasia Journal* 16, no. 2 (1990): 71–80.

Wilson, Rob, and Arif Dirlik. "Asian/Pacific as Space of Cultural Production." *boundary 2* 21, no. 1 (1994): 1–14.

Wong, Sau-ling Cynthia. "Autobiography as Guided Chinatown Tour? Maxine Hong Kingston's *The Woman Warrior* and the Chinese American Autobiography Controversy." Pp. 248–79 in *Multicultural Autobiography: American Lives,* ed. James Robert Payne. Knoxville: University of Tennessee Press, 1992.

Wright, Richard. *The Outsider.* New York: Harper and Brothers, 1953.

Yamada, Mitsuye. "Masks of Women." Pp. 89–91 in *Desert Run: Poems and Stories.* Latham, N.Y.: Kitchen Table: Women of Color Press, 1988.

3

Personal Criticism and the Academic Personality

The incidence of scholars—most notably academic feminists—speaking about voice, identity, and positionality, among other personal topics, has greatly increased in the last decade. One opponent to such voicing identified herself as a "skeptical, secular humanist, Jewish, feminist, intellectual lawyer, currently residing in the Ivy League," an identification she hurriedly described as a joke. Yet the joke has found its target: When did it become necessary for critics to signal *all* the groups to which they belong, to announce the intellectual and social framework they see as characterizing their positions? What underlies this practice that Linda Alcoff calls the "problem of speaking for others," a problem she describes as deriving from identity politics, of "speaking from" a particular position (7)?[1]

Some skeptics argue that the emphasis in the current academic scene on personal criticism is a way of establishing the academic personality within institutional contexts that often erase professorial differences. Most recently, scholars have felt the need to assert their individuality, their difference, within a social context that identifies people by groups, ethnicities, genders, and sexualities and that superficially equates ideas with subject positions. Yet I would argue that the recent concern for voice is a way of asking another question: What *effect* can the "I"—the individual professor—have in a world in which effects are often lost? What authority can "I" claim in a world where the very concept of authority (let alone feminist authority) has been rendered problematic and undermined? Asking this question shifts the emphasis from the personal to the rhetorical, what I see as the struggle to speak authoritatively. While this emphasis on the personal can be read as an assertion of individualism, it can also be seen as redirecting the effects of ideas in *and* on the world. In the search for an authenticity that might be authoritative, the necessity is to avoid producing "personal" criticism with the same predictability—and perhaps irrelevance—as the analysis of water imagery in *The Mill on the Floss.*

One source of this predictability is the overwhelming sameness of the bourgeois experience and the dullness of aspiration that goes into the formation of the academic personality. For some reason, professors resist seeing themselves as part of a group, although they may see themselves as belonging to a subgroup that insists on both their difference and the difference they could make. Imagine, for instance, how startled we are to learn that, despite our special efforts at class preparation and the ways we particularize our readings, many of our students think that we are virtually interchangeable. Their greatest praise on a course evaluation is that this professor is truly different, a shocked recognition of our humanity, because in general we seem all too drearily alike. Our anxiety compels us to individuate ourselves— like the sibling rivalry that underlies so much of the pettiness and bitterness of departmental politics—when we try to shore up our ambivalence about the "difference" we make, narcissistically imagining that we are in the academic world but not of it. It is easy to imagine this intellectual distance since there no longer seems to be a shared, public discursive arena, except perhaps through the authenticating power of private experience made public. This ostensible absence of a shared public discourse leads scholars to the recourse of the personal. Writing about the personal aims to recapture the immediacy of context and to suggest an authoritative experiential stance but which, no surprise here, seems only to reify the personal.

My questions for this essay concern this very recent discourse about academic feminist voice, especially as that voice is sounded as a reaction to institutionalization, although it is often more coded in academic writing than it is in student prose (but not always). What might the voice of professorial resistance be? What forms might it take? Can professorial resistance learn something from the student voice of resistance, perhaps not in kind, but in intensity? The need for students to speak authoritatively about their own cultures has informed many essays on student learning and resistance; these essays claim that students talk back when faced with what Paulo Freire has called the banking model of education, whereby teachers invest knowledge in the empty vessels of their students and students cash in on this revered wisdom.

Whether it be from critical or feminist pedagogies, one of the blithe assumptions of these educational theories is that resistance is good and that we ought to be fostering student resistance as a form of critical thinking, teaching students the value of their own cultural authority, and thereby bolstering what critical pedagogy theorists like Henry Giroux call "transformative authority." As Giroux states, "The discourse of student experience supports a view of pedagogy and empowerment that allows students to draw upon their own experiences and cultural resources and that also enables them to play a self-consciously active role as producers of knowledge within the teaching and learning process" (148). Giroux and others have argued that fostering a climate for student voices allows students to resist whatever co-optation they see in the schooling process while also encouraging them to transform that process. While students were urged in the 1980s to take critical control of their education, the very professors who have been urging this agency or critical resistance seem to have been silenced themselves—whether by attacks for or against political correctness, by institutional co-optation, or by sheer exhaustion from the academic speedup and specialization that have hit every discipline.[2] How would professors themselves gain a transformative authority, offering a voice that is not merely personal but also productive of dialogue?

In this essay, I want to discuss a particular example of student voice and compare it to some examples of academic feminists making claims for their political differences and their ambivalence about the academy. In a decade dominated by identity politics and communities of consensus, it is no accident that students and professors alike are proclaiming their individual differences from peers and colleagues. This move provides both groups with a form of resistance to the overwhelming emphasis on identity (and the assumption of a certain sameness of interest and politics), but it does not yet develop the rhetorical model of identification I will be charting here.

Identification is defined in various contexts as a rhetorical strategy: "You persuade a man only insofar as you can talk his language by speech, gesture, tonality, order, image, attitude, idea, *identifying* your ways with his" (Burke 55); as a mode of personal alliance or recognition, "identification—the very process by which subjects say, '*I am like* him or her' [in contrast to] object choice—the process by which subjects say '*I like* him or her'" (Williams 215); or as a form of political commitment, "strong group-identification across politically charged boundaries, whether of gender, of class, of race, of sexuality, of nation" (Sedgwick 59). While the use of personal voice is a claim of individual identity, it is also a rhetorical move, as the quotations from Kenneth Burke, Linda Williams, and Eve Sedgwick suggest. In identification, we recognize our alterity from the subject we see as "like" (but not the same as) the self and, in doing so, we can imagine a political or affective investment in others, not based on identity but on difference.

For example, many women's studies students must negotiate their identification with feminist ideals against their peers' resistance to "being a feminist." One student spoke about her negotiation with feminism in the following way:

> I felt that the class has helped me to a very comfortable medium between extreme leftist feminism and stuffy conservatism. The most important, and most amusing conclusion I came to was that you can still be a feminist without being a "feminist." Understand?
> . . . The entire institution of feminism has gotten a somewhat negative name in our society. I never hear the end of "Why are you taking that rideculous [*sic*] man hating class?" Through these comments I have learned to defend my ground, often turning my defense into a battleground by heated debates. . . . I was never aware of the closed mind [of the] society in which we live until taking this class. With my new found knowledge from this course I have tried many times to pass it along to others, sometimes unsuccessfully, other times I have simply been asked, "Who is brainwashing you?"

This student negotiates her peers' resistance to feminism and her own ambivalence about "leftist feminism" and "stuffy conservatism" by differentiating herself from "feminism" (in scare quotes) and the feminist debate in which she has learned to engage. While confronting both the "closed mind" of contemporary society and the "brainwashing" her friends fear, the student carves out a spot for herself by testing herself through debate and conversation about sexuality, gender equity, and equality versus difference. She first defends, then "passes along" her beliefs, a mode of resistance to feminism's "negative name" that enables her to resist, then to identify her commitment. The women's studies class becomes a place to distinguish herself and her beliefs dialogically from the conservative mainstream while also affirming the particular content of feminist commitments she has undertaken.

Do professors voice their attitudes toward institutions, institutionalization, or their resistance to conservatism and brainwashing (that is, co-optation) in the same way? Ellen Rosenman, a feminist teacher at a state university in the South, said this about working as a joint-appointed faculty member in two departments, English and women's studies: "The whole network of public/private metaphors, like 'home' department, the 'woman's work' of advising and mentoring, colleagues as 'sisters' or 'mothers' or 'daughters,' has been very confusing for me and other women I know. . . . Even though most of my intellectual and emotional network is in women's studies, . . . the family metaphors at work *there* are equally damaging in the expectations for endless nurturing and accessibility that they confer on women faculty" (personal correspondence, Dec. 9,1992). Rosenman writes about the failure of home departments to be centers of "political advocacy" for marginalized faculty members. But what prevents professors from voicing their resistance to institutional co-optation or from engaging in political advocacy? Why is professorial resistance—whether from left-, center-, or right-leaning academics—so often limited, at worst ineffectual, and at best ambivalent?

This ambivalence manifests itself in a variety of ways. One professor I know circulated a departmental memo showing how the amount of research on Maxine Hong Kingston was not surpassing that on "dead white males." Her memo stated that there have been 64 CD-ROM entries for Kingston in the last eleven years; entries on "Living White American Authors" (one of the "four playfully named categories not meant to offend anyone") have accumulated 445 on Thomas Pynchon and 112 on Norman Mailer (Anne Tyler has 33; Ann Beattie has 18). This professor's memo explained that colleagues who were anxious about the overwhelming rate of scholarly production on women and ethnic writers need not fear; "dead white male authors"—versus dead and living white female and "ethnic" writers—retain their prominence in CD-ROM citations (and elsewhere). While this memo invoked the general fear about the waning of traditional scholarship only to disprove its justifications by measuring the relative inconsequentiality of the work on Kingston as "a drop in the bucket," it also—perhaps unconsciously—revealed the professor's own desire to mark her difference from her colleagues who assume *their* marginality in the profession and remain silent about it. Albeit ambivalent, hers is an important gesture because it seeks to counter an (often) unspoken dismissal of the significant work on women and ethnicity being undertaken in departments across the country.

It is hard to miss the irony of the female complaint lodged here, no matter how whimsical the categories about "dead white males." This attempt at professorial resistance—or defense—is significant insofar as it is lodged in mock aggression against the traditional canonical authors, who are symbolic substitutes for the colleagues with whom this scholar is really waging battle but whom she cannot acknowledge as her opposition (unlike the student who named her reluctant peers as her antagonists). Often, in professorial resistance, an inability to define the locus of one's ambivalence, the result of a diffusion of bureaucratic power, leads to an internalization of defeat. For instance, when I became associate chair of women's studies in 1992, I found the following directions to new women's studies administrators at the end of a memo: "If you ever did any rat psych you'll do okay. But this time you're the rat and there's no pellet of food at the end." Again, this joke marks a resistance to—or at least ironic recognition of—the ambivalent state of institutional bureaucracies, but where does this ambivalence go? What happens to ambivalence left unresolved? One scholar I know skips every third department meeting, if only to show the effect of her absence, a strategy that we could call "willed illness." Others find their strength in opposition to the home department's status quo in practicing their counterstance. Still others need to uphold the existing power relations within their departments in order to continue their oppositionality.

In response to the continued opposition of students and of many administrations, academic feminists are facing up to their internalization of attack from the outside and from within, especially from self-identified feminists like Katie Roiphe and Christina Hoff Sommers. Feminist scholars have always been aware of the need to anticipate such trouble; two prominent examples come to mind, one from bell hooks's *Talking Back* (1989) and the other from queer theorist Eve Sedgwick's *Epistemology of the Closet* (1990). These examples emerge both from the authors' experiences as feminist teachers and from their struggle with authority in the classroom. First, hooks describes her classroom style:

> My classroom style is very confrontational. . . . I encourage students to work at coming to voice in an atmosphere where they may be afraid or see themselves at risk. . . . [Many students] do not usually come away from my class talking about how much they enjoyed the experience. . . . Often I did not feel liked or affirmed and this was difficult for me to accept. (53)

Second, Sedgwick describes her confessed discomfort in the classroom:

> I think, for instance, of a graduate class I taught a few years ago in gay and lesbian literature. Half the students in the class were men, half women. Throughout the semester all the women, including me, intensely uncomfortable with the dynamics of the class and hyperconscious of the problems of articulating lesbian with gay male perspectives, attributed our discomfort to some obliquity in the classroom relations between ourselves and the men. But by the end of the semester it seemed clear that we were in the grip of some much more intimate dissonance. . . . it appeared that each woman in the class possessed (or might, rather, feel we were possessed by) an ability to make one or more of the other women radically and excruciatingly doubt the authority of her own self-defi-

nition as a woman; as a feminist; and as the positional subject of a
particular sexuality. (61)

These examples demonstrate the fears about professional vulnerability
that are the inevitable result of academic personalities and personal criticism in the classroom. Regardless of their critical strengths, both hooks
and Sedgwick feel the dissonance of negotiating their critical work with
their personal boundaries. On the right, too, there is a legion of examples about the dissonance of classroom life, especially in Martin Anderson's *Impostors in the Temple* (1992) or Thomas Sowell's *Inside American
Education* (1993), which offers a catalogue of abuses in classrooms.
These adversarial duels, however, reveal how both the right and the left
are feeling the heat of the classroom in particular and how both sides
lament the lack of professorial resistance in general.

The general resistance to the status quo is based on many professors' senses of being outside of power and beyond identification with
the institution. Moreover, in her own show of ambivalence, bell
hooks's desire to be liked and affirmed suggests how the institution
forces her into conflicted goals of seeking personal affirmation while
confronting student complacency. While hooks and Sedgwick may
prefer the "liking and affirming" part of their pedagogies, their testimonies are important insofar as they recognize their difference from
their students and the difficulty of constructing community in the
classroom based on any singular notions of identity. Indeed, as Sedgwick suggests, professorial resistance is bound up with classroom confrontation, making the yearning for "likeness" and "liking" harder to
abandon for the importance of forging more political identifications,
generally across differences.

In the personal criticism of other feminist critics, too, context and
personal voice are also invoked in order to recapture political circumstances of conversion, persuasion, and individual transformation or to
bolster a sense of commitment to feminism. Jane Gallop writes that
reading Jean-Jacques Rousseau's *Julie* (1761) in graduate school made
her cry; reading the Marquis de Sade moved her to masturbate (18).
Nancy Miller argues that giving up the "masterful" position of authority in the classroom, "in favor of a more ambiguous and less predictable pedagogy" (41), made her question the "seductions" involved in
traditional pedagogy. She challenges the value of asking students to
identify with her, whether as a form of "female narcissism," "psychic
miming," or "role modeling" (39). Confessing her dissatisfaction with
the academic mode, Jane Tompkins wants more intimate connections
in her student-centered classrooms; she is tired of the "performance

model" of teaching and academic life, preferring to express her grief over the suicide of her friend Janice and her interest in the birds outside her window ("Me and My Shadow").

Linda Kauffman tells her history of life on the road with her father, a Bible salesman and grifter, and her own stint as a janitor in Orange County, showing how these experiences led her to become the kind of feminist she is. After five pages of writing about her identification as an academic feminist, Kauffman argues: "Writing about yourself does not liberate you, it just shows how ingrained the ideology of freedom through self-expression is in our thinking" (269). In this ironic play, Kauffman enacts exactly what she is criticizing. Or is her confessing unselfconscious, though no less moving for being so? Kauffman's confusion in writing academic personal criticism as a form of professorial resistance to business as usual has her "straining"—a word she repeats in the course of her essay (262, 266). She wants to make "being a feminist" politically useful, which she qualifies by saying, "I have not everything to do, but something. . . . My happiness, frankly, is not very important in the grand scheme of things. I never thought feminism was about happiness" (273–74). The desperate longing for a sense of purpose—whether personal, academic, or social—underwrites all of these rhetorical turns in feminist criticism.

In short, I have just catalogued some of the best-known academic feminists confessing their grief, pain, and despair over teaching feminism in the academy. Yet even as I say this, I fear my tone will be misunderstood, and I want to be careful not to dismiss each critic's invocation and enactment of the personal in her writing. I have read persuasive pieces arguing against Gallop's, Tompkins's, and Miller's integrations of the personal in academic prose. A host of detractors in the pages of *College English* (53, no. 4 and 5 [1991] and 54, no. 4 [1992]), which published Tompkins's much maligned "Pedagogy of the Distressed," attacked her in tones ranging from indignation over her privilege in the academy (Carroll 600) to the ironic judgment— "Poor Jane Tompkins!" (Martin 356). The rage against Tompkins's call for personal voice in academic writing and teaching is telling, a vehemence that Gallop, Miller, Sedgwick, and hooks have also had directed against them. (It is no coincidence that Miller spends the first thirty pages in *Getting Personal* defending Tompkins's incorporation of grief, melancholia, and mourning into her "academic" prose.) This fury indicates their criticism's effectiveness and the fear (on the right) that academic feminism is again driving up the stakes of professional commitment.

What is clear from this trend in academic feminist discourse and the response to it is that the classroom no longer seems the place to contain one's politics; the new trend is to look beyond the academy for an ever larger identification with larger audiences and larger venues for political commitment. Thus, the question of who can speak in the public realm (as opposed to the academic arena) has recently dominated feminist debates, an argument in large part sparked by the ready access to the media afforded to counterfeminists like Christina Hoff Sommers. As Susan Friedman suggests in "Making History," Sommers's self-identification as a feminist is belied by her attacks on women's studies and her claim to "greater objectivity" when "she laments the contamination of reasonable feminism by the destructive distortions of irrational excess" (7, 10).

Sommers certainly indicts personal criticism as an example of the excess of academic feminist discourse. I disagree. In this light, the drive for personality in criticism especially can be understood as not really personal at all but a very structured rhetorical move. If anything, the tendency—and its popularity—shows the social formation of the academic personality and the academic's dissatisfaction, in our criticism, with pleading our case to a public of like-minded professors (hence, even Sommers sells her book to a publisher that will move her out of traditional academic circles). The yearning for a truly public audience beyond the classroom or departmental experience might happen through a change in our discourse and the way we cast issues, not merely through personal disclosures or identity claims about our tentative individual or group associations. Although this seems the logical first step, for too many it becomes the only step. In the personal confession lies the logic of privatization, for the confession only veils the bourgeois academic personality's desire for public acceptance. Such recognition is indeed the goal of feminist discourse, but for the recognition of political commitment, not the confessor. In this sense, the confession of personal experience yokes together the rhetoric of individualism with the desire for a public audience.

When we hear the charges against PC rhetoric (whether PC means "political correctness" or "personal confession"), we can also interpret those contentions as resistance to the greater ironic distance and division that mark the professorial life. We have an excess of ethical calls, from Quaker Oats commercials ("It's the right thing to do") to Spike Lee's exhortation (*Do the Right Thing*), seemingly locating all these pleas on the same plane.[3] It is not the scarcity of personal appeals in our culture but their excess that makes feminist personal and pedagogical confessions in scholarly essays so disturbing and, at the same time, so memorable. But we hear them at a time when the culture has been so saturated with appeals to ethical choice that it is almost impossible to hear these rhetorical voices—whether from Miller, Gallop, Tompkins, hooks, or Sedgwick—without the cynical conjecture that there is nothing different about them; they are like the advertisements for the cotton industry about "the fabric of our lives," oversimplifying the democratic weaves of our identities. Simply dismissing these appeals as purely ironic or purely PC, and thus asserting our ironic distance, is to undermine our important transformative authority while trivializing the strategy of personal identifications and the important rhetorical work they are intended to perform.

The case I am making here for the rhetorical strategy of identification is crucial because the whole point of confession and personal criticism is identificatory. For better, I think, rather than worse, a whole generation of new feminist scholars looks to the previous one for models of identification. They do so not to establish their scholarly identities but to identify and align themselves with some sort of affective investment with the history of feminism and academic life. The rhetorical work of the personal confession, then, can be effective. In a culture that makes being a professor of the humanities, much less women's studies, often demoralizing, we have to show that the way we make our subjects matter is to make our subjectivity matter most. So the best kind of teaching evaluation we could receive from students is not, as I have written above, that students are startled to perceive something of our humanity and our difference, but that they recognize our investments in what Lawrence Grossberg movingly calls "the particular content of a commitment" (230). Nothing in our culture confirms what professors, for the most part, do, because in many senses we appear as the new clerics of the culture; we are even understood as a little ascetic. If we do indeed function this way, it becomes our responsibility to create a model of identification so that what we teach will be invested again in ideological and intellectual commitment.

The question is not whether we should have personal academic criticism or not; it really has always existed, and it flourishes now because feminists have been resisting our institutionalization—just as we should. Each generation of feminist scholars has had its challenge, and ours above all is to keep the discipline vital precisely at the time society, the economy, and conventional politics are making it increasingly difficult for us to thrive. Most feminist professors I know have to fight on a daily basis the temptation to give up. The level of frustration can be overwhelming. However, to surrender to frustration is to make private deals in the name that we are just too exhausted to go on and to accept our co-optation in the name of "being realistic."

Finally, I do not say that we should indulge in telling futile, quixotic stories merely to help us differentiate ourselves from the colleagues we hate to be mistaken for. I do say, however, that in our reading of the rhetoric of personal identification and autobiography we must be careful not to confuse the differentiation of personal identity with that of ideological position. An effective professorial resistance to the academy's business as usual cannot afford to invest in merely private pursuits when we need more crucial identifications, more identifications *with* than divisions *from*. In order to avoid an "affective epidemic" (Grossberg), where everyone talks about their own beliefs as though that would make them national popular celebrities, we need to be clearer about what rhetorical identifications want to persuade people *to do*. Personal testimonies and autobiographical criticism in general too often stop at the identification, rather than spell out the persuasion or commitment that is always the next step of identificatory rhetoric. Linda Kauffman is right when she says that we need to do "something," but academic feminists and others have not always named what that something is. And perhaps the "something" to which she vaguely refers, combined with the sense of longing (or nostalgia) for collectivity expressed in many academic feminist confessions, will propel us beyond the indifference with which most professors feel they are treated (reported in the 1994 Carnegie Foundation report on "The Academic Profession: An International Perspective"). At a time when we need to move beyond individual resistance to a more collective form, the question is not "Who can speak?" but "How can we speak in a culture that treats the academy indifferently, trivially, sometimes contemptuously?"

Within feminist circles, this is also a generational affair: while the first generation of academic feminists established women's studies programs through the community and through activism, there is a new generation of academic feminists working without the benefit of community activism as a background to their academic or institutional work. Some of that activist sense of purpose is gone, since the new generation of feminist scholars has learned their feminism (for the most part) from within the academy. Perhaps the confessional mode in much current feminist theorizing is a needed attempt to find community through theorizing one's experience. In this light, the attempts by Miller, Gallop, hooks, Tompkins, Sedgwick, and many others are necessary moves to establish a community that has dissipated through the institutional success, new specialization, and establishment status of women's studies. These academic feminists are dealing, then, with their ambivalence about the institutional success of the feminist movement originally designed to be countercultural rather than institutional. Personal confessions as a mark of community building, even a kind of political activism, are also a sign of our difference from a previous generation of feminists.

That is the next important phase of our critical work, I confess: we need to theorize the ambivalence in which we find ourselves, between the impasse of identity politics and the public sphere and institutional arena, where our rhetorical actions need to count most.

Dale M. Bauer

Notes

I want to thank several colleagues at the University of Wisconsin–Madison for their intellectual generosity: Jane Collins, Nancy Kaiser, Amy Ling, Mimi Orner, Gina Sapiro, Sarah Zimmerman, and Gordon Hutner. I am also grateful to Pam Matthews, Ellen Rosenman, and Elaine Orr for their comments and ongoing discussions about women's studies and feminist pedagogy.

1. In a 1993 issue of the *Nation*, Wendy Kaminer responds to the review of her critique of self-help books and self-help culture, *I'm Dysfunctional, You're Dysfunctional*, by an explanation of a witticism in her book that misfired: "When I identified myself as a 'skeptical, secular humanist, Jewish, feminist, intellectual lawyer, currently residing in the Ivy League,' I was joking. . . . As I explained when I offered it, this description of myself was a list of categories reviled by popular, religious self-help writers; it amused me to realize that I might be accused of belonging to each of them. But most of all, this categorical self-portrait satirized the postmodern academic tradition of deconstructing yourself, which seemed to me an amusing analogue to the popular recovery tradition of testifying. It still surprises me that people take such silly statements so seriously" (146). Kaminer readily dismisses identity politics as a form of self-help testifying, or confessing, intended apparently to help individuals recover from their postmodern lightness of being. Yet it is not so surprising that people—even academics—take self-categorizing seriously rather than as an "amusing" new academic trend. Whatever the reasons, the need to "testify" or confess has traversed social classes and professions, and academics (postmodern or otherwise) are not exempt. This battle has also been waged in the *Chronicle of Higher Education* between Daphne Patai (Feb. 23, 1994) and Ruth Behar (June 29, 1994), where Behar challenges Patai's claim that the academic personal voice is solipsistic.

2. Gregory Jay argues that many academics lack training in the public sphere and, indeed, in the rhetorical sphere; "expert at such media as the sophomore lecture, the graduate seminar, the job interview, the grant application, the critical article, the devastating footnote, the self-righteous polemic, the self-deceptive memo, the dazzling theoretical digression, or the arcane

treatise," Jay's ironic list suggests just how limited our sphere of influence really is (20). (In our defense, Jay claims that the "academic speedup" leaves us all struggling to "keep up.")

3. I thank Charles Harmon for his witty response to my work and for this formulation (personal correspondence).

Works Cited and Consulted

Alcoff, Linda. "The Problem of Speaking for Others." *Cultural Critique* 20 (Winter 1991–92): 5–32.

Anderson, Martin. *Impostors in the Temple.* New York: Simon and Schuster, 1992.

Bakhtin, Mikhail. "Discourse in the Novel." Pp. 259–422 in *The Dialogic Imagination.* Trans. Caryl Emerson and Michael Holquist. Austin: University of Texas Press, 1981.

Bauer, Dale M. "The Other 'F' Word." *College English* 52, no. 4 (1990): 385–96.

Bauer, Dale M., and Susan C. Jarratt. "Feminist Sophistics: Teaching with an Attitude." Pp. 149–65 in *Changing Classroom Practices,* ed. David Downing. Urbana: National Council of Teachers of English, 1994.

Behar, Ruth. "Dare We Say 'I'? Bringing the Personal into Scholarship." *Chronicle of Higher Education,* June 29, 1994.

Bernstein, Susan. "Confessing Feminist Theory: What's 'I' Got to Do with It?" *Hypatia* 7, no. 2 (1992): 120–47.

Burke, Kenneth. *A Rhetoric of Motives.* Berkeley: University of California Press, 1950.

Carroll, Michael. "A Comment on 'Pedagogy of the Distressed.'" *College English* 53, no. 5 (1991): 599–601.

Freire, Paulo. *Pedagogy of the Oppressed.* Trans. Myra Bergman Ramos. New York: Continuum, 1981.

Friedman, Susan. "Making History: Reflections on Feminism, Narrative, and Desire." In *Feminism Beside Itself,* ed. Diane Elam and Robyn Wiegman. New York: Routledge, forthcoming.

Gallop, Jane. *Thinking Through the Body.* New York: Columbia University Press, 1988.

Giroux, Henry. "Schooling as a Form of Cultural Politics: Toward a Pedagogy of and for Difference." Pp. 125–51 in *Critical Pedagogy, the State, and Cultural Struggle,* ed. Henry Giroux and Peter McLaren. Albany: State University of New York Press, 1989.

Gitlin, Todd. "From Universality to Difference: Notes on the Fragmentation of the Idea of the Left." *Contention* 2, no. 2 (1993): 15–40.

Grossberg, Lawrence. *We Gotta Get Out of This Place: Popular Conservatism and Postmodern Culture.* New York: Routledge, 1992.

Honan, William H. "Professors in 14-Nation Study Say Their Ideas Are Ignored." *New York Times,* June 20, 1994.

hooks, bell. *Talking Back.* Boston: South End Press, 1989.

Jay, Gregory S. "Knowledge, Power, and the Struggle for Representation." *College English* 56, no. 1 (1994): 9–29.

Kaminer, Wendy. Letter to the Editor. *Nation*, Feb. 8, 1993, 146.

Kauffman, Linda. "The Long Goodbye: Against Personal Testimony, or an Infant Grifter Grows Up." Pp. 258–77 in *American Feminist Thought at Century's End: A Reader*, ed. Linda S. Kauffman. Cambridge: Blackwell, 1993.

Laclau, Ernesto. "Theory, Democracy and Socialism." Pp. 197–213 in *New Reflections on the Revolution of Our Time*. London: Verso, 1990.

Martin, Robert M. "Comment on 'Pedagogy of the Distressed.'" *College English* 54, no. 3 (1992): 356–58.

Miller, Nancy. *Getting Personal: Feminist Occasions and Other Autobiographical Acts*. New York: Routledge, 1991.

Penley, Constance. "Feminism, Psychoanalysis, and the Study of Popular Culture." Pp. 479–500 in *Cultural Studies*, ed. Lawrence Grossberg, Cary Nelson, and Paula Treichler. New York: Routledge, 1992.

Sedgwick, Eve Kosofsky. *Epistemology of the Closet*. Berkeley: University of California Press, 1990.

Sowell, Thomas. *Inside American Education*. New York: Free Press, 1993.

Tompkins, Jane. "Me and My Shadow." *New Literary History* 19, no. 1 (1987): 197–200.

———. "Pedagogy of the Distressed." Pp. 169–78 in *Changing Classroom Practices*, ed. David Downing. Urbana: National Council of Teachers of English, 1994.

Van Leer, David. "Beast of the Closet: Homosociality and the Pathology of Manhood." *Critical Inquiry* 15 (1989): 758–63.

Williams, Linda. *Hard Core*. Berkeley: University of California Press, 1989.

4

A Black Man's Place(s)
in Black Feminist Criticism

The main theoretical task for male feminists, then, is to develop
an analysis of their own position, and a strategy for how their
awareness of their difficult and contradictory position in relation
to feminism can be made explicit in discourse and practice.

    —Toril Moi, "Men Against Patriarchy"

She had been looking all along for a friend, and it took her a
while to discover that a [male] lover was not a comrade and
could never be—for a woman.

    —Toni Morrison, *Sula*

Critics eternally become and embody the generative myths of
their culture by half-perceiving and half-inventing their culture,
their myths, and themselves.

    —Houston A. Baker, Jr., *Afro-American Poetics*

Many essays by male and female scholars devoted to exploring the
subject of male critics' place(s) in feminism generally agree about the
uses and usefulness of the autobiographical male "I." Such essays suggest that citing the male critical self reflects a response to (apparent)
self-difference—on the one hand, an exploration of the disparities between the masculine's antagonistic position in feminist discourse and,
on the other, the desire of the individual male critic to represent his
differences with and from the traditional androcentric perspectives of
his gender and culture. Put another way, in male feminist acts, to
identify the writing self as biologically male is to emphasize the desire
not to be ideologically male; it is to explore the process of rejecting
the phallocentric perspectives by which men traditionally have justified the subjugation of women.[1]

In what strikes me as a particularly suggestive theoretical fo
tion, Joseph Boone articulates his sense of the goals of such ma.. ....
inist autobiographical acts:[2]

> In exposing the latent multiplicity and difference in the word
> "me(n)," we can perhaps open up a space within the discourse of
> feminism where a male feminist voice can have something to say
> beyond impossibilities and apologies and unresolved ire. Indeed, if
> the male feminist can discover a position *from which* to speak that
> neither elides the importance of feminism to his work nor ignores
> the specificity of his gender, his voice may also find that it no longer
> exists as an abstraction . . . but that it in fact inhabits a body: its own
> sexual/textual body. (159)

Given their awareness that androcentric perspectives are learned and
transmitted by means of specific (and, at this point, well-identified)
sociocultural practices in such effective ways that they appear natural, male feminists such as Joseph Boone believe that, through an informed investigation of androcentric and feminist ideologies, individual men can work to resist the lure of the normatively masculine. That
resistance for the aspiring male feminist requires, in Boone's phrase,
the exposure of "the latent multiplicity and difference in the word
'me(n),'" in other words, the (dis)rupturing of unproblematized perceptions of monolithic and/or normative maleness (as villainous, antagonistic "other," for feminism, and, for androcentricism, powerful,
domineering patriarch). At this early stage of male feminism's development, to speak self-consciously—autobiographically—is necessarily
to explore, implicitly and explicitly, why and how the individual male
experience (the "me" in men) has diverged from and created possibilities for a rejection of the androcentric norm.

While there is not yet agreement as to what constitutes an identifi-
ably male feminist act of criticism or about the usefulness of such acts
for the general advancement of the feminist project, at least one possible explanation for a male critic's self-referential discourse is that it
is a response to palpable mistrust—emanating from some female participants in feminism and perhaps from the writing male subject himself—about his motives. A skeptical strand of opinion with regard to
male feminism is represented by Alice Jardine's "Men in Feminism:
Odor di Uomo or Campagnons de Route?" Having determined that the
most useful measure of an adequately feminist text is its *"inscription of
struggle—even of pain,"* Jardine finds such inscriptions absent from
most male feminist acts, perhaps because "the historical fact that is the
oppression of women [is] . . . one of their favorite blind spots" (58).

She admits to some confusion about the motivations for males' willing participation: "Why . . . would men want to be in feminism if it's about struggle? What do men want to be in—in pain?" (58).

In addition to seeking to cure its blindness (if such blindness still generally exists) where the history of female oppression is concerned, a male feminism must explore the motivations for its participation in what we might call, in keeping with Jardine's formulations, a discourse of (en)gendered pain. If one of the goals of male feminist self-referentiality is to demonstrate to females that individual males can indeed serve as allies in efforts to undermine androcentric power—and it seems invariably that this is the case—the necessary trust cannot be gained (if this type of trust is at all possible) by insisting that motivation as such does not represent a crucial area that must be carefully negotiated. For example, I accept as generally accurate and, indeed, reflective of my own situation Andrew Ross's assertion that "there are those [men] for whom the *facticity* of feminism, for the most part, goes without saying . . . who are young enough for feminism to have been a primary component of their intellectual formation" (86). However, in discussions whose apparent function is a foregrounding of both obstacles to and possibilities of a male feminism, men's relation to the discourse can never go "without saying"; for the foreseeable future at least, this relation needs necessarily to be rigorously and judiciously theorized and grounded explicitly in, among other places, the experiential realm of the writing male subject.

No matter how illuminating and exemplary we find self-referential inscriptions of a male feminist critical self, if current views of the impossibility of a consistently truthful autobiographical act are correct, there are difficulties implicit in any such attempt to situate or inscribe that male self. While recent theorizing of the autobiographical subject has demonstrated that acts of discursive self-rendering unavoidably involve the creation, for the duration of the writing process at least, of what is in some ways an idealized version of a unified or unifiable self (a self structured around what Georges Poulet calls, in another context and without the skepticism implicit in contemporary studies of self-disclosure, an "identity theme" [45]), we can be certain only of the fact that the autobiographical impulse yields but part of the truth of the male feminist critic's experiences. As is also the case for female participants, a male cannot—can never—be in possession of or able to tell the whole truth and nothing but the truth about his relationship to feminist discourse and praxis.

While autobiographical criticism, like the autobiographical genre itself, is poised tenuously between the poles of closure and disclosure, between representation and re-presentation, between a lived life and an invented one, I believe that even in the recoverable half-truths of my life are some of the materials that have shaped my perceptions, beliefs, and the self and/or selves that I bring to the interpretive act. In these half-truths is the source of my desire to inscribe both a black male feminism and myself as a self-consciously racialized version of what Jardine considers a potentially oxymoronic entity (male feminist) whose literal, if not ideological and/or performative, "blackness" is indisputable and whose adequacy vis-à-vis feminism must be determined by others outside of my self/selves. By examining discussions of the phenomenon of the male feminist—that is to say, by reading male and female explorations of men's place(s) in feminist criticism—and exploring responses of others to my own professional and personal relationships to feminism, I will identify autobiographically and textually grounded sources for my belief that while gendered difference might be said to complicate the prospect of a nonphallocentric black male feminism, it does not render such a project impossible.

At the outset, I acknowledge my own full awareness of the fact that, in this elaboration, mine is a necessary participation with regard to black feminist criticism in the half-invention, half-perception which, in Houston Baker's compelling formulation, represents every scholar's relationship to cultural criticism. Such an acknowledgment is not intended to indicate that my (male) relationship to feminism is naturally that of an illegitimate child, as it were. Rather, it is meant to suggest, like Elizabeth Weed's insistence on "the impossibility" of both men's and women's "relationship to feminism," my belief that while feminism represents a complex, sometimes self-contradictory, "utopian vision" that no one can fully possess, a biological male can "develop political, theoretical [and, more generally, interpretive] strategies" (Weed 75). While at most perhaps half true to all that feminist ideologies are, these strategies nevertheless can assist—in unison both with more voluminous and productive female myths and with other emerging antipatriarchal male acts—a movement toward the actualization of the goals of feminism.

*   *   *

I have been forced to think in especially serious ways about my own relationship to feminist criticism since I completed the first drafts of *Inspiriting Influences*, my study of Afro-American women novelists. I questioned neither the explanatory power of feminism nor the essential importance of developing models adequate to the analysis of black female-authored texts, as my book—in harmony, I believe, with the black feminist project concerned with recovering and uncovering an Afro-American female literary tradition—attempts to provide on a limited scale. Instead, I have been confronted with suspicion about my gendered suitability for the task of explicating Afro-American women's texts, suspicion that has been manifested in the form of both specific responses to my project and general inquiries within literary studies into the phenomenon of the male feminist.

For example, a white female reader of the manuscript's first draft asserted—with undisguised surprise—that my work was "so feminist" and asked how I had managed to offer such ideologically informed readings. Another scholar, a black feminist literary critic, recorded with no discernible hesitation her unease with my "male readings" of the texts of Zora Neale Hurston, Toni Morrison, Gloria Naylor, and Alice Walker, on whom the study focuses. I wondered about the possibility of my being simultaneously "so feminist" and not-so-feminist (i.e., so "male"), about the meanings of these terms both for these scholars and for the larger interpretive communities in which they participate. Consequently, in what was perhaps initially an act of psychic self-protection, I began to formulate questions for which I still have found no consistently satisfactory answers. Were the differences in the readers' perceptions of the ideological adequacy of my study a function of their own racially influenced views of feminist criticism, a product, in other words, of the differences not simply *within me* that could lead to the production of a discourse characterizable as both feminist and androcentric, but *within feminism itself?* Moreover, if the differences within feminism are so significant, could I possibly satisfy everybody with "legitimate" interests in the texts of Hurston and the others by means of my own appropriated version of black feminist discourse, my unavoidably half-true myth of what that discourse is, means, and does? Should my myth of feminism and its mobilization in critical texts be considered naturally less analytically compelling than that of a female scholar simply as a function of my biological maleness? And how could what I took to be a useful self-reflexivity avoid becoming a debilitating inquiry into a process that has come to seem for me, if not "natural" (as Cary Nelson views his relationship to feminism), then at least *necessary?*[3]

Compelled and, to be frank, disturbed by such questions, I searched for answers in others' words, others' work. I purchased a copy of the then recently published *Men in Feminism,* a collection of essays that examines the possibility of men's participation as "comrades" (to use Toni Morrison's term, which I will return to below) in feminist criticism and theory. Gratified by the appearance of such a volume, I became dismayed immediately upon reading the editors' introductory remarks that noted their difficulty in "locating intellectuals, who, having shown interest in the question, would offer, for instance, a gay or a black perspective on the problem" (Jardine and Smith vii–viii). While a self-consciously "gay . . . perspective" does find its way into the collection, the insights of nonwhite males and females are conspicuously absent.[4]

Even more troubling for me than the absence of Afro-American voices, or for that matter of general inquiries into the effects of racial, cultural, and class differences on males' relationship to feminism, was the sense shared by many of its contributors of male feminism's insurmountable obstacles. In fact, the collection's lead essay, Stephen Heath's "Male Feminism," begins by insisting that "men's relation to feminism is an impossible one" (1). Heath's formulations are insightful and provocative, if not always for me persuasive, such as when he claims: "This is, I believe, the most any man can do today: to learn and so to try to write or talk or act in response to feminism, and so to try not in any way to be anti-feminist, supportive of the old oppressive structures. Any more, any notion of writing a feminist book or being a feminist, is a myth, a male imaginary with the reality of appropriation and domination right behind" (9). Is male participation in feminism restricted to being either appropriative and domineering or not "antifeminist"? Must we necessarily agree with Stephen Heath and Robert Scholes, another contributor to *Men in Feminism*, that "a male critic . . . may work within the feminist paradigm but never be a full-fledged member of the class of feminists" (207)? To put the matter differently, is gender really an adequate determinant of "class" position?

Despite the poststructuralist tenor of Heath's work generally and of many of his perspectives, his is an easily problematized essentialist claim—that, in effect, biology determines destiny and, therefore, one's relationship to feminist ideology. In short, womanhood allows one to become feminist at the same time that manhood necessarily denies that status to men. Moreover, while Heath embraces feminism's notions of history as a narrative of male "appropriation and domination" of gendered others, he appears resistant at this point in his discourse to evidence of a powerful feminist institutional present and presence. I believe that we must acknowledge that feminism represents, at least in areas of the American academy, an incomparably productive, influential, and resilient ideology and institution which men, no matter how cunning, duplicitous, or culturally powerful, will neither control nor overthrow in the foreseeable future, one whose perspectives have proven and might continue to prove convincing even to biological males. In other words, in surveying the potential implications of the participation of biological men in feminism, we must be honest about feminism's current persuasiveness and indomitability, about its clarifying, transformative potential, and about the fact that the corruptive possibility of both the purposefully treacherous and the only half-convinced male is, for the present at least, slight indeed. Surely it is neither naive, presumptuous, nor premature to suggest that feminism as ideology and reading strategy has assumed a position of exegetical and institutional strength capable of withstanding even the most energetically masculinistic acts of subversion.

I want to focus specifically on the question—on the "problem," as the editors of *Men in Feminism*, among others, might put it—of a black male feminism. Rather than seeing black male feminism necessarily as an impossibility or as a subtle new manifestation of and attempt at androcentric domination, I want to show that certain instances of Afrocentric feminism provide Afro-American men with an invaluable means of rewriting—of *re-vis(ion)ing*—our selves, our history and literary tradition, and our future.

*   *   *

Few would deny that black feminist literary criticism is an oppositional discourse constituted in large part as a response against black male participation in the subjugation of Afro-American women. From Barbara Smith's castigation of black male critics for their "virulently sexist . . . treatment" of black women writers and her insistence that they "are, of course, hampered by an inability to comprehend Black women's experience in sexual as well as racial terms" (172) to, more recently, Michele Wallace's characterization of the "black male Afro-Americanists who make pivotal use of Hurston's work in their most recent critical speculations" as "a gang" (18), Afro-American men are generally perceived as nonallied others of black feminist discourse. Not only are Afro-American males often so regarded, but, as is evident in Wallace's figuration of male Hurston scholars as intraracial street warriors, they are viewed at times as already damned and unredeemable, even when they appear to take black women's writing seriously. We—I—must accept the fact that black male investigations informed by feminist principles—including this essay—may never be good enough or ideologically correct enough for some Afro-American women who are feminists.

This sense of an unredeemable black male critic/reader is in stark contrast to perspectives offered in such texts as Sherley Anne Williams's "Some Implications of Womanist Theory." In her essay, she embraces Alice Walker's term "womanist"—which, according to Williams, connotes a "commit[ment] to the survival and wholeness of an entire people, female and male, as well as a valorization of women's works in all their varieties and multitudes"—because she considers the black feminist project to be separatist in "its tendency to see not only a distinct black female culture but to see that culture as a separate cultural form" from "the facticity of Afro-American life" (304).

I believe that a black male feminism, whatever its connections to critical theory or its specific areas of concern, can profit immensely from what female feminists have to say about male participation. For example, Valerie Smith's suggestion that "black male critics and theorists might explore the nature of the contradictions that arise when they undertake black feminist projects" (68) seems to me quite useful, as does Alice Jardine's advice to male feminists. Speaking for white female feminists and to white males who consider themselves to be feminists, Jardine urges: "We do not want you to mimic us, to become the same as us; we don't want your pathos or your guilt; and we don't even want your admiration (even if it's nice to get it once in a while). What we want, I would even say what we need, is your *work*. We need you to get down to serious work. And like all serious work, that involves struggle and pain" (60). The womanist theoretical project that has been adopted by Williams, Smith, and others provides aspiring Afro-American male feminists with a useful model for the type of self-exploration that Smith and Jardine advocate. What Williams terms "womanist theory" is especially suggestive for Afro-American men because, while it calls for feminist discussions of black women's texts and for critiques of black androcentricism, womanism foregrounds a general black psychic health as a primary objective. For instance, Williams also argues that "what is needed is a thoroughgoing examination of male images in the works of black male writers"; her womanism, then, aims at "ending the separatist tendency in Afro-American criticism," at leading black feminism away from "the same hole The Brother has dug for himself—narcissism, isolation, inarticulation, obscurity"—toward the creation and/or continuation of black "community and dialogue" (307).

If a black man is to become a useful contributor to black feminism, he must, as Boone argues, "discover a position *from which* to speak that neither elides the importance of feminism to his work nor ignores the specificity of his gender" (159). However multiply split we perceive the subject to be or deeply felt our sense of "maleness" and "femaleness" as social constructions, however heightened our sense of the historical consequences and current dangers of black androcentricism, a black male feminism cannot contribute to the continuation and expansion of the black feminist project by being so identified against or out of touch with itself as to fail to be both self-reflective and at least minimally self-interested. A black male feminist self-reflectivity of the type I have in mind necessarily would involve, among other things, examination of both the benefits and dangers of a situatedness in feminist discourse. The self-interestedness of a black male feminist would be manifested in part by his concern with exploring "a man's place." Clearly if, as several feminists insist, convincing mimicry of female-authored concerns and interpretive strategies (or, in the words of a long-standing debate, speaking *like* a female feminist) is not in and of itself an appropriate goal for aspiring male participants (and I am not fully convinced that such mimicry is avoidable at present, at least as an initiatory moment of a male feminist's development), then a male feminism necessarily must explore, among other matters, males' various situations—in the (con)texts of history and the present—as one of its central concerns.

Perhaps the most difficult task for a black male feminism is striking a workable balance between male self-inquiry and self-interest and an adequately feminist critique of patriarchy. To this point, especially in response to the commercial and critical success of contemporary Afro-American women's literature, scores of black men have proven unsuccessful in this regard. As black feminist critics such as Valerie Smith and Deborah McDowell have argued, the contemporary moment of black feminist literature has been greeted by many Afro-American males with hostility, self-interested misrepresentation, and an apparent lack of honest intellectual introspection. McDowell's "Reading Family Matters" is a useful discussion for black male feminism primarily as an exploration of what such a discourse ought not do or be. Of widely circulated androcentric male analyses of Afro-American feminist texts by writers such as Toni Morrison and Alice Walker, McDowell says:

> Critics leading the debate [about the representation of black men in black women's texts] have lumped all black women writers together and have focused on one tiny aspect of their immensely complex and diverse project—the image of black men—despite the fact that, if we can claim a center for these texts, it is located in the complexities of black female subjectivity and experience. In other words, though black women writers have made black women the subjects of their own family stories, these male readers/critics are attempting to usurp that place for themselves and place it at the center of critical inquiry. (84)

Although I do not believe that "the image of black men" is as microscopic an element in Afro-American women's texts as McDowell claims, I agree with her about the reprehensible nature of unabashed androcentricism found in formulations she cites by such figures as Robert Staples, Mel Watkins, and Darryl Pinckney. Nevertheless, where the potential development of a black male feminism is concerned, I am troubled by what appears to be a surprisingly explicit element of turf-protection manifest in her perspective. In their unwillingness to grant that analysis of the depiction of Afro-American males by contemporary black female novelists is a legitimate response to this "immensely complex and diverse project," McDowell's formulations echo in unfortunate ways those of antifeminist male critics of the last two decades, white and black, who consider feminism to be an unredeemably myopic and unsupple interpretive strategy incapable of offering subtle readings of canonical (largely male-authored) texts. Despite the existence and circulation of reprehensibly masculinist responses to Afro-American women's literature, black feminist literary critics do not best serve the discourses with which they are concerned by setting into motion homeostatic manuevers intended to devalue all forms of inquiry except those they hold to be most valuable (in this particular case, a female-authored scholarship that emphasizes Afro-American women's writings of black female subjectivity). If the Afro-American women's literary project is indeed as "immensely complex and diverse" as McDowell claims, the incorporation of other angles of vision, including antipatriarchal male ones, can assist in—among other things—the analysis of aspects of that complexity.

While the views of Staples and others are clearly problematic, those problems do not arise specifically from their efforts to place males "at the center of critical inquiry" any more than feminism is implicitly flawed because it insists, in some of its manifestations, on a gynocritical foregrounding of representations of women. Rather, these problems appear to result from the fact that the particular readers who produce these perspectives do not seem sufficiently to be, in Toril Moi's titular phrase, "men against patriarchy." Certainly, in an age where both gender studies and Afro-American women's literature have achieved a degree of legitimacy within and outside of the academy, it is unreasonable for black women either to demand that black men not be concerned at all—or even centrally, if this is their wish— with the ways in which they are depicted by Afro-American women writers or necessarily to see that concern as intrinsically troubling in feminist terms. If female feminist calls for a nonmimicking male feminism are indeed persuasive, then black men will have very little of substance to say about contemporary Afro-American women's literature if we are also to consider as transgressive any attention to figurations of black manhood. It seems to me that the most black females in feminism can insist upon in this regard is that examinations that focus on male characters treat the complexity of contemporary Afro-American women novelists' delineations of black manhood with an antipatriarchal seriousness, which the essays cited by McDowell clearly lack.

From my perspective, what is potentially most valuable about the development of a black male feminism is not its capacity to reproduce black feminism as it has been established and is being practiced by black females who focus primarily on "the complexities of black female subjectivity and experience." Rather, its potential value lies in the possibility that, in being antipatriarchal and as self-inquiring about their relationships to feminism as Afro-American women have been, black men can expand the range and utilization of feminist inquiry, that they will be able to explore other fruitful applications for feminist perspectives, including such topics as obstacles to a black male feminist project and new figurations of "family matters" and black male sexuality.

For purposes of this essay—for theorizing about a black male feminism—perhaps the most provocative, enlightening, and inviting moment in womanist scholarship occurs in Hortense Spillers's "Mama's Baby, Papa's Maybe: An American Grammar Book." Indeed, Spillers's essay represents a fruitful starting point for new, potentially nonpatriarchal figurations of family and of black males' relationship to black females. Toward the end of this illuminating theoretical text, which concerns itself with slavery's debilitating effects on the Afro-American family, among other matters, Spillers envisions black male identity formation as a process whose movement toward successful resolution seems necessarily to require serious engagement of black feminist principles and perspectives. Spillers asserts that as a result of the specific familial patterns that functioned during and after American slavery and that "removed the African-American male not so much from sight as from *mimetic* view as a partner in the prevailing social fiction of the Father's name, the Father's law," "the African-American male has been touched . . . by the *mother, handed* by her in ways that he cannot escape." Because of separation from traditional American paternal name and law, "the black American male embodies the *only* American community of males which has had the specific occasion to learn *who* the female is within itself. . . . It is the heritage of the *mother* that the African-American male must regain as an aspect of his own personhood—the power of 'yes' to the 'female' within" (80).

Rather than seeing the "female" strictly as other for the Afro-American male, Spillers's Afrocentric revisioning of psychoanalytic theory insists that we consider it as an important aspect of the repressed in the black male self.[5] Employing Spillers's analyses as a starting point, we might regard Afro-American males' potential "in-ness" vis-à-vis feminism not, as Paul Smith insists in *Men in Feminism,* as a representation of male heterosexual desires to penetrate and violate female spaces (33), but as an acknowledgment of what Spillers considers the distinctive nature of the Afro-American male's connection to the "female." If Afro-American males are ever to have anything to say about or to black feminism beyond the types of reflex-action devaluations and diatribes about divisiveness that critics such as Deborah McDowell and Valerie Smith rightly decry—diatribes that have too often marked our discourse and patently ignore the extent to which the practice of patriarchy has already divided us—the investigative process of which womanist acts by Spillers and Williams speak is indispensible. Such a process, if pursued in an intellectually rigorous manner, offers a means by which black men can participate usefully in and contribute productively to the black feminist project.

Black womanism demands neither the erasure of the black gendered other's subjectivity, as have male movements to reacquire a putatively lost Afro-American manhood, nor the relegation of males to prone, domestic, or other limiting or objectifiable positions. What it does require, if it is indeed to become an ideology—a worldview—with widespread cultural impact, is a recognition on the part of both black females and males of the nature of the gendered inequities that have marked our past and present as well as a commitment to working for change. In that sense, black feminist criticism has not only created a space for an informed Afro-American male participation but it heartily welcomes—in fact, insists upon—the joint participation of black males and females as *comrades,* to invoke, with a difference, this essay's epigraphic reference to *Sula.*

* * *

Reading "Mama's Baby, Papa's Maybe" was of special importance to me in part because, as nothing I have read previously or since, it has helped me to clarify and articulate my belief that my relationship to feminism need not mark me necessarily as a debilitatingly split subject.[6] The source of that relationship can only be traced autobiographically, if at all. I was raised by a mother who, like too many women of too many generations, was the victim of male physical and psycho-logical brutality—a brutality which, according to my mother, resulted in large part from my father's frustrations about his inability to par-take in what Spillers calls masculinity's "prevailing social fiction." Thus, my earliest stories, my familial narratives, as it were, figured "maleness" in quite troubling terms. My mother told me horrific sto-ries, one of which I was, in a sense, immediately involved in: my fa-ther—who left us before I was one year old and whom I never knew—kicked her in the stomach when my fetal presence swelled her body because he believed that she had been unfaithful to him and that I was only "maybe" his baby.

As a youth, I pondered this and other such stories often and deeply in part because of the pain I knew these incidents caused my mother, in part because, as someone largely without a consistent male familial role model, I actively sought a means by which to achieve a gendered self-definition. As one for whom maleness as manifested in the sur-rounding inner-city culture seemed to be represented only by vio-lence, familial abandonment, and the certainty of imprisonment, I found that I was able to define myself with regard to my gender pri-marily in oppositional ways. I had internalized the cautionary intent of my mother's narratives, which also served as her dearest wish for me: that I not grow up to be like my father, that I not adopt the defi-nitions of maleness represented by his example and in the culture generally. Because the scars of male brutality were visibly etched—lit-erally marked, as it were—on my mother's flesh and psyche, male-ness, as figured in both my mother's stories and my environment, seemed to me not to be a viable "mimetic" option. I grew up, then, not always sure of what—or who—I was with respect to prevailing social definitions of gender but generally quite painfully aware of what I could not become.

In order to begin to understand who my mother was, perhaps also who my father was, what "maleness" was, and what extra-biological relationship I could hope to have to it, I needed answers that, for a variety of reasons, my mother was unable to provide. I found little of value in the black masculinist discourse of the time which spoke ceaselessly of Afro-American male dehumanization and castration by white men and black women—our central social narrative for too long—for this rhetoric seemed, perhaps because of my particular fa-milial context and maturational dilemma, simplistic and unselfcon-sciously concerned with justifying domestic violence and other forms of black male brutality.

Afro-American women's literature, to which I was introduced in

1977 as a sophomore at Brandeis University along with black feminism, helped me to move toward a comprehension of the world, of
aspects of my mother's life, and of what a man against patriarchy
could be and do. These discourses provided me with answers nowhere
else available to what had been largely unresolvable mysteries. I work
within the paradigm of black feminist literary criticism because it explains elements of the world about which—for strictly autobiographical reasons—I care most deeply. I write and read what and as I do
because I am incapable of escaping the meanings of my mother's narratives for my own life, because the pain and, in the fact of their enun-
ciation to the next generation, the sense of hope for better days that
characterize these familial texts are illuminatingly explored in many
narratives by black women. Afro-American women's literature has
given me parts of myself that—incapable of a (biological) "fatherly
reprieve"—I would not otherwise have had.

I have decided that it is ultimately irrelevant whether these autobiographical facts—facts which, of course, are not, and can never be,
the whole story—are deemed by others sufficient to permit me to call
myself "feminist." Like Toril Moi, I have come to believe that "the
important thing for men is not to spend their time worrying about
definitions and essences ('am I *really* a feminist?'), but to take up a
recognizable anti-patriarchal position" (184). What is most important
to me is that my work contribute, in however small a way, to the
project whose goal is the dismantling of phallocentric rule by which
black females—and, I am sure, countless other Afro-American sons—
have been injuriously "touched."

*   *   *

My indebtedness to Spillers's and other womanist perspectives is,
then, great indeed, as is my sense of their potential as illuminating,
originary moments for a newborn—or not-yet-born—black male feminist discourse. However, utilizing these perspectives requires that we
be more inquiring than Spillers is in her formulations, not in envisioning liberating possibilities of an acknowledgment of "the 'female'
within" the black community and the male subject but in noting potential dangers inherent in such an attempted embrasure by traditional and/or historically brutalized Afro-American men whose relationship to a repressed "'female'" is not painstakingly (re)defined.

Clearly, more thinking is necessary not only about what "the 'female' within" is but also about what it can be said to represent for
black males, as well as serious analysis of useful means and methods
of interacting with a repressed female interiority and subject. Spillers's

theorizing does not perform this task, in part because it has other, more compelling interests and emphases, including the righting/ (re)writing of definitions of "woman" so as to reflect Afro-American women's particular, historically conditioned "female social subject" status (80). But a black male feminism must be especially focused on exploring such issues if it is to mobilize Spillers's suggestive remarks as a means of developing a fuller understanding of the complex formulations of black manhood found in many (con)texts, including Afro-American women's narratives.

I will discuss these matters a bit more fully, in order to build on Spillers's provocative theorizing about the black male's maturational process and situation on American shores. To this end, I will briefly look at an illuminating moment in Toni Morrison's *Sula*, a text that is not only an unparalleled Afro-American woman's writing of what McDowell calls "the complexities of black female subjectivity and experience" but also of black males' relationship to "the 'female' within" as a consequence of their limited access to "the prevailing social fiction" of masculinity. In this novel, the difficulty—the near impossibility—of negotiating the spaces between black male absence and black female presence is plainly manifested in such figures as: the undifferentiated deweys; BoyBoy, whose name, in contrast to most of the authorial designations in *Sula*, speaks unambiguously for him; and Jude, whose difficulty in assuming the mantle of male provider leads him to view his union with Nel as that which "would make one Jude" (71).

The response of Plum, the most tragic of *Sula*'s unsuccessful negotiators of the so-called white man's world, vividly represents some of the contemporary dangers of black male "in-ness" vis-à-vis the "female." Despite (because of?) a childhood characterized by "float[ing] in a constant swaddle of love and affection" (unlike Hannah, who is uncertain whether her mother ever loved her, Eva's son did experience traditional manifestations of maternal love, reflecting a gender-determined disparity in treatment) and his mother's intention to follow the Father's law by "bequeath[ing] everything" to him (38), Plum appears incapable of embracing hegemonic notions of masculinity. Instead, he returns from World War I spiritually fractured, but, unlike a similarly devastated Shadrack, he lacks the imaginative wherewithal to begin to theorize or ritualize a new relationship to his world. Consequently, he turns to drugs as a method of anesthetizing himself from the horrors of his devastation and, in his mother's view, seeks to compel her resumption of familiar/familial patterns of caretaking. In the following passage, Eva explains to Hannah her perception of Plum's desires, as well as the motivation for her participation in what amounts to an act of infanticide:

> When he came back from that war he wanted to git back in. After all that carryin' on, just gettin' him out and keepin' him alive, he wanted to crawl back in my womb and well . . . I ain't got the room no more even if he could do it. There wasn't space for him in my womb. And he was crawlin' back. Being helpless and thinking baby thoughts and dreaming baby dreams and messing up his pants again and smiling all the time. I had room enough in my heart, but not in my womb, got no more. I birthed him once. I couldn't do it again. He was growed, a big old thing. Godhavemercy, I couldn't birth him twice. . . . [A] big man can't be a baby all wrapped up inside his mamma no more; he suffocate. I done everything I could to make him leave me and go on and live and be a man but he wouldn't and I had to keep him out so I just thought of a way he could die like a man not all scrunched up inside my womb, but like a man. (62)[7]

What is significant about this passage for a theorizing of the possibilities of a nonoppressive black male relationship to feminism—to female experience characterized by a refusal to be subjugated to androcentric desire—is its suggestiveness for our understanding of the obstacles to a revised male view of the repressed "female" that result in large part from black males' relative social powerlessness. If black feminism is persuasive in its analysis of the limitations of an Afro-American masculinist ideology that has emphasized the achievement of black manhood at the expense of black female subjectivity, if, as a growing body of social analyses indicates, we can best describe an overwhelming number of Africa's American male descendants as males-in-crisis, the question a black male feminism must address is: On what basis, according to what ideological perspective, can an Afro-American heterosexual male ground his notions of the female? Beyond its (hetero)sexual dimension, can the "female" truly come to represent for a traditional black male-in-crisis more than a protective maternal womb from which he seeks to be "birthed" again and a site upon which to find relief from or, as in the case of Jude's relationship to Nel, locate frustrations caused by an inability to achieve putatively normative American male socioeconomic status? If embracing normative masculinity requires a movement beyond, indeed, an escape from the protection and life-sustaining aspects symbolized by maternal umbilical cords and apron strings, and an achievement of an economic situation wherein the male provides domestic space and material sustenance for his dependents (including "his woman"), black manhood generally is, like Plum, in desperate trouble. And if, as has often been the case, a black female can be seen by a black male-in-crisis only if she has been emptied of subjectivity and selfhood, if she becomes visible for the male only when she is subsumed by male desires, then the types of refiguration and redefinition of black male subjectivity and embrasure of the "female" central to Spillers's formulations are highly unlikely.

This question of seeing and not seeing, of the male gaze's erasure and re-creation of "the 'female,'" is central to *Sula*'s general thematics. It seems to me that Morrison's figuration of black female subjectivity in all of her novels is largely incomprehensible without some serious attention both to her representation of black manhood and to her exploration of the relationships between socially constructed gendered (and racial) positions. To return explicitly to the case of Eva: what Eva fears, what appears to be her motivation for murdering her son, is that Plum's pitiful, infantile state has the potential to reduce *her* to a static female-function—self-sacrificing mother—which, according to Bottom legend, had already provoked her decision to lose a leg in order to collect insurance money with which to provide for her children. Having personally lost so much already, Eva chooses, instead of sacrificing other essential parts of her self, to take the life of her self-described male heir. Moreover, if Plum dies "like a man" in Eva's estimation, his achievement of manhood has nothing to do with an assumption of traditional masculine traits, nothing to do with strength, courage, and a refusal to cry in the face of death. Instead, that achievement results from Eva's creation of conditions that have become essential components of her definition of manhood: death forces him to "leave" her and to "keep . . . out" of her womb. It would appear that manhood is defined here not as presence (as it is represented typically in Western thought) but—by and for Eva at least—as liberating (domestic and uterine) absence.

* * *

One of the intentions of this essay is to suggest that feminism represents a fruitful, potentially nonoppressive means of reconceptualizing, of figuratively "birth[ing] . . . twice" the black male subject. But, as a close reading of the aforementioned passage from *Sula* suggests, interactions between men and women motivated by male self-interest, such as necessarily characterizes an aspect of male participation in feminism, are fraught with possible dangers for the biological/ideological female body of an enactment of or a capitulation to hegemonic male power. Indeed, if it is the case that, as Spillers has argued in another context, "the woman who stays in man's company keeps alive the possibility of having, one day, an unwanted guest, or the guest, deciding 'to hump the hostess,' whose intentions turn homicidal" ("Protocol"), then male proximity to feminism generally creates the threat of a specifically masculinist violation. If, as I noted earlier, the dangers of a hegemonic, heterosexual Euroamerican male's "in-ness" vis-à-vis feminism include (sexualized) penetration and domination, then those associated with a heterosexual black male's interactions with the ideological female body are at least doubled and potentially involve an envisioning of the black female body as self-sacrificingly maternal and/or self-sacrificingly sexual. Because of a general lack of access to the full force of hegemonic male power, Afro-American men could see in increasingly influential black female texts not only serious challenges to black male fictions of the self but also an appropriate location for masculine desires for control of the types of valuable resources that the discourse of black womanhood currently represents.

But a rigorous, conscientious black male feminism need not give into traditional patriarchal desires for control and erasure of the "female." To be of any sustained value to the feminist project, such a discourse must provide illuminating and persuasive readings of gender as it is constituted for Afro-Americans—sophisticated, informed, and contentious critiques of phallocentric practices in an effort to redefine our notions of black male (and female) textuality and subjectivity. And in its differences with black feminist texts produced by individual Afro-American women—and surely there will be differences, for such is the nature of intellectual and political life—a black male feminism must be both rigorous in its engagement of these texts and self-reflective enough to avoid, at all costs, the types of patronizing, marginalizing gestures that have traditionally characterized Afro-American male intellectuals' responses to black womanhood. A black male feminism must strive for, above all else, the envisioning and enactment of the possibilities signaled by the differences that feminism has exposed and created. Being an Afro-American male in black feminist criticism does not mean attempting to invade an/other political body like a lascivious soul snatcher or striving to erase its essence in order to replace it with his own myth of what the discourse should be. Such a position for black men means, above all else, an acknowledgment and celebration of the incontrovertible fact that "the father's law" is no longer the only law of the land.

Michael Awkward

Notes

An earlier version of this chapter appears in Michael Awkward, *Negotiating Difference: Race, Gender, and the Politics of Positionality* (Chicago: University of Chicago Press, 1995), 43–58. © 1995 by The University of Chicago. Reprinted by permission of The University of Chicago Press.

1. For example, Joseph Boone's and Gerald MacLean's essays in *Gender and Theory* assume that foregrounding gendered subjectivity is essential to the production of a male feminist critical practice. Consequently, in a effort to articulate his perspectives on the possibilities of a male feminist discourse, Boone shares professional secrets: specifically, he writes of his disagreement with the male-authored essays that begin Alice Jardine and Paul Smith's *Men and Feminism*, and of being excluded, because of his gender, from a Harvard University feminist group discussion of Elaine Showalter's "Critical Cross-Dressing: Male Feminists and the Woman of the Year." Moreover, MacLean's essay discloses painful personal information about his difficult relationship with his mother, his unsatisfying experience with psychoanalysis, and an incident of marital violence (his essay was composed as epistolary discourse—letters to Jane Tompkins—which, as a response to Tompkins's response to Ellen Messer-Davidow's "The Philosophical Bases of Feminist Literary Criticisms," assumes an at least doubly supplemental position vis-à-vis female-authored feminist discourse).

2. For my purposes here, Boone's remarks are suggestive despite their employment of language that might seem to mark them as a (hetero)-sexualization of men's participation in feminism ("open up a space," "discover a position"). I believe that Boone's passage implies less about any desire for domination on his part than it does about the pervasiveness in our language of terms that have acquired sexual connotations and, consequently, demonstrates the virtual unavoidability—the seeming naturalness, if you will—of the employment of a discourse of penetration to describe interactions between males and females. But it also appears to reflect a sense of frustration motivated by Boone's knowledge that while feminism has had a tremendous impact on his thinking about the world he inhabits, many of the discourse's practitioners do not see a place in it for him or other like-minded males. In order to make a place for himself in the face of female opposition to his involvement in feminism, violation and transgression seem unavoidable to Boone. Also, his self-consciousness about the implications of using a discourse of penetration to describe male participation in feminism is further evidence that we should not read his statement as possessing a (hetero)sexualized subtext. For example, toward the end of his essay, he argues that "a recognition of the presence and influence of gay men working in and around feminism has the potential of rewriting feminist fears about 'men in feminism' as a strictly heterosexual gesture of appropriation" (174).

3. About his own relationship to feminism, Nelson writes: "Feminism is part of my social and intellectual life, has been so for many years, and so, to the extent that writing is ever 'natural,' it is natural that I write about femi-

nism" (153). Nelson's "Men, Feminism: The Materiality of Discourse" is, in my estimation, a model for self-referential male feminist inquiries that assume—or at the very least seek to demonstrate—a useful place for males in the discourse of feminism.

4. It is hard for me to believe that Jardine and Smith's difficulty reflected a lack of interest among Afro-Americans in exploring the relationship of men to black feminism. Texts such as a special issue of *Black Scholar* (1979) devoted to investigating black feminism as manifested primarily in Ntozake Shange's *for colored girls* and Michele Wallace's *Black Macho and the Myth of the Superwoman*, Mel Watkins's and Darryl Pinckney's essays, and more recent essays by Valerie Smith and Deborah McDowell from which I have drawn and which, among other things, critique such black male investigations of feminism, offer clear evidence of Afro-American interest in "the problem." Jardine and Smith's difficulties, it would appear, at least where inclusion of Afro-American male perspectives was concerned, might have stemmed from the fact that (1) most of the men who had spoken publicly on the subject were open about their hostility to black feminism, and (2) they generally did not speak the language of contemporary theory, a high academic idiom which demonstrates that the contributors to *Men in Feminism* are, despite significant differences between them, members of the same speech community.

5. In this sense, Spillers's perspective complements that of Sherley Anne Williams, who demands, in effect, that we consider the extent to which black male repression of the "female" results from an attempt to follow the letter of the white father's law.

6. "Whose Canon Is It, Anyway?" served as an enabling pretext to this essay because it introduced me to Spillers's formulations and because of its (apparently controversial) discussion of connections between black mothers and sons expressed by a self-consciously male critical voice employing elements of black feminist methodology. Henry Louis Gates, Jr., states that his initial encounter with Spillers's essay was a crucial, illuminating moment—the point at which he began to understand that "much of my scholarly and critical work has been an attempt to learn how to speak in the strong, compelling cadences of my mother's voice" (45). The autobiographical elements of my essay were inspired not only by what Gates might call his own "autocritographical" moment but as importantly by Houston Baker's recent call for an Afro-American autobiographical criticism and by the self-referential dimension in much feminist criticism and theory (especially, because of my own positionality, that which appears in the work of male feminists). These acts convinced me of the crucial nature of self-referentiality in this initial effort on my part to theorize about a black man's place(s)—or, perhaps more accurately, *my* place—in black feminist criticism.

7. At least one other reading of Eva's murder of her son is possible: as protection against the threat of incest. In a section of her explanation to Hannah—very little of which is contained in my textual citation of *Sula*—Eva discusses a dream she has had concerning Plum: "I'd be laying here at night and he be downstairs in that room, but when I closed my eyes I'd see him . . . six

feet tall smilin' and crawlin' up the stairs quietlike so I wouldn't hear and opening the door soft so I wouldn't hear and he'd be creepin' to the bed trying to spread my legs trying to get back up in my womb. He was a man, girl, a big old growed-up man. I didn't have that much room. I kept on dreaming it. Dreaming it and I knowed it was true. One night it wouldn't be no dream. It'd be true and I would have done it, would have let him if I'd've had the room but a big man can't be a baby all wrapped up inside his mamma no more; he suffocate" (72–73). In this construction, Morrison reverses to some extent the traditional dynamics of the most prevalent form of intergenerational incest. Instead of the physically and psychologically irresistible male parent creeping to the bed and spreading the legs of his defenseless female child, in Eva's dream, her large manchild Plum is the active agent of violation. Eva's emphasis on Plum's physical immensity and her own uterus's size—and, clearly, the obvious intent of this is to suggest the impossibility of a literal return of even the regressive male body to the womb—makes connections to incestuous creeping and spreading possible. It is not difficult to imagine, given Plum's constantly drugged state, that frustrations caused by an inability to reinsert his whole body into his mother's womb during what Eva views as an inevitable encounter might lead to a forced insertion of a part that "naturally" fits, his penis. At any rate, a reading of this scene that notes its use of language consistent with parent-child incest serves to ground what otherwise appear (at least in literal terms) as senseless fears on Eva's part concerning both the possible effects of Plum's desire for reentry into her uterine space and her own inability to deny her son access to that space ("I would have done it, would have let him").

Works Cited

Awkward, Michael. *Inspiriting Influences: Tradition, Revision, and Afro-American Women's Novels.* New York: Columbia University Press, 1989.

Baker, Houston A., Jr. *Afro-American Poetics: Revisions of Harlem and the Black Aesthetic.* Madison: University of Wisconsin Press, 1988.

Boone, Joseph. "Of Me(n) and Feminism: Who(se) Is the Sex that Writes." Pp. 158–80 in *Gender and Theory,* ed. Kauffman.

Gates, Henry Louis, Jr. "Whose Canon Is It, Anyway?" *New York Times Book Review,* Feb. 26, 1989, 1, 44–45.

Heath, Stephen. "Male Feminism." Pp. 1–32 in *Men in Feminism,* ed. Jardine and Smith.

Jardine, Alice. "Men in Feminism: Odor di Uomo or Compagnons de Route." Pp. 54–61 in *Men in Feminism,* ed. Jardine and Smith.

Jardine, Alice, and Paul Smith, eds. *Men in Feminism.* New York: Methuen, 1987.

Kauffman, Linda, ed. *Gender and Theory: Dialogues on Feminist Criticism.* New York: Blackwell, 1989.

MacLean, Gerald. "Citing the Subject." Pp. 140–57 in *Gender and Theory,* ed. Kauffman.

McDowell, Deborah. "Reading Family Matters." Pp. 75–97 in *Changing Our Own Words*, ed. Wall.

Moi, Toril. "Men Against Patriarchy." Pp. 181–88 in *Gender and Theory*, ed. Kauffman.

Morrison, Toni. *Sula*. New York: Plume, 1973.

Nelson, Cary. "Men, Feminism: The Materiality of Discourse." Pp. 153–72 in *Men in Feminism*, ed. Jardine and Smith.

Owens, Craig. "Outlaws: Gay Men in Feminism." Pp. 219–32 in *Men in Feminism*, ed. Jardine and Smith.

Pinckney, Darryl. "Black Victims, Black Villains." *New York Review of Books*, Jan. 29, 1987, 17–20.

Poulet, Georges. "Criticism and the Experience of Interiority." Pp. 41–49 in *Reader-Response Criticism*, ed. Tompkins.

Ross, Andrew. "No Question of Silence." Pp. 85–92 in *Men in Feminism*, ed. Jardine and Smith.

Scholes, Robert. "Reading as a Man." Pp. 204–18 in *Men in Feminism*, ed. Jardine and Smith.

Showalter, Elaine, ed. *The New Feminist Criticism*. New York: Pantheon, 1985.

——, ed. *Speaking of Gender*. New York: Routledge, 1989.

Smith, Barbara. "Toward a Black Feminist Criticism." Pp. 168–85 in *The New Feminist Criticism*, ed. Showalter.

Smith, Paul. "Men in Feminism: Men and Feminist Theory." Pp. 33–46 in *Men in Feminism*, ed. Jardine and Smith.

Smith, Valerie. "Gender and Afro-Americanist Literary Theory and Criticism." Pp. 56–70 in *Speaking of Gender*, ed. Showalter.

Spillers, Hortense J. "Black, White, and In Color, or Learning How to Paint: Toward an Intramural Protocol of Reading." Paper presented at the "Sites of Colonialism" retreat, Center for the Study of Black Literature and Culture, University of Pennsylvania, 1990.

——. "Mama's Baby, Papa's Maybe: An American Grammar Book." *Diacritics* (1987): 65–81.

Staples, Robert. "The Myth of Black Macho: A Response to Angry Black Feminists." *Black Scholar* 10 (Mar./Apr. 1979): 24–36.

Tompkins, Jane P., ed. *Reader-Response Criticism: From Formalism to Post-Structuralism*. Baltimore: Johns Hopkins University Press, 1980.

Wall, Cheryl, ed. *Changing Our Own Words: Essays on Criticism, Theory, and Writing by Black Women*. New Brunswick, N.J.: Rutgers University Press, 1989.

Wallace, Michele. "Who Dat Say Dat When I Say Dat? Zora Neale Hurston Then and Now." *Village Voice Literary Supplement*, Apr. 1988, 18–21.

Watkins, Mel. "Sexism, Racism, and Black Women Writers." *New York Times Book Review*, June 15, 1986, 1, 35–36.

Weed, Elizabeth. "A Man's Place." Pp. 71–77 in *Men in Feminism*, ed. Jardine and Smith.

Williams, Sherley Anne. "Some Implications of Womanist Theory," *Callaloo* 9 (1986): 303–8.

Part Two

Speaking Parts

Partially Speaking

Authority is the privilege to speak as author, as an originator. Such a privilege is often understood to come from some wisdom, insight, or experience of the author. If authority is claimed on the basis of personal experience, then authority becomes a matter of interpreting one's own life, often without reference to the assumptions, beliefs, or methods by which that interpretation is accomplished. When personal experience is the basis for critical knowledge, such knowledge may be premised on a fairly unexamined opinion, whose rhetorical force comes from its appeal to the "authentic." When opinion claims to be unassailable because it is based on experience, authority becomes tautological—it is because I say it is and who are you to question my life? This tautology fixes ultimately on the person of the speaker who becomes both the subject and object of critical attention while criticism becomes an extension of personal essence. Although the "in se" authority of self appears to grant a certain kind of experiential authority, it also limits that authority.

Aren't both the object and subject also defined here according to certain hegemonic assumptions about the relation between self and the cultural categories to which that self is believed to belong? For instance, African Americans are always assumed to be African Americanists, as though the ontological scripting of blackness in Western culture is the only intellectual category, the only site of analysis that whites think would be interesting to them. Or worse, blackness is the only notable experience an African American critic can have. In this, ontological determinations that adhere to race (as well as national and perhaps to a lesser extent gender) categories become both the precondition for and discursive grounds of academic speech and authority. This is disturbing and hardly a "privilege"; it is a ruse, allowing an individual an authority to speak forever as other, the native informant to all the other others.

The connection between experience and identity as a basis for critical authority is shaky. Linking the two results in a reiteration of certain dominant ideologies (about race, sexuality, gender, class, age, ethnicity) perpetuated through an assumption of experiential privilege. In this sense experience as ground for authority substitutes for and masks reasoning and logic, while preventing critics from certain ontologically defined groups from assuming authority in any other way. Hence, women can only speak about/for women, lesbians about/for lesbians, and so on. Authority becomes a matter of propriety, of a seemly match between identity and critical object.

By propriety, can we assume the significatory codes and historical formations of the subject that have coincided with the ability to be public—a legitimate citizen—in the West? In other words, the propriety you speak of points to those requirements of citizenship that have underwritten the seemingly universal entitlements offered by democratic social organizations. Such requirements have always been more specific, more corporeal, and more monied than the ideologies of democracy reveal. . . . But I've missed your point, haven't I? You are trying to turn my attention more to the idea of the "real," of the "experience," as a way of establishing the problem of essence that underlies issues of authority—those essences that, in the theory of the democratic public, would discount specific individual and group authorizations. In particular, you seem to want to explore how *questions about a speaker's authority and ethics (based on an idea of experience as arising from a particular social location [locution]) arise when conventions of propriety are broken.* For example, what happens, in terms of ethics and the politics of authority, when Q tries to speak as, of, or for X, or even when Q tries to speak as, of, or for every Q?

But pointing to the mechanism by which it is proper to speak only as oneself or from one's own unassailable experience also points to the impropriety of speaking as, of, or for others. The categorical logic that authorizes speaking from experience also suggests that such experience might be generalized to all those in the same category. Thus, speaking for those presumably like one is not a dilemma. But is Q for every Q really less of a problem? The impropriety caused by a misalignment between subject and group position happens between every subject and its group, indeed between every subject and herself.

Questioning the relation between identity, experience, and authority and their ties to representation makes visible the ideologies of subjectivity and knowledge that govern contemporary critical speech and the authority for it. On what bases do we assume Q can speak as, for, or of Q? Why do we assume

Q cannot speak as, for, or of X? What concept of the subject makes it difficult, problematic, or desirable for Q to speak as, of, or for every Q? Why do we think that Q would know Q enough to speak about Q at all? What is the difference between a "Q" identity and identifying with Q? And if the responses to all of these questions indicate that authority is impossible or no longer desirable, or only ever partial, then should we, and how can we, speak anyway?

5

The Problem of Speaking for Others

Consider the following true stories:

1. Anne Cameron, a very gifted white Canadian author, writes several first person accounts of the lives of Native Canadian women. At the 1988 International Feminist Book Fair in Montreal, a group of Native Canadian writers asks Cameron to, in their words, "move over" on the grounds that her writings are disempowering for indigenous authors. She agrees (Maracle 1989).

2. After Manuel Noriega overturns the 1989 elections in Panama, U.S. President George Bush declares in a public address that Noriega's actions constitute an "outrageous fraud" and that "the voice of the Panamanian people have spoken. . . . The Panamanian people want democracy and not tyranny, and want Noriega out." He proceeds to plan the invasion of Panama.

3. At a recent symposium at my university, a prestigious theorist was invited to lecture on the political problems of postmodernism. The audience, which includes many white women and people of oppressed nationalities and races, waits in eager anticipation for his contribution to this important discussion. To the audience's disappointment, he introduces his lecture by explaining that he cannot cover the assigned topic because as a white male he does not feel that he can speak for the feminist and postcolonial perspectives that have launched the critical interrogation of postmodernism's politics. Instead he lectures on architecture.

These examples demonstrate the range of current practices of speaking for others in our society. While the prerogative of speaking for others remains unquestioned in the citadels of colonial administration, among activists and in the academy it elicits a growing unease and, in some communities of discourse, it is being rejected. There is a strong, albeit contested, current within feminism which holds that speaking for others—even for other women—is arrogant, vain, unethical, and politically illegitimate. Feminist scholarship has a liberatory agenda that almost requires that women scholars speak on behalf of other women; yet the dangers of speaking across differences of race, culture, sexuality, and power are becoming increasingly clear. Articles and letters in which the author states that she can only speak for herself are commonly found in feminist magazines such as *Sojourner.* In her important essay, "Dyke Methods," Joyce Trebilcot offers a philosophical articulation of this view. She renounces for herself the practice of speaking for others within a lesbian feminist community, arguing that she "will not try to get other wimmin to accept my beliefs in place of their own" on the grounds that to do so would be to practice a kind of discursive coercion and even a violence" (1).[1]

Feminist discourse is not the only site in which the problem of speaking for others has been acknowledged and addressed. In anthropology there is similar discussion about whether it is possible to speak for others either adequately or justifiably. Trinh T. Minh-hà explains the grounds for skepticism when she says that anthropology is "mainly a conversation of 'us' with 'us' about 'them,' of the white man with the white man about the primitive-nature man . . . in which 'them' is silenced. 'Them' always stands on the other side of the hill, naked and speechless . . . 'them' is only admitted among 'us,' the discussing subjects, when accompanied or introduced by an 'us'" (65, 67).[2] Given this analysis, even ethnographies written by progressive anthropologists are a priori regressive because of the structural features of anthropological discursive practice.

The recognition that there is a problem in speaking for others has followed from the widespread acceptance of two claims. First, there has been a growing awareness that where an individual speaks from affects both the meaning and truth of what she says and thus she cannot assume an ability to transcend her location. In other words, a speaker's location (which I take here to refer to her *social* location or social identity) has an epistemically significant impact on that speaker's claims and can serve either to authorize or de-authorize her speech. Women's studies and African American studies departments were founded on this very belief: that both the study of and the advocacy for the oppressed must be done principally by the oppressed themselves and that we must finally acknowledge that systematic divergences in social location between speakers and those spoken for will have a significant effect on the content of what is said. The unspoken premise is simply that a speaker's location is epistemically salient. I shall explore this issue further in the next section.

The second claim holds that not only is location epistemically salient but certain privileged locations are discursively dangerous.[3] In particular, the practice of privileged persons speaking for or on behalf of less privileged persons has actually resulted (in many cases) in increasing or reinforcing the oppression of the group spoken for. This was part of the argument made against Anne Cameron's speaking for indigenous women: Cameron's intentions were never in question, but the effects of her writing were argued to be harmful to the needs of indigenous authors because it is Cameron rather than they who will be listened to and whose books will be bought by readers interested in indigenous women. Persons from dominant groups who speak for others are often treated as authenticating presences that confer legitimacy and credibility on the demands of subjugated speakers; such speaking for others does nothing to disrupt the discursive hierarchies that operate in public spaces. For this reason, the work of privileged authors who speak on behalf of the oppressed is becoming increasingly criticized by members of those oppressed groups.[4]

As social theorists, we are authorized by virtue of our academic positions to develop theories that express and encompass the ideas, needs, and goals of others. We must begin to ask ourselves whether this is ever a legitimate authority, and if so, what are the criteria for legitimacy? In particular, is it ever valid to speak for others who are unlike us or who are less privileged than us?

We might try to delimit this problem as only arising when a more privileged person speaks for a less privileged one. In this case, we might say that I should only speak for groups of which I am a member. But this does not tell us how groups themselves should be delimited. For example, can a white woman speak for all women simply by virtue of being a woman? If not, how narrowly should we draw the categories? The complexity and multiplicity of group identifications could result in "communities" composed of single individuals. Moreover, the concept of groups assumes specious notions about clear-cut boundaries and "pure" identities. I am a Panamanian American and a person of mixed ethnicity and race: half white/Angla and half Panamanian mestiza. The criterion of group identity leaves many unanswered questions for a person such as myself, since I have membership in many conflicting groups but my membership in all of them is problematic. Group identities and boundaries are ambiguous and permeable, and decisions about demarcating identity are always partly arbitrary. Another problem concerns how specific an identity needs to be to confer epistemic authority. Reflection on such problems quickly reveals that no easy solution to the problem of speaking for others can be found by simply restricting the practice to speaking for groups of which one is a member.

Adopting the position that an individual should only speak for herself raises similarly difficult questions. If I don't speak for those less privileged than myself, am I abandoning my political responsibility to speak out against oppression, a responsibility incurred by the very fact of my privilege? If I should not speak for others, should I restrict myself to following their lead uncritically? Is my greatest contribution to *move over and get out of the way?* If so, what is the best way to do this—to keep silent or to deconstruct my own discourse?

The answers to these questions will certainly depend on who is asking them. While some of us may want to undermine, for example, the U.S. government's practice of speaking for the "third world," we may *not* want to undermine someone such as Rigoberta Menchu's ability to speak for Guatemalan Indians.[5] So the question arises about whether all instances of speaking for should be condemned and, if not, how we can justify a position that would repudiate some speakers while accepting others.

In order to answer these questions we need to become clearer on the epistemological and metaphysical issues involved in the articulation of the problem of speaking for others, issues that most often remain implicit. I will attempt to clarify these issues before discussing some of the possible responses to the problem and advancing a provisional, procedural solution of my own. But first I need to explain further my framing of the problem.

In the examples above, there may appear to be a conflation between the issue of speaking for others and the issue of speaking about others. This conflation was intentional on my part, because it is often difficult to distinguish speaking about from speaking for. There is an ambiguity in the two phrases: when A is speaking for B, A may be describing B's situation and thus also speaking about B. In fact, it may be impossible to speak for another without simultaneously conferring information about them. Similarly, when A is speaking about B, or simply trying to describe B's situation or some aspect of it, A may also be speaking in place of B, in other words, speaking for B. Thus, I would maintain that if the practice of speaking for others is problematic, so too must be the practice of speaking about others.[6] This is partly the case because of what has been called the "crisis of representation." For in both the practice of speaking for and the practice of speaking about others, I am engaging in the act of representing the other's needs, goals, situation, and in fact, *who they are*, based on my own situated interpretation. In poststructuralist terms, I am participating in the construction of their subject positions rather than simply discovering their true selves.

Once we pose it as a problem of representation, we see that, not only are speaking for and speaking about analytically close, so too are the practices of speaking for others and speaking for myself. For, in speaking for myself, I am also representing my self in a certain way, as occupying a specific subject position, having certain characteristics and not others, and so on. In speaking for myself, I (momentarily) create my self—just as much as when I speak for others I create them as a public, discursive self, a self that is more unified than any subjective experience can support. And this public self will in most cases have an effect on the self experienced as interiority.

The point here is that the problem of representation underlies all cases of speaking for, whether I am speaking for myself or for others. This is not to suggest that all representations are fictions: they have very real material effects, as well as material origins, but they are always mediated in complex ways by discourse, power, and location. However, the problem of speaking for others is more specific than the problem of representation generally and requires its own particular analysis.

There is one final point I want to make before we can pursue this analysis. The way I have articulated this problem may imply that individuals make conscious choices about their discursive practices free of ideology and the constraints of material reality. This is not what I wish to imply. The problem of speaking for others is a social one, the options available to us are socially constructed, and the practices we engage in cannot be understood as simply the results of autonomous individual choice. Yet to replace both "I" and "we" with a passive voice that erases agency results in an erasure of responsibility and accountability for one's speech, an erasure I would strenuously argue against (there is too little responsibility-taking already in Western practice!). When we sit down to write or stand up to speak, we experience ourselves as making choices. We may experience hesitation from fear of being criticized or from fear of exacerbating a problem we would like to remedy, or we may experience a resolve to speak despite existing obstacles, but in many cases we experience having the possibility to speak or not to speak. On the one hand, a theory that explains this experience as involving autonomous choices free of material structures would be false and ideological, but, on the other hand, if we do not acknowledge the activity of choice and the experience of individual doubt, we are denying a reality of our experiential lives.[7] So I see the argument of this chapter as addressing that small space of discursive agency we all experience, however multilayered, fictional, and constrained it in fact is.

Ultimately, the question of speaking for others bears crucially on the possibility of political effectivity. Both collective action and coalitions would seem to require the possibility of speaking for. Yet influential postmodernists such as Gilles Deleuze have characterized as "absolutely fundamental: the indignity of speaking for others" (209), and important feminist theorists have renounced the practice as irretrievably harmful. What is at stake in rejecting or validating speaking for others as a discursive practice? To answer this, we must come to understand more clearly the epistemological and metaphysical claims that are implicit in the articulation of the problem.

*   *   *

In this century, a plethora of sources have argued that the neutrality of the theorizer can no longer, can never again, be sustained, even for a moment. Critical theory, discourses of empowerment, psychoanalytic theory, poststructuralism, feminism, and anticolonialist theories have all concurred on this point. Who is speaking to whom turns out to be as important for meaning and truth as what is said; in fact what is said turns out to change according to who is speaking and who is listening. Following Michel Foucault, I will call these "rituals of speaking" to identify discursive practices of speaking or writing that involve not only the text or utterance but also their position within a social space that includes the persons involved in, acting upon, and/ or affected by the words. Two elements within these rituals deserve our attention: the positionality or location of the speaker and the discursive context. The notion of a discursive context refers to the connections and relations of involvement between the utterance/text and other utterances and texts, as well as the material practices in the relevant environment, which should not be confused with an environment spatially adjacent to the particular discursive event.

Rituals of speaking are constitutive of the meaning of the words spoken as well as the meaning of the event. This claim requires us to shift the ontology of meaning from its location in a text or utterance to a larger space that includes the text or utterance as well as the discursive context. An important implication of this claim is that meaning must be understood as plural and shifting, since a single text can engender diverse meanings within diverse contexts. Not only what is emphasized, noticed, and how it is understood will be affected by the location of both speaker and hearer, but the truth-value or epistemic status will also be affected.

In many situations, for example, when a woman speaks the presumption is against her; when a man speaks he is usually taken seriously (unless his speech patterns mark him as socially inferior by dominant standards). When writers from oppressed races and nationalities have insisted that all writing is political, the claim has been dismissed as foolish or grounded in ressentiment or simply ignored; when prestigious European philosophers say that all writing is political, that statement is praised as a new and original "truth" (Judith Wilson calls this "the intellectual equivalent of the 'cover record'").[8] The rituals of speaking, which involve the locations of speaker and listeners, affect whether a claim is taken as a true, well-reasoned, compelling argument or significant idea. Thus, how what is said gets heard depends on who says it and who says it will affect the style and language in which it is stated. The discursive style in which some European poststructuralists have claimed that all writing is political marks the claim as important and likely to be true for a certain (powerful) milieu, whereas the style in which African American writers made the same claim marked their speech as dismissable in the eyes of the same milieu.

This point might be conceded by those who admit to the political mutability of *interpretation,* but they might continue to maintain that *truth* is a different matter altogether. Moreover, they would be right that acknowledging the effect of location on meaning and even on whether something is *taken* as true within a particular discursive context does not entail that the "actual" truth of the claim is contingent upon its context. However, this objection presupposes a particular conception of truth, one in which the truth of a statement can be distinguished from its interpretation and acceptance. Such a concept would require truth to be independent of the speakers' or listeners' embodied and perspectival location. Thus, the question of whether location bears simply on what is taken to be true or what is really true, and whether such a distinction can be upheld, involves the very difficult problem of the meaning of truth. In the history of Western philosophy, there have existed multiple, competing definitions and ontologies of truth: correspondence, idealist, pragmatist, coherentist, and consensual notions. The dominant modernist view has been that truth represents a relationship of correspondence between a proposition and an extra-discursive reality. In this view, truth is about a realm completely independent of human action and expresses things "as they are in themselves," that is, free of human interpretation.

Arguably since Kant, more obviously since Hegel, it has been widely accepted that an understanding of truth that requires it to be free of human interpretation leads inexorably to skepticism, since it makes

truth inaccessible by definition. This created an impetus to reconfig-
ure the ontology of truth from a locus outside human interpretation
to one within it. Hegel, for example, understood truth as an "identity
in difference" between subjective and objective elements. Thus, in the
Hegelian aftermath, so-called subjective elements, or the historically
specific conditions in which human knowledge occurs, are no longer
rendered irrelevant or even obstacles to truth.

In a coherentist account of truth, which is held by such philosophers as Richard Rorty, Donald Davidson, W. V. O. Quine, and (I
would argue) Hans-Georg Gadamer and Michel Foucault, truth is defined as an emergent property of converging discursive and nondiscursive elements, when there exists a specific form of integration
among these elements in a particular event. Such a view has no necessary relationship to idealism, but it allows us to understand how the
social location of the speaker can be said to bear on truth. The speaker's location is one of the elements that converge to produce meaning
and thus to determine epistemic validity.[9]

Let me return now to the formulation of the problem of speaking
for others. There are two premises implied by the articulation of the
problem, and unpacking these should advance our understanding of
the issues involved.

> *Premise 1:* The "ritual of speaking" (as defined above) in which an
> utterance is located always bears on meaning and truth such that
> there is no possibility of rendering positionality, location, or con-
> text irrelevant to content.

The phrase "bears on" here should indicate some variable amount of
influence short of determination or fixing.

One important implication of this first premise is that we can no
longer determine the validity of a given instance of speaking for others simply by asking whether or not the speaker has done sufficient
research to justify her claims. Adequate research will be a necessary
but insufficient criterion of evaluation.

> *Premise 2:* All contexts and locations are differentially related in
> complex ways to structures of oppression. Given that truth is con-
> nected to politics, these political differences between locations will
> produce epistemic differences as well.

The claim in premise 2 that "truth is connected to politics" follows
necessarily from premise 1. Rituals of speaking are politically consti-

tuted by power relations of domination, exploitation, and subordination. Who is speaking, who is spoken of, and who listens is a result, as well as an act, of political struggle. Simply put, the discursive context is a political arena. To the extent that this context bears on meaning, and meaning is in some sense the object of truth, we cannot make an epistemic evaluation of the claim without simultaneously assessing the politics of the situation.

Although we cannot maintain a neutral voice, according to the first premise we may at least all claim the right and legitimacy to speak. But the second premise suggests that some voices may be de-authorized on grounds that are simultaneously political and epistemic. Any statement will invoke the structures of power allied with the social location of the speaker, aside from the speaker's intentions or attempts to avoid such invocations.

The conjunction of premises 1 and 2 suggests that the speaker loses some portion of control over the meaning and truth of her utterance. Given that the context of listeners is partially determinant, the speaker is not the master or mistress of the situation. Speakers may seek to regain control by taking into account the context of their speech, but they can never know everything about this context. Moreover, with written and electronic communication it is becoming increasingly difficult to know anything at all about the context of reception.

This loss of control may be taken by some speakers to mean that no speaker can be held accountable for her discursive actions. The meaning of any discursive event will be shifting and plural, fragmented and even inconsistent. As it ranges over diverse spaces and transforms in the minds of its recipients according to their different horizons of interpretation, the effective control of the speaker over the meanings that she puts in motion may seem negligible. However, a *partial* loss of control does not entail a *complete* loss of accountability. Moreover, the better we understand the trajectories by which meanings proliferate, the more likely we can increase, though always only partially, our ability to direct the interpretations and transformations our speech undergoes. When I acknowledge that the listener's social location will affect the meaning of my words, I can more effectively generate the meaning I intend. Paradoxically, the view that holds the speaker or author of a speech act as solely responsible for its meanings ensures the speaker's least effective determinacy over the meanings that are produced.

We do not need to posit the existence of fully conscious acts or containable, fixed meanings in order to hold that speakers can alter their discursive practices and be held accountable for at least some of the effects of these practices. It is a false dilemma to pose the choice as one between no accountability or complete causal power.

* * *

In this section I shall consider some of the principal responses offered to the problem of speaking for others. First, I want to consider the argument that the very formulation of the problem with speaking for others involves a retrograde, metaphysically insupportable essentialism that assumes we can read off the truth and meaning of *what* we say straight from the discursive context. Let's call this response the "charge of reductionism," because it argues that a sort of reductionist theory of justification (or evaluation) is entailed by premises 1 and 2. Such a reductionist theory might, for example, reduce evaluation to a political assessment of the speaker's location where that location is seen as an insurmountable essence that fixes an individual, as if her feet are superglued to a spot on the sidewalk.

For instance, after I vehemently defended Barbara Christian's "The Race for Theory," a male friend who had a different evaluation of the piece couldn't help raising the possibility of whether a sort of apologetics structured my response, that I was motivated by a desire to valorize African American writing against all odds. In effect his question raised the issue of the reductionist/essentialist theory of justification that I have just described.

I, too, would reject reductionist theories of justification and essentialist accounts of what it means to have a location. To say that location *bears* on meaning and truth is not the same as saying that location *determines* meaning and truth. Location is not a fixed essence absolutely authorizing an individual's speech in the way that God's favor absolutely authorized the speech of Moses. Location and positionality should not be conceived as one-dimensional or static but as multiple and with varying degrees of mobility.[10] What it means, then, to speak from or within a group and/or a location is immensely complex. To the extent that location is not a fixed essence, and to the extent that there is an uneasy, underdetermined, and contested relationship between location on the one hand and meaning and truth on the other, we cannot reduce evaluation of meaning and truth to a simple identification of the speaker's location. Neither premise 1 nor premise 2 entail reductionism or essentialism. They argue for the relevance of location, not its singular power of determination, and they are noncommittal on how to construe the metaphysics of location.

While the "charge of reductionism" response has been popular among academic theorists, what I call the "retreat" response has been popular among some sections of the U.S. feminist movement. This response is simply to retreat from all practices of speaking for; it asserts that an individual can only know her own narrow individual experience and her "own truth" and thus that she can never make claims beyond this. This response is motivated in part by the desire to recognize difference and different priorities without organizing these differences into hierarchies.

Sometimes I think this is the proper response to the problem of speaking for others, depending on who is making it. We certainly want to encourage a more receptive listening on the part of the discursively privileged and to discourage presumptuous and oppressive practices of speaking for. The desire to retreat sometimes results from the desire to engage in political work but without practicing what might be called discursive imperialism. But a retreat from speaking for will not result in an increase in receptive listening in all cases; it may result merely in a retreat into a narcissistic yuppie lifestyle in which a privileged person takes no responsibility whatsoever for her society. She may even feel justified in exploiting her privileged capacity for personal happiness at the expense of others on the grounds that she has no alternative.

The major problem with such a retreat is that it significantly undercuts the possibility of political effectivity. There are numerous examples of the practice of speaking for others that have been politically efficacious in advancing the needs of those spoken for, from Rigoberta Menchu to Edward Said and Steven Biko. Menchu's efforts to speak for the thirty-three Indian communities facing genocide in Guatemala have helped to raise money for the revolution and bring pressure against the Guatemalan and U.S. governments who have committed the massacres in collusion. The point is not that for some speakers the danger of speaking for others does not arise, but that in some cases certain political effects can be garnered in no other way.

Joyce Trebilcot's version of the retreat response acknowledges these political realities. She agrees that an absolute prohibition of speaking for would undermine political effectiveness and therefore says that she will avoid speaking for others only within her lesbian feminist community. So it might be argued that the retreat from speaking for others can be maintained without sacrificing political effectivity if it is restricted to particular discursive spaces. Why might we advocate such a partial retreat? Given that interpretations and meanings are discursive constructions made by embodied speakers, Trebilcot worries that attempting to persuade or speak for another will cut off that person's ability or willingness to engage in the constructive act of developing meaning. Since no embodied speaker can produce more than a partial account, and since the process of producing meaning is necessarily collective, everyone's account within a specified community needs to be encouraged.

I agree with a great deal of Trebilcot's argument. I certainly agree that in some instances speaking for others constitutes a violence and should be stopped. But Trebilcot's position, as well as a more general retreat position, presumes an ontological configuration of the discursive context that simply does not obtain. In particular, it assumes that an individual *can* retreat into her discrete location and make claims entirely and singularly within that location that do not range over others and, therefore, that an individual can disentangle herself from the implicating networks between her discursive practices and others' locations, situations, and practices. In other words, the claim that I can speak only for myself assumes the autonomous conception of the self in classical liberal theory—that I am unconnected to others in my authentic self or that I can achieve an autonomy from others given certain conditions. But there is no neutral place to stand free and clear in which my words do not prescriptively affect or mediate the experience of others, nor is there a way to demarcate decisively a boundary between my location and all others. Even a complete retreat from speech is of course not neutral since it allows the continued dominance of current discourses and acts by omission to reinforce their dominance.

As my practices are made possible by events spatially far away from my body, so too my own practices make possible or impossible others' practices. The declaration that I "speak only for myself" has the sole effect of allowing me to avoid responsibility and accountability for my effects on others; it cannot literally erase those effects.

Let me offer an illustration of this. The feminist movement in the United States has spawned many kinds of support groups for women with various needs: rape victims, incest survivors, battered wives, and so forth; some of these groups have been structured around the view that each survivor must come to her own "truth" which ranges only over herself and has no bearing on others. Thus, one woman's experience of sexual assault, its effect on her and her interpretation of it, should not be taken as a universal generalization to which others must subsume or conform their experience. This view works only up to a point. To the extent it recognizes irreducible differences in the way people respond to various traumas and is sensitive to the genuinely variable way in which women can heal themselves, it represents real progress beyond the homogeneous, universalizing approach that maps one road for all to follow.

However, it is an illusion to think that, even in the safe space of a support group, a member of the group can, for example, trivialize brother-sister incest as "sex play" without profoundly harming someone else in the group who is trying to maintain her realistic assessment of her brother's sexual activities with her as a harmful assault against his adult rationalization that "well, for me it was just harmless fun." Even if the speaker offers a dozen caveats about her views as restricted to her location, she will still affect the other woman's ability to conceptualize and interpret her experience and her response to it. This is true simply because we cannot neatly separate our mediating praxis, which interprets and constructs our experiences, from the praxis of others. We are collectively caught in an intricate, delicate web in which each action I take, discursive or otherwise, pulls on, breaks off, or maintains the tension in many strands of the web in which others also find themselves moving. When I speak for myself, I am constructing a possible self, a way to be in the world, and am offering that, whether I intend to or not, to others, as one possible form of existence.

Thus, the attempt to avoid the problematic of speaking for by retreating into an individualist realm is based on an illusion, well supported in the individualist ideology of the West, that a self is not constituted by multiple intersecting discourses but consists in a unified whole capable of autonomy from others. It is an illusion that I can separate from others to such an extent that I can avoid affecting them. This may be the intention of my speech, and even its meaning if we take that to be the formal entailments of the sentences, but it will not be the effect of the speech and therefore cannot capture the speech in its reality as a discursive practice. When I "speak for myself," I am participating in the creation and reproduction of discourses through which my own and other selves are constituted.

A further problem with the retreat response is that it may be motivated by a desire to find a method or practice immune from criticism. If I speak only for myself it may appear that I am immune from criticism because I am not making any claims that describe others or prescribe actions for them. If I am only speaking for myself I have no responsibility for being true to your experience or needs.

Surely it is both morally and politically objectionable to structure our actions around the desire to avoid criticism, especially if this outweighs other questions of effectivity. In some cases, the motivation is perhaps not so much to avoid criticism as to avoid errors, and we may believe that the only way to avoid errors is to avoid all speaking for others. Yet errors are unavoidable in theoretical inquiry as well as political struggle, and they usually make contributions. The pursuit of an absolute means to avoid making errors comes perhaps not from a desire to advance collective goals but from a desire for personal mastery, to establish a privileged discursive position wherein we cannot be undermined or challenged and thus become master of the situation. From such a position our own location and positionality would not require constant interrogation and critical reflection; we would not have to constantly engage in this emotionally troublesome endeavor and would be immune from the interrogation of others. Such a desire for mastery and immunity must be resisted.

The final response to the problem of speaking for others that I will consider occurs in Gayatri Chakravorty Spivak's rich essay "Can the Subaltern Speak?" Spivak rejects a total retreat from speaking for others, and she criticizes the "self-abnegating intellectual" pose that Foucault and Deleuze adopt when they reject speaking for others on the grounds that their position assumes the oppressed can transparently represent their own true interests. According to Spivak, Foucault's and Deleuze's self-abnegation serves only to conceal the actual authorizing power of the retreating intellectuals, who in their very retreat help to consolidate a particular conception of experience (as transparent and self-knowing). Thus, to promote "listening to" as opposed to speaking for essentializes the oppressed as nonideologically constructed subjects. But Spivak is also critical of speaking for that engages in dangerous representations. In the end Spivak prefers a "speaking to" in which the intellectual neither abnegates his or her discursive role nor presumes an authenticity of the oppressed, but still allows for the possibility that the oppressed will produce a "countersentence" that can then suggest a new historical narrative.

Spivak's arguments suggest that the speech of the oppressed will not necessarily be either liberatory or reflective of their "true interests," if such exist. At the same time, however, ignoring the subaltern's or oppressed person's speech is, as she notes, "to continue the imperialist project" (298). I would add that, even if the oppressed person's speech is not liberatory in its content, it remains the case that the very act of speaking constitutes a subject that challenges and subverts the opposition between the knowing agent and the object of knowledge, an opposition that has served as a key player in the reproduction of imperialist modes of discourse. Thus, the problem with speaking for others exists in the very structure of discursive practice, irrespective of its content, and subverting the hierarchical rituals of speaking will always have some liberatory effects.

I agree, then, that we should strive to create wherever possible the conditions for dialogue and the practice of speaking with and to rather than speaking for others. Often the possibility of dialogue is left unexplored or inadequately pursued by more privileged persons. Spaces in which it may seem impossible to engage in dialogic encounters (e.g., classrooms, hospitals, workplaces, welfare agencies, universities, institutions for international development and aid, and governments) need to be transformed in order to do so. It has long been noted that existing communication technologies have the potential to produce these kinds of interaction even though research and development teams have not found it advantageous under capitalism to do so.

While there is much theoretical and practical work to be done to develop such alternatives, the practice of speaking for others remains the best option in some existing situations. An absolute retreat weakens political effectivity, is based on a metaphysical illusion, and often produces only an obscuring of the intellectual's power. There can be no complete or definitive solution to the problem of speaking for others, but there is a possibility that its dangers can be decreased. The remainder of this chapter will try to contribute toward the development of that possibility.

*   *   *

In rejecting a general retreat from speaking for, I am not advocating a return to an unselfconscious appropriation of the other but rather that anyone who speaks for others should only do so out of a concrete analysis of the particular power relations and discursive effects involved. I want to develop this point by elucidating four sets of interrogatory practices that are meant to help evaluate possible and actual instances of speaking for. In list form they may appear to resemble an algorithm, as if we could plug in an instance of speaking for and factor out an analysis and evaluation. Yet they are meant only to suggest the questions that should be asked concerning any such discursive practice. These are by no means original: they have been learned and practiced by many activists and theorists.

1. The *impetus to speak* must be carefully analyzed and, in many cases (certainly for academics), fought against. This may seem an odd way to begin discussing how to speak for, but the point is that the impetus to *always* be the speaker and to speak in all situations must be seen for what it is: a desire for mastery and domination. If our immediate impulse is to teach rather than to listen to a less-privileged speaker, we should resist that impulse long enough to interrogate it carefully. Some of us have been taught that by right of having the dominant gender, class, race, letters after our name, or some other

criterion, we are more likely to have the truth. Others have been taught the opposite and will speak haltingly, with apologies, if they speak at all.[11]

At the same time, we must acknowledge that the very decision to "move over" or retreat can occur only from a position of privilege. Those who are not in a position of speaking at all cannot retreat from an action they do not employ. Moreover, an individual's decision of whether or not to retreat is an extension or application of privilege, not an abdication of it. Still, it is sometimes called for.

2. We must also interrogate the *bearing of our location and context* on what we are saying, and this should be an explicit part of every serious discursive practice in which we engage. Constructing hypotheses about the possible connections between our location and our words is one way to begin. This procedure would be most successful if engaged in collectively with others, by which aspects of our location less obvious to us might be revealed.[12]

One deformed way in which this is too often carried out is when speakers offer up in the spirit of "honesty" autobiographical information about themselves as a kind of disclaimer, usually at the beginning of their discourse. This is meant to acknowledge their own understanding that they are speaking from a specified, embodied location without pretense to a transcendental truth. But as Maria Lugones and others have forcefully argued, such an act serves no good end when it is used as a disclaimer against the speaker's ignorance or errors and is made without critical interrogation of the bearing of such an autobiography on what is about to be said. All the real work is left for the listeners to do. For example, if a middle-class white man started a speech by sharing such autobiographical information and then used it as a kind of apologetics for any limitations of his speech, this would leave to the audience who do not share his social location all the work of translating his terms into their own, apprising the applicability of his analysis to their diverse situation, and determining the substantive relevance of his location on his claims. This is simply what less-privileged persons have always had to do for themselves when reading the history of philosophy, literature, and so on, which makes the task of appropriating these discourses more difficult and time-consuming (and more likely to result in alienation). Simple unanalyzed disclaimers do not improve on this familiar situation and may even make it worse to the extent that by offering such information the speaker may feel even more authorized to speak and be accorded more authority by his peers.

3. Speaking should always carry with it an *accountability and responsibility* for what an individual says. To whom we are accountable is a

political/epistemological choice contestable, contingent, and as Donna Haraway says, constructed through the process of discursive action. What this entails in practice is a serious commitment to remain open to criticism and to attempt actively, attentively, and sensitively to "hear" the criticism (i.e., understand it). A quick impulse to reject criticism must make us wary.

4. Here is my central point. In order to evaluate attempts to speak for others in particular instances, we need to analyze the *probable or actual effects of the words on the discursive and material context.* We cannot simply look at the location of the speaker or her credentials to speak; nor can we look merely at the propositional content of the speech; we must also look at where the speech goes and what it does there.

Looking merely at the content of a set of claims without looking at their effects cannot produce an adequate or even meaningful evaluation of it; this is partly because the notion of a content separate from effects does not hold up. The content of the claim, or its meaning, emerges in interaction between words and hearers within a very specific historical situation. Given this, we have to pay careful attention to the discursive arrangement in order to understand the full meaning of any given discursive event. For example, in a situation where a well-meaning first world person is speaking for a person or group in the third world, the very discursive arrangement may reinscribe the "hierarchy of civilizations" view where the United States lands squarely at the top. This effect occurs because the speaker is positioned as authoritative and empowered, as the knowledgeable subject, while the third world group is reduced, merely because of the structure of the speaking practice, to an object and victim that must be championed from afar. Though the speaker may be trying to materially improve the situation of some lesser-privileged group, one of the effects of her discourse is to reinforce racist, imperialist conceptions and perhaps also to further silence the lesser-privileged group's own ability to speak and be heard.[13] This illustrates why it is so important to reconceptualize discourse, as Foucault recommends, as an *event* that includes speaker, words, hearers, location, language, and so on.

All such evaluations produced in this way will be of necessity *indexed.* That is, they will obtain for a very specific location and cannot be taken as universal. This simply follows from the fact that the evaluations will be based on the specific elements of historical discursive context, location of speakers and hearers, and so forth. When any of these elements is changed, a new evaluation is called for.

Our ability to assess the effects of a given discursive event is limited; our ability to predict these effects is even more circumscribed.

When meaning is plural and deferred, we can never hope to know the totality of effects. Still, we can know some of the effects our speech generates: I can find out, for example, whether the people I spoke for are angry or appreciative that I did so. By learning as much as possible about the context of reception I can increase my ability to discern at least some of the possible effects. This mandates incorporating a more dialogic approach to speaking that would include learning from and about the domains of discourse my words will affect.

I want to illustrate the implications of this fourth point by applying it to the examples at the beginning of this chapter. In the case of Anne Cameron, if the effects of her books are truly disempowering for indigenous women, then they are counterproductive to Cameron's own stated intentions, and she should indeed "move over." In the case of the white male theorist who discussed architecture instead of the politics of postmodernism, the effect of his refusal was that he offered no contribution to an important issue and his audience lost an opportunity to discuss and explore it.

Now let me turn to the example of George Bush. When Bush claimed that Noriega is a corrupt dictator who stands in the way of democracy in Panama, he repeated a claim that has been made almost word for word by the Opposition movement in Panama. Yet the effects of the two statements are vastly different because the meaning of the claim changes radically depending on who states it. When the president of the United States stands before the world passing judgment on a third world government and criticizes it on the basis of corruption and a lack of democracy, the immediate effect of *this* statement, as opposed to the Opposition's, is to reinforce the prominent Anglo view that Latin American corruption is the primary cause of the region's poverty and lack of democracy, that the United States is on the side of democracy in the region, and that the United States opposes corruption and tyranny. Thus, the effect of a U.S. president's speaking for Latin America in this way is to reconsolidate U.S. imperialism by obscuring its true role in torturing and murdering hundreds of thousands of people who have tried to bring democratic and progressive governments into existence in Latin America. Moreover, this effect will continue until the U.S. government admits its history of international mass murder and radically alters it foreign policy.

Conclusion

Any discussion of discursive responsibility is complicated by the variable way in which the importance of the source, or location of the author, can be understood, a topic alluded to earlier. In one view, the author of a text is its "owner" and "originator," credited with creating its ideas and with being their authoritative interpreter. In another view, the original speaker or writer is no more privileged than any other person who articulates these views and, in fact, the "author" cannot be identified in a strict sense because the concept of author is an ideological construction many abstractions removed from the way in which ideas emerge and become material forces.[14] Does this latter position mean that the source or location of the author is irrelevant?

It need not entail this conclusion, though it might in some formulations. We can de-privilege the "original" author and reconceptualize ideas as traversing (almost) freely in a discursive space, available from many locations and without a clearly identifiable originary track, and yet retain our sense that source remains relevant to effect. Our metatheory of authorship does not preclude the material reality that in discursive spaces there is a speaker or writer credited as the author of her utterances, or that, for example, the feminist appropriation of the concept "patriarchy" gets tied to Kate Millett, a white Anglo feminist, or that the term feminism itself has been and is associated with a Western origin. These associations have an effect of producing distrust on the part of some third world nationalists and of reinscribing semiconscious imperialist attitudes on the part of some first world feminists. These are not the only possible effects. Some of the effects may not be pernicious but all must be considered when evaluating the discourse of "patriarchy."

The emphasis on effects should not imply, therefore, that an examination of the speaker's location is any less crucial. Such an examination might be called a kind of genealogy. In this sense, a genealogy involves asking how a position or view is mediated and constituted through and within the conjunction and conflict of historical, cultural, economic, psychological, and sexual practices. But it seems to me that the importance of the source of a view, and the importance of doing a genealogy, should be subsumed within an overall analysis of effects, making the central question what the effects are of the view on material and discursive practices through which it traverses and the particular configuration of power relations emergent from these. Source is relevant only to the extent that it has an impact on effect. As Gayatri Chakravorty Spivak has repeatedly pointed out, the invention of the telephone by a European upper-class male in no way preempts its being put to the use of an anti-imperialist revolution.

In conclusion, I would stress that the practice of speaking for others is often born of a desire for mastery, to privilege oneself as the one

who more correctly understands the truth about another's situation
or as the one who can champion a just cause and thus achieve glory
and praise. The effect of the practice of speaking for others is often,
though not always, erasure and a reinscription of sexual, national, and
other kinds of hierarchies. I hope that this analysis will contribute toward rather than diminish the important ongoing discussion about
how to develop strategies for a more equitable, just distribution of the
ability to speak and be heard. But this development should not be tak-
en as an absolute de-authorization of all practices of speaking for. It is
not *always* the case that when others unlike me speak for me I have
ended up worse off or that when we speak for others they end up
worse off. Sometimes, as Loyce Stewart has argued, we do need a
"messenger" to advocate for our needs.

The source of a claim or discursive practice in suspect motives or
maneuvers or in privileged social locations, I have argued, cannot be
sufficient to repudiate it, though it is always relevant. We must ask
further questions about its effects, questions that address the following: Will it enable the empowerment of oppressed peoples?

Linda Martín Alcoff

Notes

For their generous help with this chapter, I am grateful to the Eastern Society
for Women in Philosophy, the Central New York Women Philosophers' Group,
Loyce Stewart, Richard Schmitt, Sandra Bartky, Laurence Thomas, Leslie
Bender, Robyn Wiegman, Anita Canizares Molina, and Felicity Nussbaum. An
earlier version of this essay appeared in *Cultural Critique* 20 (Winter 1991–92):
5–32.

1. Trebilcot is explaining here her own reasoning for rejecting these practices, but she is not advocating that other women join her. Thus, her argument does not fall into a self-referential incoherence.

2. For examples of anthropologists' concern with this issue, see James Clifford and George E. Marcus, eds., *Writing Culture;* James Clifford, "On Ethnographic Authority"; George Marcus and Michael Fischer, eds., *Anthropology as
Cultural Critique;* and Paul Rabinow, "Discourse and Power."

3. To be privileged here means to be in a more favorable, mobile, and dominant position vis-à-vis the structures of power and knowledge in a society.
This privilege carries with it, for example, presumption in one's favor when
one speaks. Certain races, nationalities, genders, sexualities, and classes confer privilege, but a single individual (perhaps most individuals) may enjoy
privilege in respect to some parts of their identity and a lack of privilege in
respect to other parts. Therefore, privilege must always be indexed to specific
relationships as well as to specific locations.

The term privilege is not meant to include positions of discursive power achieved through merit, but in any case these are rarely pure. In other words, some persons are accorded discursive authority because they are respected leaders or because they are teachers in a classroom and know more about the material at hand. Often, of course, the authority they may enjoy by virtue of their merit combines with the authority they may enjoy by virtue of their having the dominant gender, race, class, or sexuality. It is gender, race, class, and sexuality as sources of authority that I refer to by the term "privilege."

4. See also, Maria Lugones and Elizabeth Spelman, "Have We Got a Theory For You!" In their article, Lugones and Spelman explore the way in which the "demand for the women's voice" disempowered women of color by not attending to the difference in privilege within the category of women, resulting in a privileging of only white women's voices. They explore the effects this has had on the making of theory within feminism, and they attempt to find "ways of talking or being talked about that are helpful, illuminating, empowering, respectful" (25). My chapter takes inspiration from their essay and is meant to continue their discussion.

5. See Menchu's *I . . . Rigoberta Menchu*. The use of the term "Indian" here follows Menchu's use.

6. For example, if it is the case that no "descriptive" discourse is normative- or value-free, then no discourse is free of some kind of advocacy, and all speaking about will involve speaking for someone(s) or something.

7. Another distinction that might be made is between different material practices of speaking for: giving a speech, writing an essay or book, making a movie or TV program, as well as hearing, reading, watching, and so on. I will not address the possible differences that arise from these multifarious practices and will address myself to the (fictional) "generic" practice of speaking for.

8. See Wilson's "Down to the Crossroads: The Art of Alison Saar," for a discussion of this phenomenon in the art world (especially p. 36). See also Barbara Christian, "The Race for Theory," and Henry Louis Gates, Jr., "Authority, (White) Power and the (Black) Critic."

9. I know that my insistence on using the word "truth" swims upstream of current postmodernist orthodoxies. My insistence is not based on a commitment to transparent accounts of representation or a correspondence theory of truth but on my belief that the demarcation between epistemically better and worse claims continues to operate (indeed is inevitable) and that what happens when we eschew all epistemological issues of truth is that the terms upon which those demarcations are made go unseen and uncontested. A very radical revision of what we mean by truth is in order, but if we ignore the ways in which our discourses appeal to some version of truth for their persuasiveness, we are in danger of remaining blind to the operations of legitimation that function within our own texts. The task is therefore to explicate the relations between politics and knowledge rather than pronounce the death of truth. See my *Real Knowing* (forthcoming).

10. See also my "Cultural Feminism versus Post-Structuralism." For more discussions on the multidimensionality of social identity, see Maria Lugones,

"Playfulness, 'World'-Travelling, and Loving Perception," and Gloria Anzaldúa, *Borderlands/La Frontera*.

11. See Edward Said, "Representing the Colonized" on this point. He shows how the "dialogue" between Western anthropology and colonized people has been nonreciprocal and supports the need for Westerners to begin to *stop talking*.

12. See Said, "Representing the Colonized" (212), where he encourages in particular the self-interrogation of privileged speakers. This seems to be a running theme in what are sometimes called "minority discourses": asserting the need for whites to study whiteness. The need for an interrogation of one's location exists with every discursive event by any speaker, but given the lopsidedness of current "dialogues" it seems especially important to push for this among the privileged, who sometimes seem to want to study everybody's social and cultural constructions but their own.

13. To argue for the relevance of effects for evaluation does not mean that there is only one way to do such an accounting nor does it dictate what kind of effects will be deemed desirable. How we evaluate a particular effect is left open; point number four argues simply that effects must always be taken into account.

14. I like the way Susan Bordo makes this point. In speaking about theories or ideas that gain prominence, she says: "All cultural formations . . . [are] complexly constructed out of diverse elements—intellectual, psychological, institutional, and sociological. Arising not from monolithic design but from an interplay of factors and forces, it is best understood not as a discrete, definable position which can be adopted or rejected, but as an emerging coherence which is being fed by a variety of currents, sometimes overlapping, sometimes quite distinct" (135). If these ideas arise in such a configuration of forces, does it make sense to ask for an author?

Works Cited

Alcoff, Linda. "Cultural Feminism versus Post-Structuralism: The Identity Crisis in Feminist Theory." *Signs: Journal of Women in Culture and Society* 13 (1988): 405–36.

———. *Real Knowing*. Ithaca, N.Y.: Cornell University Press, forthcoming.

Anzaldúa, Gloria. *Borderlands/La Frontera: The New Mestiza*. San Francisco: Spinsters/Aunt Lute, 1987.

Bordo, Susan. "Feminism, Postmodernism, and Gender-Skepticism." Pp. 133–56 in *Feminism/Postmodernism*, ed. Linda Nicholson. New York: Routledge, 1989.

Christian, Barbara. "The Race for Theory." *Feminist Studies* 14 (1988): 67–79.

Clifford, James. "On Ethnographic Authority." *Representations* 1 (1983): 118–46.

Clifford, James, and George Marcus, eds. *Writing Culture: The Poetics and Politics of Ethnography*. Berkeley: University of California Press, 1986.

Deleuze, Gilles, and Michel Foucault. "Intellectuals and Power." Pp. 205–17 in *Language, Counter-Memory, Practice*, ed. Donald Bouchard. Trans. Donald Bouchard and Sherry Simon. Ithaca, N.Y.: Cornell University Press, 1977.

Gates, Henry Louis, Jr. "Authority, (White) Power and the (Black) Critic: It's All Greek to Me." *Cultural Critique* 7 (fall 1987): 19–46.

Lugones, Maria. "Playfulness, 'World'-Travelling, and Loving Perception." *Hypatia* 2, no. 2 (1987): 3–19.

Lugones, Maria, and Elizabeth Spelman. "Have We Got a Theory For You! Feminist Theory, Cultural Imperialism, and the Demand for the 'Women's Voice.'" *Women's Studies International Forum* 6, no. 6 (1983): 573–81.

Maracle, Lee. "Moving Over." *Trivia* 14 (spring 1989): 9–10.

Marcus, George, and Michael Fisher, eds. *Anthropology as Cultural Critique.* Chicago: University of Chicago Press, 1986.

Menchu, Rigoberta. *I . . . Rigoberta Menchu.* Edited by Elisabeth Burgos-Debray. Trans. Ann Wright. London: Verso, 1984.

Nelson, Cary, and Lawrence Grossberg. *Marxism and the Interpretation of Culture.* Urbana: University of Illinois Press, 1988.

Rabinow, Paul. "Discourse and Power: On the Limits of Ethnographic Texts." *Dialectical Anthropology* 10, nos. 1–2 (1985): 1–14.

Said, Edward. "Representing the Colonized: Anthropology's Interlocutors." *Critical Inquiry* 15 (1989): 205–25.

Spivak, Gayatri Chakravorty. "Can the Subaltern Speak?" Pp. 271–313 in *Marxism and the Interpretation of Culture*, ed. Nelson and Grossberg.

Trebilcot, Joyce. "Dyke Methods." *Hypatia* 3, no. 2 (1988): 1–13.

Trinh T. Minh-hà. *Woman, Native, Other: Writing Postcoloniality and Feminism.* Bloomington: Indiana University Press, 1989.

Wilson, Judith. "Down to the Crossroads: The Art of Alison Saar." *Third Text* 10 (Spring 1990): 25–44.

6

Subjectivity, Experience, and Knowledge: An Epistemology from/for Rainbow Coalition Politics

The issue of difference has come to play a complex role in the theory and politics of those new social movements that have as their goal increasing democracy.[1] Feminists criticized the idea of universal man and his transhistorical rationality; what has been claimed to be true for man and reason is in fact characteristic (at best) only of men in the dominant groups in the West and their preferred view of themselves and the world. Neo-Marxists and post-Marxists have continued the older critique of "rational economic man" and his distinctively bourgeois reason. Postcolonial critics have identified the Eurocentric character of Western assumptions. Criticisms of the "straight mind" have added compulsory heterosexuality to the coercive social structures that have generated partial and distorted accounts of nature and social life (Wittig 1980).

Each of these new social movements has come to recognize that the logic of its arguments also undermines the legitimacy of generalizations from a speaker's situation to *all* women, or economically disadvantaged people, or people of third world descent, or lesbians and gays, as the case may be. If there is no universal or even typical man and his transcendental reason, then neither can there be a universal or typical woman, poor person, person of third world descent, lesbian or gay person, or her or his uniquely legitimate view of the world. Consequently, there will necessarily be legitimately different versions of feminism, postcolonialism, and any other such theory and politics that is intended to advance democracy. For these movements, there can be no single true story of a world that is out there and ready-made for reflecting in our glassy-mirror minds. When we examine feminism, for example, we find many different feminisms that have been generated from the conditions of different women's lives.

In this sense, there are many different subjects (speakers, authors) of feminist thought and politics as, apparently, there must also be for the thought and politics of other new social movements. Since mainstream Western thought has assumed a single, unitary subject, we may feel as if we had dropped through Alice's rabbit hole when we try to grasp the consequences of multiple subjectivity for conventional philosophic issues and conventional understandings of progressive politics. Assumptions that appeared unremarkable suddenly become problematic. In this essay I want to explore some consequences of this emerging logic of multiple subjects for thinking about who can make liberatory knowledge and history, as well as discuss the relationship between experience and knowledge. I shall argue that the concern to articulate the experience of the marginalized in the liberatory accounts does not function to ground knowledge in any conventional sense. Instead, this process produces the kinds of subjects who can go on to create knowledge and history. The role of marginal experience has not always been clear either in the new social movements or to critics of their claims. First, I will review a necessary reconceptualization of gender, race, class, and sexuality and the basic arguments for multiple subjects.[2]

Reconceptualizing Gender, Race, Class, and Sexuality

I begin with the observation that, in this society, each of us is located in a determinate place in gender, race, ethnicity, class, and sexuality relations.[3] That is, it is not just the marginalized who have a gender, or race, and so on. People of European descent, for example, do not escape a racial location just because they are not forced constantly to notice it or to qualify their speech by identifying the supposedly special interests, which others can see very well that it expresses. Thus, feminist analyses, for example, cannot simply be added to conventional analyses as if the latter would remain undisturbed by the addition, for the conventional analyses express special interests that are distorting: namely, the claim that a masculine perspective is identical to a gender-free and ideal human perspective.

Popular opinion, supported by the dominant tendencies in U.S. social science, conceptualizes gender, race, class, sexual orientation, and other such phenomena in ways that make it difficult to move past those misleading additive approaches to difference. In order to do so, it is helpful to keep in mind that these phenomena are fundamentally relations—structural ones—and are mutually constitutive. First, each of these phenomena should be thought of as a relation rather than as a thing or an inherent property of people. Race, gender, ethnicity, and sexuality do not designate any fixed set of qualities or properties of individuals, social or biological, such that if an individual possesses these and only these properties then he is a man, an African American, and so forth. Instead, masculinity is continuously defined and redefined as "not femininity," just as white means "not colored."

Second, these relations are deeply embedded in the structure of society. They are institutionalized relations that distribute economic, political, and social power. Contrary to popular opinion, such phenomena as racial and gender inequality have no biological causes.[4] Moreover, they are not *caused* by prejudice—by individual bad attitudes and false beliefs. The tendency to see prejudice as the cause of racial (or gender, class, or sexual) inequality tends to lodge responsibility for racism on already economically disadvantaged whites—the "Archie Bunkers" (in sociologist David Wellman's analysis)—who have not learned to avoid making overtly racist statements, as have middle-class people, and who are forced to bear a disproportionately large share of the burdens of affirmative action and equal opportunity programs. Racism is enacted in many different ways, and overt individual prejudice is just one of them. It is fundamentally a political relationship, a strategy that, in Wellman's words, "systematically provides economic, political, psychological, and social advantages for whites at the expense of Blacks and other people of color," and it is a dynamic relationship that is flexible enough to adapt to changing historical conditions (37). Similarly, sexist prejudice is the effect, not the cause, of a dynamic and flexible male supremacist social structure.

Of course, individuals *should* be held responsible for their beliefs and behaviors: it is wrong to express or enact these kinds of prejudices and thereby increase the misery of the already disadvantaged. But to rest satisfied with this individualistic and idealist analysis and its recommended remedies is to fail to come to grips with the institutional race (or gender, class, or sexuality) supremacy that appears in the beliefs and behaviors of people who do not exhibit symptoms of prejudice. An individual can be well-informed about, and not at all hostile toward, people of color, women, the poor, or gays and lesbians—that is, he or she can have the proper *mental* characteristics that constitute lack of prejudice—and nevertheless continually and effectively support beliefs and practices that maintain economic, political, and social inequality.

These two points lead to a third. Systems of political hierarchy based on differences of gender, race, class, and sexual orientation are not parallel to each other, as the preceding analysis might suggest, but interlocked, mutually created, and mutually maintaining (Mies; hooks; Collins). A setback or advance in one reverberates through the whole matrix of hierarchy creating consequences far from where such change began. This point clarifies why the new social movements can and must try to center analyses from the perspective of lives that have been marginalized within each movement. For example, there are determinate causal relations between the lives of women of European and third world descent, economically privileged and poor women, heterosexual women and lesbians, ethnic and "nonethnic" women, as well as between the men and women who have been the primary focus of feminist concern.

From the perspective of this kind of understanding, it is odd that some critics of feminism (and some feminists) have believed that starting thought from a conceptual framework that centers differences between women will have the necessary consequence of abandoning gender as an analytic category. To the contrary, it is only what we might call essential, or transcendental, gender that would have been abandoned, and that is as mythical as the transcendental man feminists have criticized. If women and men can only be found in historically determinate races, classes, and sexualities, then a gender analysis—one from the perspective of women's lives—must scrutinize gender *as it exists* from the perspective of *all* women's lives. There is no other defensible choice. The point here is not just that to insist on transcendental woman distorts the lives of marginal women. It does so, but it also distorts the lives of those at the center. I, a white Western woman, misunderstand my own life and the causes of my beliefs and actions if I cannot understand how they are shaped by institutional relations of race, class, and heterosexist supremacy as well as by male supremacy. Indeed, to understand the latter *is* to understand the former, and vice versa.

Of course racism, sexism, class exploitation, and heterosexism have their own distinctive histories, institutional forms, and dynamics; they are not identical in their histories or structures, as my account here might suggest. Nevertheless, they are widely recognized to be similar enough that they can be understood in the shared ways indicated here. Indeed, analogical reasoning from the theories and analytical strategies developed within one new social movement to the others has consistently provided important resources for grasping the logic of multiple subjects.

This brings us to the next challenge: if I must learn to understand my life from the standpoint of, say, third world women's lives, it is not so that I can speak *as* or *for* third world women. Men must learn to see themselves as they appear from the perspective of women's lives, but it is not that men can speak *as* or *for* women.

The Logic of Multiple Subjects

One main tendency in feminist epistemology has insisted that starting thought—theorizing—from women's lives decreases the partiality and distortion in our images of nature and social relations. It creates knowledge—not just opinion—that is socially situated. It is still partial in both senses of the word—interested and incomplete; but it is less distorting than thought originating in the agendas and perspectives of the lives of dominant group men. This is the feminist standpoint theory developed by Dorothy Smith, Nancy Hartsock, Hilary Rose, Alison Jaggar, myself, and others. This epistemology has been designed to account for the successes of feminist research in the social sciences and biology and to guide future research practices. Its argument is valuable in the humanities and in other natural sciences as well. Standpoint theories direct us to identify whose questions a knowledge project is asking and whose problems it has been designed to resolve. Is it asking questions that are of interest primarily to the dominant groups or to those whom the dominant groups marginalize? The disciplinary preoccupations of philosophy, sociology, biology, and literary criticism have been constructed to assist dominant institutions and individuals in their projects, not to address the concerns of the marginalized.

What does it mean to start thought from women's lives, to theorize from that location? Women lead lives different from each other; there is no typical "woman's life" from which feminists could start their thought. Moreover, in many cases women's lives are not just different from each other's but structurally opposed. In the United States, African American and Euroamerican women's lives are defined against each other by policy that is racist and sexist. African American and Euroamerican women often collude in this oppositional strategy by defining themselves as "not her"; Euroamerican women have vigorously participated in creating and maintaining racist institutions, practices, and beliefs. Nevertheless, all of these women's lives are in different respects valuable starting points for generating feminist knowledge projects. A variety of explanations for this can be gathered from mainstream social science theory.

Women's lives are the ignored and devalued missing half of human lives from which scientific problems are supposed to be generated. In important ways women are "strangers" to their own societies; their lives are not the ones the society has been designed to enable or even to fit; nor have women been as well socialized into the dominant modes of thought. Starting thought from women's lives better reveals these features of societies. Women's lives reveal the "underside" of history, the part that the "winners" of history refuse to acknowledge or name (e.g., Harding 1991, chap. 5). Thought that begins with each of these different kinds of lives can generate new scientific problems, more critical questions, and thus less partial and distorted accounts of nature and social life. Women's lives provide grounds for feminist claims not in the sense of empirically and theoretically firmer *answers* but, most importantly, of more critical empirical and theoretical *questions*. Thus, as we explored above, there is not just one unitary and coherent "speech" that is feminist thought or knowledge; instead, we have multiple and frequently contradictory knowings.

Other liberatory movements have developed similar standpoint epistemology projects, whether or not they articulate them as such. While the intellectual history of standpoint theory traces its origins to Karl Marx, Friedrich Engels, Georg Lukács, and the "standpoint of the proletariat," a social history would note that when marginalized people begin to gain voice in the dominant circles from which they had been excluded, members of the dominant group invariably begin to hear about how, from the perspective of those marginal lives, dominant assumptions and claims are distorted.

The subject/agent of feminist (or other subjugated) knowledge is multiple and frequently contradictory in a second way that mirrors the situation for women as a class. It is the thinker whose consciousness is bifurcated (Smith), the outsider within (Collins), the marginal person now also located at the center (hooks), the person who is committed to two agendas that are themselves at least partially in conflict—the liberal feminist, socialist feminist, Nicaraguan feminist, Jewish feminist— who has generated feminist sciences and new knowledge. It is thinking from a contradictory social position that generates feminist knowledge. So the logic of the directive to "start thought from women's lives" requires that we start our thought from multiple lives that in many ways conflict with each other and have multiple and contradictory commitments. In contrast, the subject of knowledge for both the conventional liberal/empiricist philosophy and for Marxism was supposed to be unitary and coherent. The condition of one kind of idealized knower—the rational man and the male proletarian, respectively—were to be created and generalized for all who would know.

In an important if controversial sense, the subject of feminist knowledge must know what every other liberatory knowledge project knows. Since at least half of the poor, racially marginalized, and gay or "queer" people are women, all feminists will have to grasp how gender, race, class, and sexuality are used to construct each other. They will have to do so if feminism is to be liberatory for marginalized women but also if feminism is to avoid deluding dominant group women about their own situations. If this were not so, there would be no way to distinguish between feminism and the narrow self-interest of dominant group women—just as conventional androcentric thought permits no criterion for distinguishing between "best beliefs" and those that serve the self-interest of men as men (bourgeois thought permits no criterion for identifying specifically bourgeois self-interest, racist thought for identifying racist self-interest, etc.).

The subject of every other liberatory movement must also learn how gender, race, class, and sexuality are used to construct each other *in order to accomplish their goals.* For example, analyses of class relations must look also at their agendas from the perspective of women's lives, since women hold class positions. Moreover, as many critics have pointed out, leftist agendas need to deal with the fact that bosses regularly and all too successfully attempt to divide the working class against itself by manipulating gender hostilities. If women are forced to tolerate lower wages and double days of work, employers can increase their profit by firing men and hiring women. Antiracist movements must conceptualize their issues from the perspective of the lives of women as well as of men of color, and so forth. We must emphasize that it is not just the women in those other movements who must know the world from the perspective of women's lives. Everyone must do so if the movements are to succeed. This requires that women be active directors of the agendas of these movements. It also requires that men in those movements be able to generate original feminist knowledge by beginning their thought from feminist understandings of women's lives, as many would argue that John Stuart Mill, Marx and Engels, Frederick Douglass, and a host of contemporary male feminists have done.

If every other liberatory movement must generate feminist knowledge, women cannot claim to be the unique generators of feminist knowledge. Nor should men claim that they are unable to produce fully feminist analyses on the grounds that they are not women or do not have women's experiences. Men, too, can contribute distinctive forms of specifically feminist knowledge *as men*—that is, from their particular social situation. Shouldn't we want men's thought to use feminist theory to think from women's lives? Men's thought, too, would start there in order to come closer to maximally critical, objective theoretical frameworks for describing and explaining their own and women's lives. Starting their thought from women's lives is necessary if men are to produce more than the male supremacist "folk belief" about themselves and the world to which female feminists object. Male feminists, like female ones, are made, not born.

If experiencing women's lives—"being a woman"—is not a necessary condition for generating feminist knowledge, what is the relation between experience and knowledge for liberatory social movements such as feminism? Is there no significant *epistemological* difference between a female feminist and a male feminist? Can whites produce "African American knowledge"? (Whether they should *claim* to do so is quite another matter!) From the perspective of conventional thought about the relations between subjectivity, experience, and knowledge, an epistemological hornet's nest appears when we follow through the logic of multiple subjects and direct *everyone,* not just women, to start their thought from women's lives.

Achieving Subjectivity and Grounding Knowledge

Some feminists and also some of their critics have assumed that feminist research and scholarship must be grounded in women's *experiences* in the sense that those experiences provide traditional kinds of foundations—clear and certain ones—for feminist claims. This assumption has been made for several apparently good reasons. To repeat well-argued points, feminists have noted that only the experiences of men in the dominant groups have grounded Western knowledge and that the generation of knowledge agendas and problematics, concepts, and interpretations of data originating in women's experiences provide a needed corrective for the distortions of androcentric thought. The shared knowledge created through such practices as consciousness-raising foregrounds women's experiences as the site where feminist knowledge processes begin. A standpoint is often assumed to be a view or perspective that is prior to the social, though standpoint theorists go to considerable effort to stress that they are talking about a location from which to generate feminist thought that is an achievement of feminist politics and theory. Women don't "naturally" have it; we have to struggle politically and conceptually to get to it. The critics are predisposed to interpret standpoint claims in this way, I wish to suggest, because mainstream empiricism assumes that the only alternative to its "objectivism" is the phenomenological approach that grounds its claims in the lived world—in "experiences."[6] Standpoint approaches are alternatives to empiricist *and* phenomenological ones and to absolutist and relativist epistemologies; but that is hard for empiricists to understand.

Standpoint approaches use the experiences of the marginalized to generate critical questions about the lives of marginalized people and of those in the dominant groups, as well as about the systematic structural and symbolic relations between them. However, I think that there is a second and crucial role that speaking one's experience plays in the generation of knowledge for marginalized people. In neither case does experience *ground* knowledge in any conventional sense. This relationship between experience and knowledge for the knowledge projects of the new social movements is troublesome precisely because the prevailing theories of experience and knowledge have been produced only from the standpoint of dominant group lives and have not recognized this second function that articulating experience plays in producing knowledge.

For women to name and describe their experiences in "their own terms" is a crucial scientific and epistemological act. Members of marginalized groups must *struggle* to name their own experiences *for* themselves in order to claim the subjectivity, the possibility of historical agency, that is given to members of dominant groups at birth (or at least, as psychoanalytic theorists report, in infancy). The Jamaican writer Michelle Cliff argues that "to write as a complete Caribbean woman, or man for that matter, demands of us retracing the African part of ourselves, reclaiming as our own, and as our subject, a history sunk under the sea, or scattered as potash in the canefields, or gone to bush, or trapped in a class system notable for its rigidity and absolute dependence on color stratification" (59). For marginalized people, to achieve subjectivity is to claim a subjugated history. Members of dominant groups are inserted into language, history, and culture as legitimate speakers and historical agents through no acts of their own, so to speak. They do not have to exert effort in order to see themselves in or as actively making history or to imagine themselves as authoritative speakers and actors. Their Dick and Jane readers, television programs, observable family and community social relations, and the structure of language itself already tell them that they are the "right stuff" to make community and history, as well as authoritative statements about reality. They simply *are* the subjectivities who *have* experiences that provide the raw material for creating dominant group conceptions of knowledge and history. For women and other marginalized groups, subjectivity and its possibility of legitimated "experience" must be achieved; subjectivity and experience are made, not born.[7] To be a recognizable subject of history and knowledge is to be permitted—indeed, expected—to have rage, anger, desire, a history, and speech, all of which are human features forbidden to marginalized people.

This denial of subjectivity is the product of material conditions. For example, it was illegal for slaves to read and write. Given formal and informal exclusionary policies, it has been difficult even for women in the dominant groups to gain access to Latin, mathematical, scientific, and other professional languages used to create and report knowledge, social theory, and public policy. It has been illegal for women to speak in public and difficult for them to publish their thoughts or travel without male chaperones. It is hard to teach philosophy without books, note several of the contributors to a special issue of the *Philosophical Forum* on apartheid (18, no. 2–3 [1987]).

But even this way of putting the point is not quite right. It is too tame. It too quickly integrates the difficult and often painful struggle of marginalized people to name their experience and so to gain a self-defined self. For marginalized people, naming their experience publicly is a cry for survival. As the African American literary critic Barbara Christian notes, "What I write and how I write is done in order to save my own life. And I mean that literally. For me literature is a way of knowing that I am not hallucinating, that whatever I feel/know *is*" (343; see also, Ellsworth; Lugones and Spelman). Henry Louis Gates, Jr., argues that Frederick Douglass, like other narrators of slave autobiographies, faced the difficult task of writing into subjectivity and history both himself and all of the other slaves whose lives would be represented by his story:

> The black slave's narrative came to be a communal utterance, a collective tale, rather than merely an individual's autobiography. Each slave author, in writing about his or her personal life's experiences, simultaneously wrote on behalf of the millions of silent slaves still held captive throughout the South. Each author, then, knew that *all* black slaves would be judged—on their character, integrity, intelligence, manners and morals, and their claims to warrant emancipation—on this published evidence provided by one of their number. (Gates x)

For Douglass, his own survival and that of millions of others depended on his ability and that of other ex-slaves to fashion their self-understandings into narratives that voiced/"created" the humanity of the silent slaves. Abdul JanMohamed notes that for Richard Wright, the

choices were literally death or the recovery/creation of his own subjectivity. The Chicana writer Gloria Anzaldúa writes of birthing herself through her writing. For a marginalized person, articulating her
or his experiences is an act of rebirthing.

Thus, marginalized people speaking their experiences is a crucial
ontological and political act, the act that creates them as the kind of
people who can make knowledge and history. Knowledge from the
perspective of women's lives could not occur without this public act
of women naming their experience in "their own terms." Subjects legitimate knowledge claims, but it takes difficult, painful, and frequently violent struggles to create such subjects. Self-created, marginal subjectivity is exactly what the dominant groups cannot permit.[8]

The naming and articulating of marginalized experience is not a
task completed at a particular moment in history. It is a continuous
process as long as oppression, exclusion, and silencing exist. Unless,
for example, African Americans have the resources to name their experiences continuously in their terms—the literacy, university positions, government consultancies, policy directorates, and so on—all of
us will lack the resources that *their* articulation of their experience
could have brought.

Let me stress that this argument does not claim incorrigibility for
expressions of marginalized experiences. As Uma Narayan has written, women's "epistemic privilege" does not include a privileged
knowledge of the *causes* of their situation.[9] What women say is not
held by feminist theorists, and certainly not by standpoint theorists,
to be immune from revision by women or anyone else. All women
have women's experiences but only at certain historical moments does
anyone ever produce feminist knowledge. We could say that our experience often "lies to us" and that the experiences of the dominant
gender, class, race, and sexuality produce more airtight, comprehensive, widely believed, and tenacious lies because these lies are used to
create institutions and ways of thinking that subsequently structure
everyone else's lives. For example, if women are excluded from education in philosophy and from participation in other institutional
forms of philosophy—conference programs, publishing, honorary
chairs, degrees, and so on—it will seem quite obvious to everyone that
"women can't do philosophy," or at least "really good" philosophy.
Thought starting from dominant group lives generates the "common
sense" of the age. Marginalized people are forced to internalize and
display what dominant groups believe of them. This is a somewhat
simplistic account of how ideology works. My point is that all of us
must live in social relations that naturalize, or seem to make neces-

sary, social arrangements that are, in fact, optional at the cultural level; they have been created and made to appear natural by the power of the dominant groups.

Transforming Subjectivities

If the subjectivities required to create knowledge can be *made* through social processes, then they can also be transformed by them. Members of the dominant groups, too, can learn how to see the world from the perspective of experiences and lives that are not theirs. After all, no woman was born with a feminist subjectivity. Women have had to learn to think from perspectives about women's lives that were not initially visible to them from "their" perspective on "their" life. Their lives and perspectives were structured by the patriarchal ideology of femininity, not by feminism. In order to transform feminine into feminist lives, they have had to listen to themselves and to other women telling about their lives, reflect on the gender (and class, race, and sexuality) aspects of their lives, undertake acts of resistance to male supremacy, reflect on the consequences of those acts, learn various feminist theories about gender relations that provide contexts into which they could insert their own experiences and perspectives . . . and so forth. They have had to *become* feminists. And, if they are, say, Euroamericans, they have had to start listening to women of color telling about their lives—and then themselves in contrast; they have had to reflect on the race aspects of their lives, undertake acts of resistance to race supremacy, reflect on the consequences of those acts, learn various theories produced by people of color about race relations and imperialism that provide contexts into which they could insert their own experiences and perspectives . . . and so forth. That is, they have had to learn how to become feminists who can function effectively as antiracists (that is, who *are* antiracist), rather than feminists who, intentionally or not, perpetuate race supremacy. They have had to learn to take historical responsibility for their race, for the white skins from which they speak and act.

There is no place in this process where it would be appropriate to say that such a white person spoke *as* or *for* women of color. Only a woman of color can speak *as* such; and women of color must be heard speaking *for* themselves. The reasons for this are many. Even though women of color's claims are not incorrigible, nor can they (anymore than anyone else) be expected to grasp the causes of their experiences, they do have a certain epistemic privilege about their own experiences. They can more easily detect the subtle forms of their marginalization and of discrimination against them. They often feel differently than do whites or the men in their own groups about what is and is not oppressive or exploitative. Furthermore, they must be heard as "equal voices" in order to *be*, to become, equal voices in discussions (Narayan). Feminists of third world descent have made such important contributions to feminist analyses in part because the necessity to theorize the connections between race, gender, class, and sexuality arises first in their lives on an everyday basis.

The logic of multiple subjects requires that all of our subjectivities be transformed in this manner, but it does not permit subjectivities to be interchangeable or, most importantly, permit members of dominant groups to speak as or for the dominated. Thus, I am not arguing that being other and "reinventing ourselves as other"—as disloyal to the dominant "civilization" and its conceptions of us—are epistemically equal social locations. They can never be so. But members of dominant groups—all of us who are Euroamerican, ethnically privileged, or masculine, economically privileged, or heterosexual—can learn to take historic responsibility for the social locations from which our speech and actions issue. This is a scientific and epistemological issue as well as a moral and political one.

Conclusion

The recognition and exploration of the existence of multiple subjects of knowledge in all of the democracy-advancing new social movements reveals that the relations between subjectivity, experience, and knowledge entrenched in conventional epistemology and political philosophy appear reasonable only from the perspective of dominant group lives. In the conventional accounts, there is an ambivalent relation to subjectivity. On the one hand, insofar as it bears the markers of its social location and, especially, of the social location of "others," it appears as something to be excluded or, at least, rigorously controlled in the production of knowledge. Socially situated subjectivity threatens to overwhelm or pollute "pure knowledge." Marginalized people are thought to be the most irretrievably mired in their social situation; women, "natives," the poor, and other others are the models for the irrationality, social passions, immersion in the bodily, and the subjective against which dispassionate reason, social justice, historical progress, "civilization," and the objective pursuit of knowledge have been defined. On the other hand, "rational man's" subjectivity is to be activated, nourished, and encouraged to range freely in the pursuit of truth, justice, and social progress.

Western science, for example, is supposedly the result of the active subjectivity of the great men of science: "In [Isaac] Newton's achievement we see how science advances by heroic exercises of the imagination rather than by patient collecting and sorting of myriads of individual facts. Who, after studying Newton's magnificent contribution to thought, could deny that pure science exemplifies the creative accomplishment of the human spirit at its pinnacle?" (Cohen 190). This double standard arises from particular historical needs: to activate dominant group subjectivity but also to suppress any sign of autonomous subjectivity in marginalized groups.

Understanding nature and social relations requires not just knowing what we think of ourselves and the world but also what others think of us and our beliefs (Mura 152). We must "reinvent ourselves as Other" in the sense of becoming "disloyal to civilization," in Adrienne Rich's memorable phrase, in order to develop the kinds of multiple subjectivities that are capable of understanding objectively their own social location, not just imagining that they understand the social locations of others.[10] This project requires the prior creation of authoritative subjectivities in the marginalized. For that, the public articulation of their different experience is a precondition. Thus, the public articulation of marginalized experience is a necessary precondition for the creation of democracy-advancing knowledge, but it is not its grounds.

The new understandings of subjectivity, experience, and knowledge offer significant possibilities for coalition politics between groups who share, at a minimum, opposition to hegemonic politics and a renegade understanding of the crucial role that articulating "experience" plays in generating and legitimating just such sciences and politics—without ever needing conventionally to "ground" them.

Sandra Harding

Notes

This essay was originally written in the spring of 1990 with the support of a fellowship in the Center for Advanced Studies at the University of Delaware. The first version appeared in *Multiple Subject: Feminist Perspectives on Postmodernism, Epistemology, and Science*, coauthored with Elvira Schieck and Maria Osietzki (Hamburg: Institute for Social Science, 1991) and in *Development and Change* 23, no. 3 (1992). That issue of *Development and Change* was subsequently reprinted as *Emancipations: Modern and Postmodern*, ed. Jan Nederveen Pieterse (London: Sage, 1992).

1. Both the feminist and antiracist/postcolonial epistemology discussions have been fast moving; a number of my claims here seem a lot less novel now than they did when I revised this esssay in late 1990 for this collection. Since I understand that other contributors to this collection are responding and referring to this second version, however, I have made only minor changes in it.

2. I have made these arguments in other places, most recently in chapter 11, "Reinventing Ourselves as Other" (*Whose Science?* 212–17, 284–88). Clarification of some of these epistemological concerns is explored in my "Rethinking Standpoint Epistemology."

3. In this chapter, the term "race" is always to be understood as in scare quotes to indicate that it is a cultural construction, not a biological given. See many of the essays in my *"Racial" Economy of Science.*

4. Indeed, race is not a useful category of biological analysis, as biologists and physical anthropologists have pointed out for decades. It is a residue from the Linnean classificatory scheme; it conflicts with evolutionary theory; and it is a social construct, as the essays in my book *"Racial" Economy* show.

5. These and other explanations are explored in chapter 5 of my *Whose Science?*

6. "Objectivism" is only "weak objectivity." Feminism and the other new social movements both demand and generate stronger standards for maximizing objectivity than objectivism's neutrality ideal permits. See chapter 6 of my *Whose Science?*, and my essay "After the Neutrality Ideal."

7. Mary Belenky and her colleagues point out that "It's my opinion" means "I have a right to my opinion" for men, but it means "It's just my opinion" for women. They also discuss the "women of silence" who do not yet "have" self, voice, or mind, whom some of their interviewees report having been.

8. Hence, I read the early feminist standpoint writings that give considerable attention to articulating the different human experiences that women have through their socially assigned activity in mothering, housework, emotional labor, and caring for others' bodies as making the following point: there is a different subjectivity from "the human" (i.e., ruling group men's), and it is created through interacting with the world in different ways than men are assigned. That is, women's experience functions in these accounts both as something to be explained and as a clue to the different social location from which much feminist research has emerged and from which everyone—not just the women who have some particular experiences or other—should start off thought. Women's experience does not function as the *grounds* for feminist claims on these standpoint accounts any more than "proletarian experience" provides the grounds for Marx's *Das Kapital.* In contrast, it does function as the grounds for knowledge in some feminist phenomenological sociology and in many radical feminist writings.

9. Narayan's illuminating arguments for the importance in the creation of knowledge of expressions of the emotions of the oppressed as they report their experiences may be read as providing additional arguments to those above for the important role that experiences play in the creation of knowl-

edge from the standpoint of oppressed lives—and without claiming that experience *grounds* that knowledge.

10. V. Y. Mudimbe argues that African philosophers must reinvent the West as a bizarre and alien tradition from which they can learn important techniques but against which they can also ambiguously define their alterity. I am arguing that Westerners—and, more generally, members of dominant social groups—can also engage in this reclamation of self and historical agency against a hegemonic culture.

Works Cited

Anzaldúa, Gloria. *Borderlands/La Frontera: The New Mestiza*. San Francisco: Spinsters/Aunt Lute, 1987.

Belenky, Mary Field, Blythe McVicker Clinchy, Nancy Rule Goldberger, and Jill Mattuck Tarule. *Women's Ways of Knowing: The Development of Self, Voice, and Mind*. New York: Basic Books, 1986.

Christian, Barbara. "The Race for Theory." Pp. 335–45 in *Making Face, Making Soul/Haciendo Caras*, ed. Gloria Anzaldúa. San Francisco: Aunt Lute Foundation, 1990.

Cliff, Michelle. "A Journey into Speech." Pp. 57–62 in *The Graywolf Annual Five: Multi-Cultural Literacy*, ed. Rick Simonson and Scott Walker. St. Paul, Minn.: Graywolf Press, 1988.

Cohen, I. Bernard. *The Birth of a New Physics*. New York: Doubleday, 1960.

Collins, Patricia Hill. *Black Feminist Thought: Knowledge, Consciousness, and the Politics of Empowerment*. Boston: Routledge, 1991.

Ellsworth, Elizabeth. "Why Doesn't This Feel Empowering? Working Through the Repressive Myths of Critical Pedagogy." *Harvard Educational Review* 59, no. 3 (1989): 297–324.

Gates, Henry Louis, Jr. "Introduction." Pp. ix–xviii in *The Classic Slave Narratives*, ed. Henry Louis Gates, Jr. New York: New American Library, 1987.

Harding, Sandra. "After the Neutrality Ideal: Politics, Science, and 'Strong Objectivity.'" *Social Research* 59, no. 3 (1992): 567–87.

———, ed. *The "Racial" Economy of Science: Toward a Democratic Future*. Bloomington: Indiana University Press, 1993.

———. "Rethinking Standpoint Epistemology: What Is 'Strong Objectivity'?" Pp. 49–82 in *Feminist Epistemologies*, ed. Linda Alcoff and Elizabeth Potter. New York: Routledge, 1993.

———. *The Science Question in Feminism*. Ithaca, N.Y.: Cornell University Press, 1986.

———. *Whose Science? Whose Knowledge? Thinking from Women's Lives*. Ithaca, N.Y.: Cornell University Press, 1991.

———. "Why Has the Sex-Gender System Become Visible Only Now?" Pp. 311–24 in *Discovering Reality*, ed. Harding and Hintikka.

Harding, Sandra, and Merrill Hintikka, eds. *Discovering Reality: Feminist Perspectives on Epistemology, Metaphysics, Methodology, and Philosophy of Science*. Dordrecht, Holland: Reidel/Kluwer, 1983.

Hartsock, Nancy. "The Feminist Standpoint: Developing the Ground for a Specifically Feminist Historical Materialism." Pp. 283–310 in *Discovering Reality*, ed. Harding and Hintikka.

hooks, bell. *Feminist Theory: From Margin to Center*. Boston: South End Press, 1983.

Jaggar, Alison. *Feminist Politics and Human Nature*. Totowa, N.J.: Rowman and Allenheld, 1983.

JanMohamed, Abdul. "Negating the Negation as a Form of Affirmation in Minority Discourse: The Construction of Richard Wright as Subject." *Cultural Critique* 7 (Fall 1987): 245–66.

Lugones, Maria, and Elizabeth V. Spelman. "Have We Got a Theory for You! Feminist Theory, Cultural Imperialism, and the Demand for the 'Women's Voice.'" *Women's Studies International Forum* 6, no. 6 (1983): 573–81.

Mies, Maria. *Patriarchy and Accumulation on a World Scale: Women in the International Division of Labor*. London: Zed Books, 1986.

Mudimbe, V. Y. *The Invention of Africa*. Bloomington: Indiana University Press, 1988.

Mura, David. "Strangers in the Village." Pp. 135–53 in *The Graywolf Annual Five: Multi-Cultural Literacy*, ed. Rick Simonson and Scott Walker. St. Paul, Minn.: Graywolf Press, 1988.

Narayan, Uma. "Working Together across Difference: Some Considerations on Emotions and Political Practice." *Hypatia* 3, no. 2 (1988): 31–48.

Rose, Hilary. "Hand, Brain, and Heart: A Feminist Epistemology for the Natural Sciences." *Signs: Journal of Women in Culture and Society* 9 (1983): 73–90.

Smith, Dorothy. *The Everyday World as Problematic: A Feminist Sociology*. Boston: Northeastern University Press, 1987.

Wellman, David. *Portraits of White Racism*. New York: Cambridge University Press, 1977.

Wittig, Monique. "The Straight Mind." *Feminist Issues* 1 (1980): 103–11.

7

Subjects, Knowledges, . . . and
All the Rest: Speaking for What?

In her essay "Subjectivity, Experience, and Knowledge" (in this volume), Sandra Harding details how feminist standpoint theory as a critique of experience offers alternative ways of thinking about the subjects and knowledge claims of feminism and other liberatory social movements. I want to highlight several of her points and relate them to some of the presuppositions in Linda Alcoff's essay, "The Problem of Speaking for Others" (in this volume), in order to delineate what I take to be the effectiveness as well as the limits of their positions. Both essays exemplify work that builds on the vision of possibility in feminist standpoint theory. While Harding explicitly acknowledges her debt to standpoint theory—she has in fact been one of its major formulators—Alcoff's ties to this critical framework are more oblique. Nonetheless, I think it is useful to read Alcoff's essay in relation to feminist standpoint theory because her emphasis on discourse and location is a Foucauldian take on many of the issues addressed by standpoint theory, a line of thinking that characterizes a growing wave of cultural studies currently pushing against and beyond the Marxist problematic within which feminist standpoint theory is rooted. Reading Alcoff and Harding in relation to each other illuminates some of what is lost to feminism in forfeiting the systemic perspective of historical materialism.

First, I want to acknowledge that I understand the process of working on the possibilities and limits of oppositional knowledge as one important facet of the philosophical and political struggle out of which a politics of resistance is forged. Affirming the possibilities of oppositional knowledge reinforces the shared vision that constitutes the basis for solidarity: a vision of social equality, shared resources, full democracy, and justice for all. While feminists take as their point of entry into the struggle to achieve these aims the particular effects of social inequality on women, they also recognize that social equity cannot be achieved without ending the exploitation and oppression of all people. Attending to the limits of what we know has also been a crucial part of the history of feminist praxis. Historically, feminists have worked on and against these limits by listening to our often divergent ways of making sense, debating their uses, and measuring the gaps between and within those knowledges against our shared commitments and the contradictions that shape our lives. This critique(al) mode of reading has been one of the movement's most valuable political resources, allowing feminists to confront the insidious ways the assumptions in our thinking sometimes can be quite at odds with our most ardent aims. Among the objectives of this collection of essays is the effort to make a space to extend this critical tradition, to expose the sites of struggle in an array of oppositional formulations of authority and identity, and to debate their limits and consequences.

For materialist feminists, struggles over knowledge are significant because they are part of the broad-ranging social contest over resources and power. However, in current feminist discussions of authority and identity, the relationship between knowledges/identities (the domain of social production I will refer to as "ideology") and "all the rest" of the social is often effaced. Sometimes in feminist analysis, discourses and knowledges substitute for *all* social relations. Of course, this is not an innocent formulation; it, too, has a history, unspoken interests, and effects. Analysis that emphasizes the cultural or ideological domain of the social and downplays or elides its relation to economic and political production has long dominated feminist thought. Socialist feminists have been the most outspoken critics of this trend (Barrett; Delphy; Hamilton and Barrett; Mies). Over the past twenty years, these socialist feminist critiques have been elaborated through the efforts of materialist feminists who recognized that accounting for the material conditions of women's oppression requires more adequate explanations of labor, subjectivity, and resistance than traditional Marxist analysis could offer. Materialist feminists have utilized postmodern theories of the subject-in-language to advance more rigorous and refined understandings of the ways patriarchal oppression is lived. But pursuing the complexities of the subject's discursive construction and location has also tended to restrict the broad systemic reach of materialist feminist analysis to cultural politics.[1] Reclaiming materialist feminism's legacy of systemic analysis can lead us to consider the limits of an exclusively cultural politics as well as the effectiveness of historical materialism as a powerful but often suppressed theory of social life.

Before turning to Harding's and Alcoff's essays, I want to offer a few brief comments on feminist standpoint theory. For many years feminists have been theorizing relations between women's lives and ways of making sense of them in terms of standpoint theory (e.g., Collins; Harding; Hartsock; Smith). Indeed, feminist standpoint theory has been one of the most significant contributions to materialist critiques of Western epistemology. Socialist feminists initially developed the notion of standpoint from the insights of Karl Marx, Friedrich Engels, Georg Lukács, and others in order to formulate a more coherent explanation of feminism's authority, who it speaks for, and the forces of oppression and exploitation it contests. Standpoint refers to a "position" in society that is affected by and in turn helps shape ways of knowing, structures of power, and divisions of labor. Feminist standpoint theorists have posited feminism as this sort of position, a way of conceptualizing reality from the vantage point of women's lives (their activities, interests, and values). Most significantly, in addressing the complex material forces that structure the relations between social positioning and ways of knowing, feminist standpoint theories have challenged the assumption that simply to be a woman guarantees a clear understanding of the world. Instead, they argue that the feminist standpoint is a position that is socially produced and so not necessarily immediately available to all women. For feminist standpoint theory, then, both the representation of a feminist perspective and its "truth" are reached through philosophical and political struggle (Jaggar 383–84).

In "Subjectivity, Experience, and Knowledge," Sandra Harding contends that by taking women's lives as a starting point for knowledge, standpoint theory confronts the "partiality and distortion" of Western thought that typically starts from the lives of men in the dominant group. Setting aside for the moment this troublesome notion of partiality, I want to look more closely at what it means to Harding that feminist critique is grounded in women's lives. First of all, her argument for women's lives as the foundation for knowledge is premised on the claim that women's lives are necessarily multiple and contradictory. Not only is there "no typical 'woman's life,'" but women's experiences of their lives are not the same as feminist knowledge of women's lives. Because women's experiences are often framed in terms of common sense, women's experiential narratives might well be as "narrow" and "distorted" as knowledge that starts from the lives of "men in the dominant groups." Harding's assertion that "women's experience" in itself is not a reliable ground for feminist knowledge is one of the key insights of standpoint theory. Since subjectivity is

made, not born, women are not the unique generators of feminist
thought but have "had to learn to think from perspectives about wom-
en's lives that were not initially visible to them from 'their' perspective on 'their' life."

Throughout her work on feminist epistemology, Harding has confronted this incoherence in feminism's correlation to women's lives,
and she has argued that feminists should replace the desire for unity
around women's common experiences with political solidarity based
on goals shared with other groups struggling against social oppression.
Harding's argument also reiterates one of the knotty problems that has
vexed feminist standpoint theory: the unexplained link between the
discursive materiality of feminist knowledge and the empirical materiality of women's lives. Poststructuralist theories of the subject-in-
language have provided feminist standpoint theorists with useful
frameworks for reconceptualizing "Woman" as a differentially and discursively constructed social position. One unfortunate effect of this
work, however, has been heightened attention to women's discursive
positionality with minimal analysis of how to understand the relationship between discursive knowledge and its presumably nondiscursive
foundation in (women's) lives. Thus, feminist standpoint theorists like
Harding, who admire the potential of postmodern theories of the subject's positionality, at times equate "subject positions" and "women's
lives" even as they hint that the lived world of women and narratives
of it are not coterminous. If the subject is theorized as an ensemble of
discursive positions, are women's lives merely discursive or more than
discursive? If they are in some way both, how are we to understand
the relation between their discursive and nondiscursive dimensions?
In that it stresses the social construction of "speaking from," standpoint theory's claim to ground its knowledges in research on wom-
en's lives is distinct from analyses that profess to speak from women's
experience. But substituting the vaguely mediated "women's lives" for
the empirical given of "women's experience" does not in itself explain
the material relation between lives and ways of making sense of them.

This problem appears in Harding's essay in the tension between
group identities and perspectives as a starting point for epistemology
from/for the rainbow coalition. At times it seems that the authority
for knowledge is grounded in group identity, as when she contends
that Western thought has started out from the lives of men in the
dominant groups or that the many different feminisms start off their
analyses from the lives of different historical groups of women. Clearly, Harding's project is to rethink the subject of knowledge as a differentiated one but without conceptualizing difference in individual or

additive terms. In this sense, she is emphatically contesting liberal plu-ralist approaches to social difference that have tended to prevail in much thinking on diversity and multiculturalism. Her aim is not a plu-ralist one—that is, to add to the dominant set of knowledges new per-spectives from the experiences of marginalized groups—but rather a more radical disruption of the dominant framework, including its sub-jects, the kinds of questions it can pose, and their implied answers. While Harding insists that membership in the group "women" does not guarantee oppositional knowledge, her argument often slides into the logic of pluralism by default, as the basis for knowledge becomes *groups of people*. If we pursue Harding's argument that knowledge is not so much a matter of group affiliation as it is a matter of critical per-spective, it seems to me that we would have to claim that the exist-ence of multiple feminist discourses is not necessarily the result of starting off their analyses from the lives of many historical *groups* of women, as Harding asserts, so much as it is the effect of multiple crit-ical *perspectives* on women's lives, whose interests may overlap or un-evenly coincide. But in what sense, then, does feminist analysis "start off" from women's lives? How are feminist perspectives differently interested? In what way are these interests part and parcel of both the materiality of women's lives and the various perspectives on them? In order to address these questions we need a critical framework, a per-spective, that can explain the complex relationship between knowledge and other social practices.

Harding's essay gestures toward this sort of perspective when she asserts that systems of social hierarchy are interlocked, mutually cre-ated, and mutually maintaining. She contends at one point that "there are determinate causal relations between the lives of women of Euro-pean and third world descent, economically privileged and poor wom-en, heterosexual women and lesbians, ethnic and 'nonethnic' wom-en." But her analysis does not then address exactly *how* these different facets of women's lives are situated in and structured by "determinate causal relations" or how perspectives on women's lives are also relat-ed to these determinate causal links among the lives of women.

Harding offers a view of social relations that is complex in its plural-ity, where persons are multiply positioned, and where thought starts from multiple lives. But the material relationship of those lives to the systemic and hierarchical workings of power is eclipsed. This eclipsing is what makes her presentation of the "partiality" of dominant knowl-edges so troublesome. Harding claims that all human thought is partial in the sense that it is "interested and incomplete" and that some par-tialities are more narrow and distorted than others. Why is this? Why is knowledge that starts from women's lives less partial than thought originating in the "agendas and perspectives of the lives of dominant group men," especially if some women make sense of their lives in terms that are coherent with those of the dominant group? If all truths are partial, isn't the pressing epistemological issue not the degree of partiality in any truth claim but the interests and effects of truth claims on the social reality they construct? In other words, isn't feminism's criterion for evaluating any knowledge not its approximation of the "whole truth" but the implicit effects of the truths it claims—for/against the oppression and exploitation of all people?

Starting thought from women's lives can expose the ways in which women are oppressed as well as how they oppress one another; it can uncover the structures of exploitation that bind women and men in suburb and ghetto, metropolis and periphery, and it can display how the contradictions in prevailing knowledges uphold these arrangements even as they work to conceal them, *but only if this project issues from a perspective that understands social relations in these systemic terms.* Systemic analysis has been standpoint theory's hallmark and its strength. Although Harding's analysis does not explain what the "determinate causal relations" it gestures toward might be and how they might affect knowledges as well as women's lives, I believe that pursuing this line of thinking is crucial to current oppositional political work. This is especially the case as the unpopularity of this critical framework marks it as a limit term, a suppressed "other" if you will, in postmodern cultural studies.

In wrestling with current criticisms of any effort to "speak for" others, Linda Alcoff resituates the question of how we know and its bearing on identity in terms that have much in common with feminist standpoint theory. She addresses the dilemma, "Is it ever a valid practice to speak for others who are unlike me or who are less privileged than me?," by acknowledging that what is at stake in this problem is much more than any notion of an experiential subject can explain. She takes as a given that the act of representation is always mediated so that speaking for oneself is not any more authentic or neutral than speaking for others. Moreover, she demonstrates the political nuances in the strategy of "not speaking for": when it is important to keep quiet and listen and when not speaking can serve to excuse an individual from examining his or her interested standpoint. As an alternative to the troublesome dynamics of "speaking for," she proposes that we try to create the conditions for dialogue—for speaking with and to rather than for—and she explores the conditions under which speaking for others might be legitimate and even necessary.

Alcoff's detailed answer to the question "Who can speak?" explicitly draws upon Michel Foucault's concept of "rituals of speaking" or discursive practices. Two elements are important in this concept: the positionality or location of the speaker and the discursive context. Throughout her analysis, Alcoff stresses the importance of "location" and "context." In keeping with Foucault's notion of discursive practices, Alcoff defines context as "the connections and relations of involvement between the utterance/text and other utterances and texts, as well as the material practices in the relevant environment." As in Foucault, the relationship between text (discourse) and all the rest—those "other material practices"—remains unexplained. It seems to me that this is another instance of the problematic relationship between *perspectives on women* and *women's lives*, except that in Alcoff's analysis the materiality of "lives" as a starting point for knowledge has itself all but disappeared, displaced by the Foucauldian starting point—discursive practices.

As many critiques of Foucault (including Alcoff's) have by now made clear, Foucault's theory of discourse, anchored as it is in his notion of power as a diffused set of force relations, is at odds with an oppositional perspective that understands power in terms of the hierarchical structures of domination and the dynamics of exploitation (whereby the surplus and privilege enjoyed by one group of people is gleaned at the expense of another). Alcoff clearly believes that power operates hierarchically. She argues, for example, that certain locations and contexts are allied with structures of oppression while others are allied with structures of resistance—in other words, all speaking positions are not equal. But here, as in Foucault, the terms of this inequality seem arbitrary. The "causal and determinate" dimension of power (that Harding at least glancingly refers to and that allows us to make connections between rich and poor, metropolis and periphery, discursive and nondiscursive practices) has disappeared almost entirely, displaced by a Foucauldian social logic of noncorrespondence that allows only for contingent, local connections or contexts.

The stress on location and context in this Foucauldian sense is reiterated in the work of many cultural theorists (Butler; de Lauretis; Diamond and Quinby; Fuss; Garber; Sawicki). It seems to me that one of the pernicious features of this local notion of context is that it can tend to keep the effects of knowledge *intransitive*. I agree with Alcoff that we need to consider the effects of knowledges; in fact, this seems to me to be one of the most important feminist contributions to the project of rethinking epistemology. But effects for what? The last paragraph of Alcoff's essay indicates that the answer to this question is for "a more equitable, just distribution of the ability to speak and be heard." As her examples demonstrate, questions about who speaks, who is able to speak, and who can be heard depend on social structures and systems of power, those "sexual, national, and other kinds of hierarchies" that speaking for others can both erase and reinscribe. However, many accounts of rituals of speaking that focus on discursive practices in very specific locations never offer any causal explanation of their connection to these hierarchies. Taking specific locations and discursive practices as the *starting point* for analysis of knowledge invariably mutes the connection between knowledges and the social hierarchies that organize people's lives: the international division of labor, differentiated but nonetheless pervasive patriarchal structures, neocolonialism, institutionalized racism, compulsory heterosexuality . . .

That these connections are obliquely referred to in Alcoff's piece indicates the *possibility* of a systemic analysis that could link rituals of speaking to configurations of state and economy. We see this when she argues that George Bush's statement that Noriega is a corrupt dictator who stands in the way of democracy in Panama has the effect of consolidating United States imperialism by obscuring its true role in Central America. Here the material effects of Bush's imperialist discourse are shown to have consequences for people's lives in Panama and the United States in that they reshape repressive policies toward Panama and reinforce images of U.S. benevolence and Latin American otherness in the national common sense.

Many other discourses that do not issue from the White House also work to consolidate (and obscure) U.S. imperialism. What about Anne Cameron's or the prominent theorist's work? They are certainly not speaking from the same location/context as George Bush, but the perspective from which Alcoff views them does not admit that their ways of making sense have effects beyond their own local situations. In order to explain why Anne Cameron should indeed "move over," we need a perspective that addresses *why* her books are "truly disempowering" for Native Canadian women but without reducing her to being in the same position as George Bush. In other words, the answer to "Who can speak?" may be so focused on the contextual contingencies shaping identity and authority that the question of "Speaking for what?" is obscured. Evaluating who can legitimately speak for others entails more than attending to the particular situation of who is speaking. Even after we situate the speaker historically, there remains the question of how we understand history—in terms of local contexts or, as I am arguing, in terms of a systemic vision of social life, a perspective that connects the circulation of knowledges in local situations to the broader social relations in which they are embedded.

* * *

Working on the limits of an only vaguely related connection between the discursive and nondiscursive from the perspective of standpoint theory's basis in historical materialism can help reformulate what is meant by "context" and make more explicit the material relations between knowledges and lives.[2] Some of the most useful advances in theorizing the materiality of language and its function in the formation of subjects have come from critical elaborations of Louis Althusser's work on ideology.[3] From a historical materialist perspective, ideologies—what is known, thought, believed, valued—operate in an interdeterminate relationship with economic and political production. In any particular historical formation, available knowledges are both shaped by and in turn help define the contradictory development and displacement of economic and political forces. Social production is not restricted to economic processes, nor is it merely a function of ideology; rather it includes the discursive production of knowledge within the complex ensemble of material production that comprises social life.

The dialectical relation between knowledge and "all the rest" is an important component of the historical materialist conception of this ensemble of relations. The discourses that constitute the material structures through which ideology works are shaped by and in turn help shape the material relations that comprise economic and political production. This means that "women's lives" have a materiality (as enactors of productive and reproductive labor, as living human bodies) that exceeds their discursive construction, but at the same time the "reality" of women's lives is only made possible through historically available knowledges. These modes of intelligibility are unevenly and contradictorily shaped in specific historical situations or contexts by divisions of labor and relations between state and civil society.

In developing theories of ideology beyond the limits of Althusser's problematic, materialist feminists have also recognized the usefulness of Antonio Gramsci's concept of hegemony for conceptualizing the complexity of the discursive face of power. Gramsci's theory of hegemony avoids the weighty determinism in Althusser's notion of the formation of subjects through ideological interpellation while still maintaining historical materialism's distinguishing global social logic.[4] Hegemony is the process whereby the interests of a ruling group come to dominate by establishing the common sense, that is, those values, beliefs, and knowledges that go without saying. Gramsci emphasizes that hegemony is forged out of social struggle. The universal appeal of the values and norms that a hegemonic formation enforces is aimed at reproducing a division of labor and power, achieved by suppressing knowledge of the struggle over knowledge, labor, and power by drawing elements from various contesting knowledges into an imaginary coherent conceptual framework. The concept of hegemony and the systemic theory of the social on which it is premised connects the materiality of people's lives and knowledges. Perspectives on people's lives, including feminist ones, are situated within and perhaps against the social order (division of labor and power) that hegemonic knowledges help reproduce. Women's lives are shaped by ideology in the sense that their lived "experiences" are never served up raw but are always made sense of from interested vantage points in some relation to hegemonic knowledges, including those of the women experiencing the events and those of the feminist critic, scholar, or theorist who appeals to women's lives as the basis for her knowledge.

Women's lives can never speak for themselves in any authentic way. The authority of an oppositional perspective's claim to make sense of them rests in its interests, by which I mean the social order it argues for, the challenge it poses to the prevailing social hierarchies, and the alternative vision of possibility it offers. Feminism contends that historically patriarchy has taken a variety of forms that give men dominance over women. Materialist feminists argue that patriarchy has succeeded by eliciting women's consent through imaginary representations that naturalize this domination. Drawing on and developing historical materialism's theory of the social, a materialist feminist standpoint sees patriarchal regimes as traversed by and embedded in capitalism's exploitative divisions of labor and expropriation of land and resources. It explores the ways in which women's lives and knowledges are shaped by and in turn affect these social systems, both in relation to men and to one another.

Understanding people's lives from a systemic materialist perspective provides a critical framework that can address how subjects are multiply positioned across systems of difference without reducing these positions to homogenized groups. It also allows us to develop oppositional analyses that acknowledge the complexity of people's lives as they are understood in the texts of culture without reducing lives to texts or to specific local contexts. From this perspective, the relationship between discourse and its contexts is a dialectical one that operates within the complex of systems that compose the social order.

Conceptualizing discourse (à la Foucault and Alcoff) as an event that includes context, where "context" consists of "speaker, words, hearers, location, language, and so on," limits "context" to only the most specific and discursive social arrangements, and it is these local situations that Alcoff stresses. She argues that evaluation of the effects of a set of claims should pay most attention to the "discursive arrangement" in order to understand its full meaning. One effect of this emphasis on the discursive is that power dynamics, between for example "first" and "third" world speakers, can be seen as merely the effect of "the structure of the speaking practice." Restricting oppositional analysis to a perspective that evaluates only from the vantage point of "a very specific location" closes off recognition of the nondiscursive material relations that underlie claims to authority and knowledge between "first" and "third world" speakers, material relations that at other times Alcoff seems very well aware of. Certainly consideration of these contingencies is important, and I want to underscore this point. Yet in itself it is not sufficient for evaluating the effects of our ways of making sense.

Consider the example of middle-class women in the 1990s. Increasingly they are invited to perceive themselves as equal to men, even as on a daily basis they confront constructions of the feminine that contradict this message. Some postmodern knowledges that focus only on the local context of middle-class urban culture encourage us to read the emergence of more flexible gender codes as an indicator that patriarchy is no longer useful as an explanatory concept. The critique of a static and universal notion of patriarchy has often led to the substitution of more specific and local stories of gender formation for patriarchy as an organizing social system. One result is that the more flexible gender ideologies in the lives of middle-class women get isolated not only from reformed, postmodern structures of patriarchal dominance but also from their place in a global capitalist system in which the labors of women "elsewhere" help make possible the new gender formations of postindustrial societies.

In part because the various facets of the social remain unconnected in our theories even as the triumph of capitalism relies on an interdependent world system, the regimes of power that regulate knowledges and people's lives are able to persist. It is this dynamic that makes a systemic analysis ever more compelling for political resistance. Advocating the appropriation of historical materialism's systemic analysis, however, means going against the grain of much work in postmodern cultural studies that equates the critique of social totalities, such as capitalism, imperialism, or patriarchy, with a reductive totalizing logic. I want to be quite clear that in arguing for the systemic analysis implicit in standpoint theory's historical materialist understanding of the social I am not

calling for a return to master narratives that universalize and homoge-
nize from a disinterested, transcendent perspective. Nor do I think we
need to forfeit the rich and important insights into the nuanced workings of power in specific locations that cultural studies has developed in
the past decade. In taking as its starting point the ensemble of productive relations that make up social life, historical materialist analysis does
not abandon attention to the ways discourses operate in specific historical contexts, but it does set out to explain the relationship of these
knowledges to broad-ranging social structures.

When the Lakota people issued a Declaration of War in September
1993 against the appropriation of their culture and spiritual traditions
by white profiteers, at issue in their statement was not simply a matter of privileged persons speaking for the less privileged but of the
exploitative social arrangements that "speaking for" is caught up in
and supports, in this case knowledge stolen and profits reaped at a
particular group's expense. In protesting the commodification of Lakota culture, whether by crass New Age consumers or well-inten-
tioned writers, the declaration powerfully makes explicit the connection between speaking for and its effects. The Lakotas' aim is not for
nonnative people to "move over" so that more authentic Lakota voices may enter the market place but to question the capitalist and imperialist commodification of knowledge. We need not be Lakota to
speak to this situation, nor would speaking for these Lakota concerns
violate political solidarity with their objectives.

If grappling with questions of authority and critical identity directs
us to think about power discursively, we need to consider that the
history of the discursive construction of knowledge (like the answer
to the question "Who can speak?") cannot be severed from the consequences of knowledge or the question "Speaking for what?" This
second question is a crucial gauge of oppositional authority because it
points to the vision of possibility that drives a politics of resistance. A
vision directed toward social equity and full democracy requires that
we make connections between the workings of power in particular
historical situations and the larger structures that organize social life,
between *who can speak* and for *what kind of world.*

Rosemary Hennessy

Notes

1. Terry Lovell offers a useful critical anthology of these developments in
British feminist thought. In addition, see my *Materialist Feminism and the Politics of Discourse* on materialist feminism's relation to cultural politics.

2. The argument in the following section is elaborated much more fully in my essay, "Women's Lives/Feminist Knowledge," and in chapter three of my book.

3. *Lenin and Philosophy* and *Reading Capital* are the most complete presentations of Althusser's theory of ideology.

4. Often the economic dimension in Gramsci's systemic framework is suppressed. The most notable example of this post-Marxist rewriting of Gramsci is Ernesto Laclau and Chantal Mouffe, *Hegemony and Socialist Strategy.*

Works Cited

Alcoff, Linda. "Feminist Politics and Foucault: The Limits to a Collaboration." Pp. 69–86 in *Crises in Continental Philosophy.* ed. Arlene Dallery and Charles Scott. Albany: State University of New York Press, 1990.

Althusser, Louis, and Etienne Balibar. *Lenin and Philosophy and Other Essays.* Trans. Ben Brewster. New York: Monthly Review Press, 1971.

————. *Reading Capital.* Trans. Ben Brewster. London: NLB, 1970.

Barrett, Michele. *Women's Oppression Today: Problems in Marxist Feminist Analysis.* London: Verso, 1980.

Butler, Judith. *Gender Trouble: Feminism and the Subversion of Identity.* New York: Routledge, 1990.

Collins, Patricia Hill. *Black Feminist Thought: Knowledge, Consciousness, and the Politics of Empowerment.* New York: Routledge, 1990.

de Lauretis, Teresa. *Technologies of Gender: Essays on Theory, Film, and Fiction.* Bloomington: Indiana University Press, 1987.

Delphy, Christine. *Close to Home: A Materialist Analysis of Women's Oppression.* London: Hutchinson, 1984.

Diamond, Irene, and Lee Quinby, eds. *Feminism and Foucault: Reflections on Resistance.* Boston: Northeastern University Press, 1988.

Fuss, Diana, ed. *Inside/Out: Lesbian Theories, Gay Theories.* New York: Routledge, 1991.

Garber, Marjorie. *Vested Interests: Cross-Dressing and Cultural Anxiety.* New York: Routledge, 1992.

Gramsci, Antonio. *Selections from the Prison Notebooks.* Trans. Quentin Hoare and Geoffrey Nowell Smith. Newark: International, 1971.

Hamilton, Roberta, and Michele Barrett, eds. *The Politics of Diversity.* London: Verso, 1987.

Harding, Sandra. *Whose Science? Whose Knowledge? Thinking from Women's Lives.* Ithaca, N.Y.: Cornell University Press, 1991.

Hartsock, Nancy C. M. *Money, Sex, and Power: Toward a Feminist Historical Materialism.* Boston: Northeastern University Press, 1985.

Hennessy, Rosemary. *Materialist Feminism and the Politics of Discourse.* New York: Routledge, 1993.

————. "Women's Lives/Feminist Knowledge: Feminist Standpoint as Ideology Critique." *Hypatia* 8, no. 1 (1993): 14–34.

Jaggar, Alison M. *Feminist Politics and Human Nature.* Totowa, N.J.: Rowman and Allenheld, 1983.

Laclau, Ernesto, and Chantal Mouffe. *Hegemony and Socialist Strategy: Towards a Radical Democratic Politics.* London: Verso, 1985.

Lovell, Terry, ed. *British Feminist Thought: A Reader.* Oxford: Blackwell, 1990.

Mies, Maria. *Patriarchy and Accumulation on a World Scale: Women in the International Division of Labour.* London: Zed Books, 1986.

Sawicki, Jana. *Disciplining Foucault.* New York: Routledge, 1991.

Smith, Dorothy E. *The Everyday World as Problematic: A Feminist Sociology.* Boston: Northeastern University Press, 1987.

Part Three

Political Grammar

Objects without Subjects

As the academy's attention turns to minor literatures and cultures—to postcolonial texts, African American texts, literature by lesbians and homosexuals, by Asian and Latino Americans, American Indian texts, and, in short, the broadly alternative literary traditions—what was once a minority report on major American culture increasingly has become canonical. Hence a paradox ensues: while in their own way these texts seek imaginative routes to social change, the structures of authority through which they are channeled and distributed are the very structures against which such social change should work. From this perspective, the absolutely necessary authority to speak must be dismantled in order for social organization to achieve the kind of egalitarian state that various "minority" texts and authors imagine and desire with real and purposeful intensity.

In this sense, canonization is akin to both colonization and commodification, and it is no accident that the essays in this volume have taken up this specific conjunction. Identities, after all, are not metaphysical but socially produced, and such production is always historically situated. But current formulations of the problematic of identity often occlude the historically specific context of capitalism in which the commodification of identities includes not only overtly economic mechanisms but also the ideological mapping of a multicultural face that masks the appearance of various dominant hegemonies. Canonization of the margins authorizes, in short, the very formulation of domination that now adheres to academic speech.

We must recognize that in a majority of these situations the other participates in this project, in this relegation of the self to a position of frame for or mirror of the dominant subject(s). There is no use of force, no strong-arm tactics. In return for being adopted as a token member and for gaining entry into the privileges of the canon and/or scholarly authority, the representative of the subordinate group complies with a variety of critical demands, including acting true to "type." After all, it is the exhibition of differences that had initially vouchsafed the subordinate member's access to the privileges of dominant discourses and their canonical formations.

What of the performance of difference within already marginalized groups and discourses? Think, for instance, of marginal masculinities, both racial and sexual, and of the difficulties of their inclusion, presence, even significations within feminism. Here, the turn toward an autobiographical act, an incipient and always reductivist "I," often becomes the political grammar for such different and difficult negotiations. What identity, what performance of self, is possible in the confessional gesture that already pretends to be the performance of self? In identifying the writing self as biologically male, can we emphasize—or enact—the desire not to be ideologically male? And can feminism not read this act, this desire, as the move toward a feminism without women?

These questions are of course the stuff of current conversations about difference as multiple and contradictory and about power as diffuse and nonbinary. In these conversations, where the theorization of difference is wrenched from the falsities of either/or, more attention is usually devoted to furthering the concept that we can shuttle between identities than to how we can go about it or what it means to make the attempt. Yet, political allegiances within the determinations of identity-based discourses continue to pivot on forging just such choices: am I an Asian Americanist or feminist? To what extent does allegiance to one cast suspicion on placement within the other, and how does this dynamic indicate the limitations of the concept of free and shifting positionalities? Must we settle for the assertion that no speaking situation is simple, that all of them in some way violate the dignity or integrity of those for whom and about whom they speak?

Or is the answer no longer to be found in identity politics but in identification—an identification that turns us toward political action and the end of an inactive, unable to act, liberal discourse? After all, assuming that our interests are always aligned with—and never against—our identity is the problem of identity politics. But from what position can we say this? Are all identities, all formations of identity politics, the same? Perhaps it is only a scholar, only a member of an oppressed group, who could feel trapped enough to intellectualize herself beyond the collective psyche of her group. Or is just such an intellectualization the negotiatory privilege of those situated closer to the dominant than to the historically oppressed? On what basis can we even begin to distinguish, to continue to differentiate, to highlight, to canonize, to resist this thing underlying identity and identification, this thing we might want, politically speaking, to believe in: the human "group"?

8

Fetishism, Identity, Politics

Toward the end of *The Predicament of Culture,* James Clifford poses questions he considers central to the current realignment of knowledge in the postmodern academy: "On what basis may human groups accurately (and we must add morally) be distinguished?" Moreover, "how does one represent other cultures? Is the notion of a distinct culture (or race, or religion, or civilization) a useful one?" (273, 274). These questions are crucial not only to how we think about those groups Clifford explicitly considers (those that Western ethnography has traditionally marked as "distinct" and "other"), but also to how we think about largely metropolitan lesbians and gays as they continue to work toward a more effective visibility and disciplinarity within the academy and without it. The academic analysis of lesbians and gay men, like the population such study claims to address and represent, has begun to insist upon itself as a distinct facet of human culture, able to resist the marginalization that has tended to mark it only as the scandalous or pathological other. It is no accident that lesbian and gay studies has become important in postmodern discourses by analogy to other "species" of difference like race, class, and gender; and while the exact dialectical relations among these aspects of culture are seldom explored as carefully as they might be, we seem currently in agreement that the fate of heterosexuality has been and remains indissolubly linked to the fate of patriarchy, capital, and the master race. But what is the value of claiming a specificity for lesbian and gay culture and identity? Can we really read that claim as self-fashioned?

We have been witness in the late 1980s to what we might call the canonical moment in lesbian and gay studies: conferences, papers, books, even our own incipient star system; all of this attests to our successful intrusion into academic business as usual, and we should be especially pleased with this given the ignorant virulence that characterizes discourses about homosexuality in our more public debates as a nation. But we must also remember that canonical moments are not the fruition of some natural cultural process; they do not innocently mirror some object that precedes the attention of their critical gaze, and we must say this despite the fact that in this case our discourse seems spurred by a "real" population of "real" gays and lesbians beginning to be visible in American society. But if we think of canonicity not just as the generation of a list of validated texts but as the politically inflected codification of fantasies about collective origin or identity, then we can see that *this* canonical moment, *this* fantasy (like all others), has a dual function. It allows something to be entertained that otherwise would remain illicit (reading Henry James and Robert Mapplethorpe together, for instance), but it also occurs only at the cost of some repression.

Apposite here is F. O. Matthiessen's repression of homoeroticism in what many take to be the canonical moment of American studies. As Jonathan Arac has pointed out, in writing *The American Renaissance* Matthiessen disciplined his response to Walt Whitman so as to erase the very thing Whitman signified in the correspondence between Matthiessen and his lover: the legitimation of homosexual love. (Matthiessen, like Hart Crane and other gay men of the 1920s in the United States, lived a contradiction between homosexuality and male friendship that Whitman's text seems to have promised to solve for them.) Repression functioned in this case to make homosexuality invisible, but the episode should remind us that disciplinarity requires repression and that our own shaping of the discipline of gay and lesbian studies might no doubt find the structure of its insights coaxial with certain blindnesses.

It may seem strange to think about homosexuality in terms of what it represses: same-sex desire has functioned almost as synecdoche for the repressed in our culture (thus, people now "come out" about anything once held secret), and we sometimes imagine that by freeing it, nothing remains unsaid. That is not necessarily the case. As Michel Foucault suggests in *The History of Sexuality,* the historical irony of our discourse about sexuality may well be that we imagined our political liberation to be somehow dependent upon what we could say about sexual desire as the ground of our subjectivity. If we take Foucault's notion of power and knowledge seriously, we have to be fairly skeptical about the level of subversiveness we want to read into the recent appearance of gays and lesbians as self-defined people in Western culture (and we might add, I think, in democratic culture). In light of such a skepticism, how might we more critically read the disciplinary or canonical moment of lesbian and gay studies? If many of those who identify as lesbian or gay do so within discourses and practices marked by an access to power and hence are "visible" or acceptable only within politically centrist terms, what could possibly constitute the political transgressivity of studying same-sex desire in our culture? On the other hand, isn't the demand that we signify always as politically earnest exactly what Foucault intends to reject when he calls us the "other Victorians," those who are determined to make sexuality and pleasure answer to ethics?

To return to repression: is there anything displaced or forgotten in our move from margin to center? If we think not, we have invoked a strangely monolithic structure of collective homosexual self-awareness uncontaminated by any trace of difference from itself, and that seems theoretically untenable. If we think so, we need to ask how our construction of a field to be known as gay studies might be changed by our knowledge that material has been lost or repressed in the process of coming to recognize ourselves as a distinct and specific facet of contemporary culture. In Foucault's words,

> sexuality must not be thought of as a kind of natural given which power tries to hold in check, or as an obscure domain which knowledge tries gradually to uncover [but] as the name that can be given to a historical construct . . . in which the stimulation of bodies, the intensification of pleasures, the incitement to discourse, the formation of special knowledges, the strengthening of controls and resistances, are linked to one another, in accordance with a few major strategies of knowledge and power. (105–6)

That is, our discourse and our being are not organic appearances but arise at the nexus of other forms of knowledge, power, and pleasure, and our analysis of homosexuality or homophobia needs always to inquire into this structural density.

Perhaps the most obvious place to begin this analysis is with the question of gender and the screen of equality implied in the phrase "lesbian and gay": as my own prose demonstrates, lesbian and gay studies slips all too easily and all too often into simply "gay studies," yet never into "lesbian studies." This asymmetry should concern us, for among other things it suggests that "our" canonical moment is itself gendered and that perhaps what we have witnessed is the canonical moment of gay studies but not the canonical moment of lesbian studies—that lesbian studies may in fact be more powerfully configured under the rubric of feminism than under any accommodations gay men will ever collectively and institutionally be able to make to it. We might also interrogate the moment of our appearance for its attention to the social text of race: Marlon Riggs, the creator of *Tongues Untied* and other videos about African American gay men, offered a plenary address at this year's gay, bisexual, and lesbian conference at Harvard University. There has been an increased interest recently in making visible the lives and texts of gay men of color, as there has historically been an interest in race in the discourse marked lesbian.

But when much of the political energy of the summer of 1992 was taken up with an absolutely necessary defense of Robert Mapplethorpe's work, the issue of Mapplethorpe's racial politics was forced into the background or evoked apologies for his photographs of black men on the grounds that he was making visible a certain kind of "beauty" that was taboo in American culture. In the need for solidarity in that encounter with Jesse Helms and the right, race within the gay community became a difference legible in terms that did not offer any sustained attention to current and historical fetishizations of black men according to their "difference." In that, an unassimilable debate has escaped the mainstream in relation to Mapplethorpe's work, a debate centered on the charge of its appropriation of African American men as an erotic fantasy for white consumers (Julien and Mercer, and I have addressed this question). In the end, however, we need to decide about these images less whether they are or are not racist in some final or definitive way than how and why they present to us a discursive formation and representation of race that is difficult to acknowledge under the regime of desire that produced and reproduces them. In other words, we all know that there is racism within gay formations—the question is not "Is it there?" but "Why are we unable to address and change it?"

To have framed both of these issues in this way is already to mark them as issues for democratic inclusivity, as terms within a discourse where representation becomes the "answer" to political oppression, thinking that if we take everyone into account in our own discourse, or give everyone voice, we will have evaded any oppressive practice. This is the logic behind cultural studies paradigms of race, class, gender, sexuality, age, ability, and so forth. We can generate that list and live in that logic, but this has rapidly become the most pointless of academic exercises—pointless not because the systems of social intelligibility marked by these terms have ceased to be crucial in the articulation of political power and control, but because the regime of representation into which they most often lead us has its base in a logic of liberal pluralism that we have by now sufficient history and reason to mistrust. Identity politics has lately gotten a deservedly bad rap all around. Although Diana Fuss argues at times for its strategic effectiveness, she has generally dismissed identity politics for its essentialist assumptions. Moreover, Judith Butler has noted how feminism can no longer retain the category of a unified (and ultimately masculine) subject as the base of its intervention, working for and in the name of a "woman" understood to be on her way home from the cultural exile of male oppression, moving toward her "true" self.

The same issues must arise for gay and lesbian studies. There is no such thing as "the homosexual and his/her truth," and if we imagine that as the project of lesbian and gay studies, we have surrendered to a lie at the outset. What we perhaps need to think about here is fetishism, as it has been defined in psychoanalysis *not* as the overvaluation of some part-object but as the denial of lack. All identity is fetishistic in that it is structured on the denial of self-difference and absence; that is, identity cannot occur except through fundamental (and generative) misrecognitions. In the case of gay identity, the constructed fiction and denial of lack at the heart of subjectivity occurs through recognition of the tropes and practices of sexuality, offering sex as a center for an otherwise decentered being. This is perhaps doubly fetishistic since we understand desire itself to be decentering, to be driven by lack. Thus, the trajectory of gay identity politics may read as follows: first, we stabilize desire (itself a move of considerable cultural violence) and then we attach the self to that desire almost as effect to cause, creating a second order violence of identification.

Identity politics is the reigning philosophy of the popular gay press, however, and that should not surprise us since that press exists only as it can identify and exploit a demographic market. In that press's debate about Jonathan Demme's film *The Silence of the Lambs* (1991), we can begin to see some of the implications of this as a practice for generating critique. In that debate, I was struck by the fact that the "pro-gay" position called for an end to homophobic stereotypes and for more positive representations of homosexuality, and that this was done in a way that imagined that we know and agree on what those "positive" images might be. In other words, a charge about the misrecognition of homosexuality is leveled against Demme by people who claim not to misrecognize but to "know" it and to be therefore fully able to speak as and for homosexuals. There are a number of problems here, not the least of which is that we have no idea what kind of homosexuals will be considered representative in such discourse. Bruce Benderson has written in *Outweek* (Feb. 27, 1991) about his boredom and impatience with the sanitization of gay culture, with the exclusion of the more violent and excessive vision of writers like John Rechy, William S. Burroughs, and Jean Genet from the mainstream-

ing of gay culture in the 1970s and 1980s, and this seems to me a salutary point. Furthermore, if Bill, the serial killer in *Silence of the Lambs*
who is explicitly identified as someone without a conventional sexual
identity, as a man who only imagines himself transsexual because he
would otherwise have no identity whatsoever (he is, if you will, Gilles
Deleuze and Felix Guattari's deterritorialized or schizo being), is considered an image dangerous to homosexuals (the claim is that this film
will promote gay bashing), then why is Divine—in all her cross-dressing glory, eating dog shit at the end of *Pink Flamingoes* (John Waters,
director)—considered an outrageous, humorous, and ultimately liberatory figure?

My point is not that we ought to consider Bill a liberatory figure as
well but that there is a contradiction in demanding "positive" images
from mainstream culture while simultaneously embracing the strange
and unusual in our own cultural space. In other words, if we need to
get rid of Demme's film on political grounds, do we also need to get
rid of Divine, since homophobes could conceivably find her image
confirmatory of themselves in their misrecognition of her? The very
notion that someone could say—in the discourse of identity politics—
what homosexuals do or do not, should or should not look, sound,
and be like is a potentially dangerous trap we may not be able to escape from once we decide to enter it. Moreover, as theorists of desire
from Sigmund Freud and Georges Bataille to Leo Bersani have noted,
sexuality seems always destined to be determined as much by misrecognition as by anything we might term an accurate cognition *and* to
remain in excess of any theoretical or political moves to enlist it in
the service of cultural mobility. Sexuality is imbricated with violence
and death in virtually all its manifestations, and to attempt to find or
articulate a clean, acceptable desire—especially a homosexuality imagined in this way—should be nearly unthinkable. If we are to build a
critique of culture and an active alternative community based in the
rejection of those terms and practices that have heretofore constituted the disciplinary or canonical formation of desire along unswerv-
ingly heterosexual lines, we must strenuously reject the wisdom of
institutionalizing a counterdiscipline or alternative list of acceptable
and unacceptable sexualities.

This would seem to be the impetus behind the new politically fashionable use of the term "queer" to designate things nonheterosexu-
al—as in Queer Nation or what a cover of the *Advocate,* referring to
Poison and *Paris Is Burning,* coined as "cinema queerité." This word
works so well because it appropriates a former badge of shame and
because it suggests that it is not our business or duty to appear accept-

able, that there is something unassimilable in nonheterosexuality and only its queerness—its difference—can define it. A similarly differential definition of identity is powerfully articulated in Judith Butler's recent work, particularly *Gender Trouble*. Although her final paean to performance has left some unsatisfied with her work's political implications, it is clear that there is something to ponder in the notion that identity (and sex/gender identity in particular) is performative rather than substantive, especially if we remember that a strong sense of discipline would inform any theory of performance, making instantiations or performances of sexuality (queer or straight) more than self-expression.

My point here is not to defend *Silence of the Lambs*. Its homophobia is apparent *if* by that we mean that it constructs the category of homosexuality within the symbolic as one marked by pathological lack. In the terms offered by feminist film theory, we have no feminine object at the center of this spectacle since Jodie Foster's on-screen presence secures identification rather than specularity, and since the moments of castration are Bill's—when he puts a ring through his breast, when he dances with his penis pulled back between his legs. We have here a spectacle that equates the homosexual with a desire to be a woman and "woman" with castration, and all of that adds up to a pretty oppressive vision of male homosexuality. But how could we expect a narrative about coming of age as an FBI agent to offer anything else? To note this film's homophobia is only to say that it was produced in America. The point in all parables of the law (and this film is nothing if not parabolic of the law of the father) is that no one is free of the implications of anyone else's desire or behavior *except* as the mechanisms of identification with the law allow one to fantasize and occupy a social niche securely on this side of transgression. The truly radical response to Demme's film, then, would not be to proclaim its unfairness and misrecognition of homosexual desire (only offered to us through highly coded moments anyway), but rather to suggest that all sexuality is caught within intricate networks of desire and violence, that desire—if never consciously a desire to dismember—always nevertheless dismembers.

Juridically we are subjects marked by our relation to a state that defines us through the criminalization of our sexual behavior—that is one way in which the gay and lesbian struggle is historically different from the struggle of other "minorities." Until those definitions are no longer in force, we cannot forgo the difficult work of identity politics, which must include our critique of images from Hollywood and other unenlightened sources. But identity politics as a discourse about juridical subjects keeps us in a definition of power and the political that is monarchical in its origin, keeping us still within what Foucault identifies as "the repressive hypothesis," the notion that power holds in check certain beings—or certain cultural forces like sexuality. In *The History of Sexuality*, Foucault writes that "we must at the same time conceive of sex without the law, and power without the king" (91). The twofold emphasis here is quite important: just as we must think of sexuality without some oppressive law of the father, we must also think it without our own counterlaw. There simply is not some proper, true, pure, or real sexuality waiting to appear once we remove the obstacles of social oppression. Perhaps more crucial to us is Foucault's suggestion that we cannot think power only through "the system of Law-and-Sovereign which has captivated political thought for such a long time" (97). Rather, he writes,

> we need to go one step further, do without the persona of the Prince, and decipher power mechanisms on the basis of a strategy that is immanent in force relations. . . . In short, it is a question of orienting ourselves to a conception of power which replaces the privilege of law with the viewpoint of objective, the privilege of prohibition with the viewpoint of tactical efficacy, the privilege of sovereignty with the analysis of a multiple and mobile field of force relations, wherein far-reaching, but never completely stable, effects of domination are produced. (102)

We could think of Foucault's paradigm for the political as postmodern: replacing such stable or foundational discursive politics as Marxism and liberalism (neither of which has been able to formulate a theory of sexuality capable of challenging the privilege of patriarchal masculinity since the sovereign and his law remain the final referent of all discourse and all bodies in both of these systems) with a reading of power as generalized and diffuse, as immanent in all social relations and therefore variable and reversible. What interests me here is not just the antifoundationalism that drives Foucault's critique of traditional notions of political power but also that his theory deploys itself in terms wholly in accord with contemporary discourses of desire. Power becomes multiple, dispersed, labile, moving across bodies and points of orientation or recognition, marking a struggle between law and aim; this could be Jacques Lacan on desire, but it is Foucault: "a multiple and mobile field of . . . relations, wherein far-reaching, but never completely stable, effects . . . are produced." Foucault challenges us to move out of a stable, dyadic, and ultimately imaginary understanding of power (including Louis Althusser's reading of ideology and the mirror stage), one that assures subjectivity through the overdetermined presence of a sovereign, transcendent subject *and into* a symbolic universe of discourse where power flows through relations and infuses discourse, knowledge, and subjectivity along channels that are under constant negotiation and renegotiation. Part of what I would like to do here is move beyond an Althusserian notion of the subject and her relation to culture, for as Pierre Bourdieu reminds us, social reality is not simply the reproduction of structures housed in the subject:

> Action is not the mere carrying out of a rule, or obedience to a rule. Social agents, in archaic societies as well as in ours, are not automata regulated like clocks, in accordance with laws they do not understand. In the most complex games, matrimonial exchange for instance, or ritual practices, they put into action the incorporated principles of a generative habitus. . . . This "feel for the game," as we call it, is what enables an infinite number of "moves" to be made, adapted to the infinite number of possible situations which no rule, however complex, can foresee. (9)

Thus, identity politics fetishizes not only identity but also politics to the extent that it imagines social agency as a compulsion within the subject to implicitly obey and act out the power structures that define it *and* to the extent that it essentializes power as the content rather than the generative effect of social relations. What Foucault offers, then, is not just the notion that power is erotic or that sex is ideological (Freud had done that much), but a way of reading power that is fully congruent with our theory of the erotic. His work forces us to consider the important question of whether or not homosexual subjectivity—once understood as a self-evidently erotic category—has become part of a taxonomy whose self-evidence is political rather than erotic. Moreover, if any identity politics is bound by the conventions of law rather than desire, then we need to ask whether we have produced in gay and lesbian identity politics a model for thinking about desire that cannot allow desire to operate within it, that cannot (finally) allow for desire. We have to take seriously the possibility that perhaps it has been transgression against sanctioned legal and social identity that has constituted the erotic and seductive appeal of homosexual behavior for many and that in mapping out new criteria for identification as homosexual, we erase the erotic edge that supposedly is the content of this new subjectivity. In other words, we must face the possibility that the repressed of our canonical moment is erotic pleasure itself (and this is reported as well by older friends who have attended recent Gay Pride activities in New York City only to find that the erotic carnival in the 1970s in which they had participated—and I mean carnival in the European, Bakhtinian sense—has become a political carnival without the explosive edge of erotic abandon it once allowed).

The final issue I would like to consider here is the question of agency and how we will think about it in the future. Not just through the defunct categories of essential or constructed subjects, not just as automata under a discursive grid more or less hostile to same-sex adventure, but a far more difficult task lies ahead: to explain our negotiation of the cultural space as a site always still unforeclosed by law, to read in our cognition of ourselves not just the recognition and misrecognition of ourselves and others, but to continue to ask ourselves what—and not just who—queer studies is for. All our profit lies in that asking.

Thomas Yingling

Note

This manuscript was incomplete at the time of the author's death. The editors have added citations where possible.

Works Cited

Althusser, Louis. "Ideology and Ideological State Apparatuses (Notes Towards an Investigation)." Pp. 121–73 in *Lenin and Philosophy and Other Essays*. Trans. Ben Brewster. New York: Monthly Review Press, 1971.

Arac, Jonathan. "F. O. Matthiessen: Authorizing and American Renaissance." Pp. 90–112 in *The American Renaissance Reconsidered*, ed. William Benn Michaels and Donald Pease. Baltimore, Md.: Johns Hopkins University Press, 1985.

Butler, Judith. *Gender Trouble: Feminism and the Subversion of Identity*. London: Routledge, 1990.

Clifford, James. *The Predicament of Culture*. Cambridge, Mass.: Harvard University Press, 1988.

Foucault, Michel. *The History of Sexuality*. Vol. 1. Trans. Robert Hurley. New York: Vintage, 1990.

Fuss, Diana. *Essentially Speaking: Feminism, Nature, and Difference*. New York: Routledge, 1989.

Julien, Isaac, and Kobena Mercer. "True Confessions: A Discourse on Images of Black Male Sexuality." *Ten.8* 22 (1986): 4–8.

Matthiessen, F. O. *The American Renaissance: Art and Expression in the Age of Emerson and Whitman*. New York: Oxford University Press, 1968.

Yingling, Thomas. "How the Eye Is Caste: Robert Mapplethorpe and the Limits of Controversy." *Discourse* 12, no. 2 (1990): 3–28.

9

Speaking with the Dead

What AIDS shows us is the limits of tolerance, that it's not
enough to be tolerated, because when the shit hits the fan you
find out how much tolerance is worth. Nothing.
  —Tony Kushner, *Angels in America*

I feel that my speaking is also disrespectful because it flies in the
face of the absoluteness of Tom's death and all the other deaths,
as if in the face of that my words could give a sense of closure, of
significance, of comfort. In fact, another AIDS death signifies
nothing and there isn't or shouldn't be any comfort. So I've
made a vow that this is the last memorial at which I will speak.
  —Robert Rafsky, at fellow AIDS
    activist Tom Cunningham's memorial

I want to begin by commenting briefly on the epigraphs I have se-
lected to begin my response to Thomas Yingling's contribution to this
anthology. Both epigraphs are public performances—one in the theater, the other at an AIDS memorial service—that call attention to the
discursive challenges surrounding our relationship to the social phenomenon we call AIDS. In the first, from Tony Kushner's *Angels in
America*, Louis (a Jewish gay male who reads Walter Benjamin in bed)
speaks to Belize (a black gay man who is a registered nurse and former
drag queen). Louis is angry; his lover, Prior, has recently been diagnosed with AIDS. Louis cannot handle Prior's illnesses, but rather than
dealing with that directly, he chooses to hold Belize captive in a long
exegesis on the problems facing America; his complaint begins with
this discussion of the limits of tolerance and his quote on AIDS. As
the play continues, it becomes clear that Louis, while insightful, is a
talkaholic; Belize tells him so. Louis's main response to AIDS is excessive speech.

The second quote, from Tom Cunningham's memorial service, is spoken by the nationally recognized AIDS activist Robert Rafsky, who died of complications due to AIDS a few weeks later. Rafsky, too, invests in speech. In the memorial to Rafsky published in the *Village Voice*, he is cited as having been one of ACT UP/New York's "most eloquent, and fearless voices" ("Age of AIDS"). Unlike Louis, Rafsky has demonstrated how speech and silence must continually be negotiated in response to AIDS.[1] As his final tribute to Tom Cunningham, Rafsky offers him, and all the others lost to AIDS, his silence. His speaking with the dead is a public performance—indeed, an articulation—of his silence.

I think my responses to AIDS are more often than not caught somewhere between paralysis and agency, between Louis and Rafsky. Beginning about 1980, I started spending time in the theater, and about 1985 I began volunteering for various community AIDS organizations. Both experiences inform how I think and speak, and from both—I don't always separate them so distinctly—I have learned about the function of performativity—that is, of enacting and signifying tactical positions—and about my need for the communal, what Stephen Greenblatt calls, a "felt community" (5). In other words, I too want to speak with the dead. I also want to offer some type of tribute to Thomas Yingling. But I'm not sure how to do either without having my response be, in Rafsky's words and context, "disrespectful." Still, this essay is an attempt to respond to Yingling's ideas, writings, and contributions to lesbian and gay studies, AIDS studies, and American studies. Since it exists in publication, it is also a type of public performance, a performative ritual offered with respect and in recognition of the power of some of those voices now silenced by AIDS but who, despite AIDS, continue to speak to me.

*   *   *

For well over two decades, scholars in all fields—and many with no institutional affiliation (read employment)—have set the groundwork and often the theoretical foundations for the current outpouring of research in lesbian and gay studies. The historian John D'Emilio, among others, has written extensively on these early years of lesbian and gay studies, documenting the various contributions of community-based scholars and their efforts to break down what he sees as the "class-based distinction between intellectual activity and the rest of life" (167).[2] D'Emilio cites a number of interventions—in academic journals, campus life, research institutions, and professional organizations—that have catalyzed the community-based movement of lesbian and gay studies since the 1970s. D'Emilio's history of lesbian and gay studies in the United States forcefully demonstrates that the origins of lesbian and gay studies are unequivocally linked with the post-Stonewall lesbian and gay liberation movement.

Like D'Emilio, Yingling, in "Fetishism, Identity, Politics" (in this volume), writes about this parallel growth of the lesbian and gay movement in and out of American universities and raises serious concerns about the (re)emergence of lesbian and gay studies in the late 1980s. Specifically, Yingling asks us to consider how we might "more critically read the disciplinary or canonical moment of lesbian and gay studies." I suggest we begin to respond to this question by stepping back and speculating on the existence of a "canonical moment" in the first place. I think if we are to understand the current state of gay and lesbian studies, it makes sense to consider the current localized instances of "canonicity" and their relation to the continuing fight for lesbian and gay rights. We need, in short, to account for the locations of lesbian and gay studies: In what departments, institutions, and communities are lesbian and gay studies emerging? If its main harbor is in departments of English or the humanities, what are the limits of this canonical moment?[3] Who and what speaks for lesbian and gay studies in this its most recent manifestation? In what ways do lesbian and gay studies correspond to the national movement for lesbian and gay rights?[4] Undoubtedly, in the 1990s there is more interest in, and tolerance of, the growing industry around lesbian and gay scholarship than twenty years ago but, as various lesbian and gay scholars and theorists have recently argued, the moment seems anything but canonical.

Lesbians, as usual, run the risk—if not the reality—of being left out of the current wave of interest. Yingling points to this quite clearly when he states that "lesbian and gay studies slips all too easily and all too often into simply 'gay studies,' yet never into 'lesbian studies.'"[5] Julie Abraham goes one step further when she claims that this slippage is a nearly irreparable dilemma intrinsic to the discipline as it was formulated in the 1980s: "A gay/lesbian studies identified with the subject of sexuality will inevitably favor gay subjects, even when the emphasis is on the perverse and the queer, because the culture's discussion of sexual dissidence has been so consistently a discussion of the homosexual male" (21). She joins Elizabeth Grosz who, in "Bodies and Pleasures in Queer Theory" (in this volume), also questions why lesbianism has been "so decidedly ignored."

If we are left to wonder, as Yingling insists we must, what is being repressed in the canonical moment of lesbian and gay studies, it may well be lesbians or, as Sue-Ellen Case explains, certain kinds of lesbians. Case argues that whatever new lesbian visibility there is in the

1990s is premised on the "lesbian with phallus-as-fetish," the lesbian
with a dildo who is "born out of the rib of gay male subcultural images" (2). This lesbian, according to Case, emerges out of the cultural
logic of phallic (re)production. Such a normalizing logic allows for the
location of the newfound lesbian visibility in a limited representation-
al economy that can only reabsorb her within the specific agendas of
its ideological authority. Case explains the illusion of power created
by this process: "While the dyke believes she is finally appearing, she
is actually disappearing into the market" (13). Thus, she concludes,
"when the dyke enters the class/room she is on the stage of dominant
practices" (13), a stage with little room for, or tolerance of, the order
of lesbian politics.

In an essay that shares some of these concerns but focuses primarily on the need to address issues of race and ethnicity in lesbian and
gay studies, Yvonne Yarbro-Bejarano explains how lesbians of color—
both in and out of the classroom—stand outside of this representa-
tional and critical commodification process, unimagined at worst or
visualized only within the normative racialized discourses of white
fetishistic erotics at best. Like Abraham and Case, Yarbro-Bejarano
raises serious and as yet unanswered concerns regarding the idea of a
"canonical moment" in lesbian and gay studies. Yarbro-Bejarano calls
for a lesbian and gay studies that includes more than "just white, middle-class gays and lesbians" (78). By offering a means for imagining
such a field (see also Román), she challenges us to recognize and "emphasize the contribution of lesbians of color to this theoretical project
of categorical expansion, in part because of the appropriation of their
work by some white feminists, and also because they have provided a
significant piece of the theoretical groundwork that could and should
serve as the foundation of Lesbian and Gay Studies" (87). Yarbro-
Bejarano, for example, cites the work of a number of Chicana lesbians—Cherríe Moraga, Gloria Anzaldúa, Chela Sandoval—who provide a new paradigm for understanding marginality and oppression by
theorizing their "multiple and shifting identities/identifications, consciousness, and agency" (91). Yarbro-Bejarano's project begins to enact the more critical readings of lesbian and gay studies suggested in
Yingling's essay, demonstrating, along with Abraham, Case, and Grosz,
the type of work lesbian and gay scholars have yet to do.

More to the point, these diverse lesbian theorists call into question
the by now commonplace assumption that lesbian and gay studies has
found its niche in academic institutions. The fact that there is *already*
in place a location from which to challenge the critical authority
emerging within (as) lesbian and gay studies in no way undermines

the significance of their concerns. To speak about lesbian and gay studies, especially within academic forums such as this one, more often than not presupposes an unproblematic positionality for the field. The act of speaking, seemingly validated with publication, suggests the illusion of an arrival at once welcome and stable—despite the subjectivity and concerns of the speaker—simply on the basis that something has been said, even if this something is actually a critique of the very process that allows its articulation in the first place. Therefore, lesbian voices such as these—the malcontents at the annual cashbar—may be expected, perhaps even tolerated, but not without some price for both speaker and listener. "Can we talk?" asks Marlon Riggs, "but of course we can, queer diva darling, if you abide by the rules of dominant discourse, which means in short, you must ultimately sing somebody else's tune to be heard" (101). The apprehensions voiced by white lesbian theorists and lesbian and gay theorists of color—each with distinct relationships to the university—suggest both the limits of the "canonical" and the complexity of effects associated with the practice of lesbian and gay studies.

This is especially true if we consider the position of lesbian and gay studies for students. I imagine that Riggs's comments hold particular resonance for queer graduate students of all genders and colors who must practice what he calls "verbal drag schtick," the haunting self-conscious activity of second guessing and performing critical authorities in order to legitimate one's own speaking position: "But does she comprehend discursive intertextual analysis, can she engage in post-feminist, neo-Marxist, postmodern deconstructionist critique? Does she understand the difference between text, subtext, and metatext?" (Riggs 103).

Despite what Michael Warner describes as the "boom point" (19) in the field, out lesbian and gay scholars negotiating graduate exam reading lists, dissertation committees, research grants, reappointment and tenure rulings are continually vulnerable to the muscle of individual and institutional homophobia prevalent throughout the academy. A career based in lesbian and gay studies still holds no guarantees. A simple perusal of recent Modern Language Association's (MLA) joblists will counter any notions of canonicity. Are two or three joblistings a year advertising for an *interest* in lesbian and gay studies enough to constitute a significant breakthrough? I remember how quickly my enthusiasm for these few positions dissipated when I noticed how many other institutions were not searching for their "queer theorist." D'Emilio claims that with the new market interest in lesbian and gay scholarship, "a young lesbian and gay scholar may have difficulty finding a job, but she or he is increasingly likely to have a dissertation published" (168). True, perhaps, but notice too the scholar's "difficulty finding a job." Only here does publication without employment threaten the possibility of actually landing a teaching position.[6]

Even those who have established the critical vocabularies of the profession and been rewarded with tenure are not exempt from constant surveillance and attack. The public gay-baiting of Professor David Halperin (an internationally respected scholar and pioneer in the field) in response to slanderous and unsubstantiated accusations against him by a disgruntled colleague at MIT demonstrates the vulnerability we all face in practicing and promoting lesbian and gay studies on our campuses.[7] Capitalizing on that campaign of vilification, Roger Kimball bashed Halperin in the *Wall Street Journal* while covering the 1992 MLA conference: "A great deal that Prof. Halperin had to say about sex that afternoon cannot be printed in a family newspaper. But it is worth reminding ourselves that his students at MIT regularly receive his unedited reflections on this and other subjects in his classes. Tuition at MIT is $18,000 a year. I wonder if the parents of MIT students think they are getting value for their money." While many would want to dismiss such a personal attack as typical of a certain extremist position in the popular press, Kimball's comments suggest the kinds of attitudes gay and lesbian scholars continually confront.[8]

The fundamental point I want to make is that the current interest in, and controversies around, lesbian and gay studies cannot be understood in isolation from other discursive practices addressing lesbians, gays, and queers. Just as the emergence of a critical practice identified as "lesbian and gay studies" and the theoretical arsenal now readily understood as "queer theory" needs to be seen in conjunction with other political and social movements in gay and lesbian life in the 1990s, as D'Emilio suggests, so must the attacks against gay and lesbian scholars and scholarship be viewed as yet one more salient display of bias and hatred informing the national debates on lesbian and gay civil rights.

D'Emilio explains the importance of understanding the dynamics of the university as a social space informed by and participating in the ideological practices of its day. He writes:

> One of the signal achievements of the campus turmoil of the 1960s was the recognition that universities are not ivory towers where individuals engage in the disinterested, dispassionate, and detached pursuit of knowledge and truth. Rather, universities are intimately connected to the society of which they are a part. They are capable of producing change, to be sure, but they also reflect, and repro-

duce, the dominant values, beliefs, habits, and inequalities of their society. (162)

The current status of lesbians and gays in the United States remains under serious debate. The "boom" in queer theory, and in lesbian and gay studies in general, is in many ways symptomatic of these debates, as Grosz explains in her contribution to this anthology. To identify the moment in gay and lesbian studies as "canonical" invents a legitimating space not always available for many of the lesbian and gay scholars I have cited. It presupposes secured political positions for gays and lesbians inside and outside of the university and imagines commodity fetishism and the rhetoric of tolerance as viable sites for lesbian and gay agency. The task at hand is to critically locate sites of agency in order to challenge the commodification and depoliticization of lesbian and gay studies within institutional movements based on tolerance or market trends.

While Yingling sees the late 1980s as the canonical moment in lesbian and gay studies and introduces this theme by citing the cultural anthopologist and theorist James Clifford, I view the late 1980s and early 1990s as a liminal moment in lesbian and gay studies. I want to cite a different anthropologist, Victor Turner, to make my point. Turner explains that "the attributes of liminality are necessarily ambiguous, since the condition and the persons elude or slip through the networks of classifications that normally locate states and positions in cultural space" (95). Liminality suggests the neither here nor there; it insists on the *process* of social initiation, the ways in which cultures enact legitimacy and authority and acculturate subjects into the social fabric of its reigning ideology. Turner, of course, builds upon the ideas of Arnold Van Gennep, who introduces the concept of the liminal to theorize social "rites of passage." For both Van Gennep and Turner, the liminal is the transitional moment between

> [an] earlier fixed state in the social structure, from a set of cultural conditions (a "state"), or from both. During the intervening "liminal" period, the characteristics of the ritual subject (the "passenger") are ambiguous; he passes through a cultural realm that has few or none of the attributes of the past or coming state. In the third phase (reaggregation or reincorporation), the passage is consummated. The ritual subject, individual or corporate, is in a relatively stable state once more and, by virtue of this, has rights and obligations vis-à-vis others of a clearly defined and "structural" type; he is expected to behave in accordance with certain customary norms and ethical standards binding on incumbents of social position in a system of such positions. (Turner 94–95)

I invoke the less fashionable ideas of Van Gennep and Turner because it may be precisely within this border space of the liminal that pleasure itself can be recuperated for lesbian and gay studies—recuperated, that is, if we agree with Yingling that erotic pleasure has been repressed in lesbian and gay studies. Yingling worries that "we must face the possibility that the repressed of our canonial moment is erotic pleasure itself" and cites both the institutionalization of lesbian and gay studies and the political investment in identity politics as complicit in this process. His suggestion that we more critically examine the "canonical moment" must involve then a process of locating the erotic and pleasurable in lesbian and gay studies.

Some have found pleasure in the dynamics of the classroom. For Joseph Litvak, for example, pleasure may be recuperated through the teaching of lesbian and gay studies.[9] Working within the Foucauldian model that frames Yingling's essay, Litvak reminds us that the same system that produces discipline must also produce "'perversions,' if only to encrypt them in each and every good middle-class subject as so many stages (suggestive term) through which he or she must pass" (10). Litvak suggests that it is precisely at this moment of encrypting that lesbian and gay studies can intervene: teaching gay studies "seems, that is, to offer a way of prying open the crypts that have already been sealed, of keeping others from forming too quickly, of bringing out, or educing, or even educating loves, pleasures, and desires that education otherwise serves to put away" (11). Litvak's goal for lesbian and gay studies is to recognize the ideological processes that produce surveillance and transgression, including the university and the classroom, and to identify and extend the moments—what I would call liminal moments—when these positions are negotiated.[10]

If the liminal performs the not yet disciplined, the almost disciplined, the about to be disciplined, it makes sense for us to exploit it. Rather than aiming toward the canonical, it may be worthwhile to protract the liminal moment of lesbian and gay studies. Judith Butler has taught us that it is often politically efficacious for us *as* lesbians and gays to "proliferate and intensify the crisis of identity politics" (*Force of Fantasy* 121), to allow for and revel in the anxieties or pleasures produced by the "uncontrollability" of the categorial terms established by regulatory disciplines and institutions. I find Butler's response to the crisis of identity politics remarkably useful in thinking through the current status of lesbian and gay studies. If lesbian and gay studies is in the liminal phase—a process that gestures toward, and at times even aspires to, the canonical—and if the liminal is defined inherently as uncategorical, then the possibilites of our scholarship and pedagogy and their effects are endless. It is precisely in the intensification of the liminal where the proliferation of multiple subjectivities, multiple *kinds* of lesbian and gay studies, and multiple pleasures become available to us. The liminal phase always enacts the move toward canonicity: it produces the illusion of assimilation while still holding license to remain temporarily outside of disciplinary control, even as it presupposes a narrative that will conclude in the initiation of customary norms.

From this perspective, the current crisis in lesbian and gay studies seems less about the anxiety of who and what queer studies is for or about. Rather it seems to me that the crisis is located in the institutional demands that insist upon responses to such questions: institutional demands that arrive in the form of justifications for new programs, courses, and hires from not always sympathetic deans, chairs, and colleagues. These demands are further exacerbated by the local governing bodies of higher education, especially for publicly funded state schools and institutions with religious affiliations. Lesbians and gays know only too well that there are few, if any, discursive ways out of inquiries pertaining to sexuality that are not already predetermined and contained within dominant discourse or, in Yingling's words, "unforeclosed by law." How can we possibly answer these questions—who and what queer studies is for and about—without falling into either the trap of defensive rhetoric or the universalizing, but well-intended, impulse of bourgeoise liberalism?

It is not possible to escape these questions: Who is queer studies for? What is queer studies for? Yingling concludes his essay by challenging us with his proposal that "all our profit lies in that asking." The multiple, shifting identities that each of us may bring at any time to our classrooms, institutions, and communities, with students, peers, and colleagues—whether queer or straight and with differing degrees of homophobia and homoignorance—suggest that these questions will always be asked and answered differently depending upon the local circumstances and specific dynamics of the exchange. This is not to say that these questions are trivial. I agree with Yingling that it is to our profit that we consider the purposes of our practices. But these questions can only be addressed locally and always in consideration of the materiality of who can speak. Our responses will never be choral and will differ according to our own specific circumstances and subject positions.

Yet, what are the limits of celebrating the liminal if as lesbians and gays we continue to aspire to a type of acculturation, with all the customary norms—domestic partnership, antidiscrimination, and other civil rights—available and intact? I think Yingling offers us a way to conceptualize a response that allows for both the radical capacities of the liminal and the securing comforts of the canonical when he writes that "our discourse and our being are not organic appearances but arise at the nexus of other forms of knowledge, power, and pleasure, and our analysis of homosexuality or homophobia needs always to inquire into this structural density." Lesbian and gay studies, to prove successful in the long run, must continue to recognize and explore what Yingling refers to and what Yarbro-Bejarano explicates more fully: that our identities and our desires, while based historically in marginalization and oppression, are dynamic processes that escape the construction of a "distinct culture."

While Yingling and Yarbro-Bejarano, among others, provide the theoretical framework for lesbian and gay studies, it is important to note that AIDS activists have provided a menu of available tactics that may enable social change for gays and lesbians inside and outside of the university. While AIDS, according to Kushner, has shown us the limits of tolerance, AIDS activists have demonstrated the efficacy of local interventions against the systemic processes that discriminate against people with AIDS and contribute to the growing epidemic (Crimp, *AIDS*). Such "local resistances" contest the systems of power that construct and, in the process, control marginal identities. As Cindy Patton explains:

> The idea of local resistances, taken seriously and in specific contexts, means that coalition, especially geographically understood, is not a coherent idea. What the emergence of ACT UP through the silence = death symbols suggests is that sparks are given off through attempts to "unleash" power within the power/discourse gap. Resistance in other locales may be ignited by these sparks, but must spring from an analysis of the local situation, finding leverage points within the narrow space offered differently by different localities. (163)

Patton's ideas on the local claim highlight the necessity to intervene on multiple fronts differently—perhaps even in contradiction or, using her term, "incoherent[ly]"—*and* to recognize that there are always multiple, distinct sites of contestation. She recommends that activists focus on tactics and locality and then strategize accordingly. This is good advice and an excellent program for lesbian and gay studies if we are to make a dent in the always different institutional biases leveled against us. There is no reason, as D'Emilio has argued consistently, for scholars to view the university as any more accommodating than any other social institution or discipline. For those who work in lesbian and gay studies, the task remains both to exploit and maintain the liminal phase of lesbian and gay studies and to work directly in our local environments to systematically challenge and contest institutional regimes that, at best, tolerate our presence and scholarship.[11] Such a simultaneous endeavor, while employing particular tactics of resistance for different localities, only demonstrates the need to engage the multiple sites of contestation within the university.

But there is more at stake for lesbian and gay studies at this point than simply replicating and appropriating the tactics of AIDS activists in order to challenge the local instances and dynamics of regulatory violence normalized against queers in the 1990s. We must also keep the focus on AIDS as a priority agenda of lesbian and gay studies, for as Simon Watney explains, "we should not define lesbian and gay studies in a way which marginalizes an epidemic that is undoubtedly the worst single catastrophe in 'our' history, however we theorize 'ourselves'" (72). A thorough and interdisciplinary analysis of AIDS is still needed if we are to understand the often contradictory ways AIDS is both constructed and encountered in different locales and communities, the effective and noneffective counterstrategies of local resistances employed to fight AIDS, and the various power networks (including the university and its production of knowledge) by which their effects are extended. Such work necessitates, as Butler explains in her support of Watney's position, "an important set of dialogues among those who work between the academy and the movement to think about priorities" ("Letter"). These dialogues among people with different and multiple positionalities, subjectivities, and desires will facilitate both our understanding of and response to AIDS, as well as serve as a tribute to the dead, especially to those who helped establish initially the lesbian and gay studies we profess to practice.

*   *   *

I never met Thomas Yingling, although we were scheduled to meet at the MLA in New York in 1992. I had organized a panel, through the Gay and Lesbian Caucus of the MLA, on "AIDS: Politics and Pedagogies in the University" and Yingling was set to deliver a paper on teaching with AIDS. He died some months before the meeting. Our only immediate connection during his life was through our correspondence. I think, although I'm not really sure, that we may have gotten along, but the possibility of a conversation, never mind a friendship, is now foreclosed by AIDS. Or is it? How peculiar is it for me to continue responding to Tom (can I call him Tom?) knowing, of course, all along that he is dead. How, after all, can we speak, indeed argue, with the dead? Because of our overlapping and nearly historical conjunction as gay men in the academy interested in lesbian and gay studies, and despite our significant differences—in rank and status, race and ethnicity, professional interests and training, and most acutely, our relationship to AIDS—I want to claim an affinity with him. I realize, of course, that in the process of identification I run the risk of enacting the very violence of misrecognition he has argued so effectively against. This, for me, is an acceptable and worthwhile risk, for how else can I convey and indulge my romantic impulse for what could have been and my relentless rage for what will never be?

To speak and identify as someone who is not living with AIDS assumes, inevitably and unfortunately, a desire to differentiate from people with AIDS. For a gay man (and one of color) to announce publicly his seronegativity (however tenuous this may be[12]) plays into a dynamic established by the dominant discursive strategies that constructs people with AIDS as other. It perpetuates the very problematic and omnipresent binarism (usually at the expense of people with AIDS) that insistently categorizes people as with AIDS or without.[13] This is not my aim. I am left wondering what means are available to me to speak with the dead—to claim an identification—without enacting the violence of misrecognition. Can there be recognition without violence? Is my mourning only a narcissistic performance of survival? Or, if I am speaking with the dead, who is listening and what is the response? All my profit lies in this asking.

David Román

Notes

This essay was written in the spring of 1993. Discussions with Carolyn Dinshaw, Yvonne Yarbro-Bejarano, Robyn Wiegman, and David Norton have helped shape some of these ideas. I would also like to thank Sue-Ellen Case, Yvonne Yarbro-Bejarano, Brad Epps, and Joe Litvak for sharing with me the drafts of their essays.

1. For me, the most useful discussions of this negotiation are Eve Kosofsky Sedgwick's "White Glasses," Douglas Crimp's "Right On, Girlfriend!," and Phillip Brian Harper's "Eloquence and Epitaph."

2. See also "Inside the Ivory Closet," by Jeffrey Escoffier, who constructs a less dynamic history of the field by insisting on the binarism not only between two, for him, distinct generations of scholars but also between those inside and outside of the academy.

3. See Brad Epps, for example, who discusses this in relation to Spanish traditions, and Richard Easton, who provides a thorough discussion of gay and

lesbian studies and art history. This is not to suggest, by any means, that the social sciences and other disciplines have not engaged lesbian and gay issues. It is precisely the question as to how this work is eclipsed by the humanities, and more specifically "English," that I wish to raise.

4. On this point, see the interview with Martin Duberman where he recounts how in Vermont, a conservative politican after reading Duberman's coedited anthology, *Hidden from History: Reclaiming the Lesbian and Gay Past,* helped rally support for the success of the lesbian and gay state civil rights bill.

5. Although Yingling calls attention to the "repression" of the lesbian in *lesbian and* gay studies, his essay simultaneously enacts it by claiming a canonical moment for lesbian and gay studies.

6. Yingling refers to this problem in his earlier essay, "Sexual Preference/ Cultural Reference," where he writes: "To be openly gay or lesbian in the academy, to be working on gay and lesbian literature and theory (despite what seems to be something of a revolution in manners), is still to find oneself all too often embattled, belittled, and un(der)employed" (185).

7. For a detailed discussion of Halperin's situation, see Martha Nussbaum. Unfortunately Nussbaum, in an otherwise brilliant argument, does not factor in lesbian studies.

8. In a letter to the editor of the *Wall Street Journal* (Jan. 27, 1993), Timothy B. Peters, a former student of Halperin's, protested against Kimball's insinuations: "Mr. Kimball makes a leap by assuming that radical scholarship automatically translates into radical and/or bad teaching. . . . To suggest that radical fields of inquiry discredit a scholar's ability to teach (an often altogether different pursuit) makes the criticism personal and mean-spirited and, therefore, inappropriate."

Degrees of homophobia are also omnipresent in the publishing world. Richard Mohr, for example, sees this as the central problem he encountered in his attempts to find a university press to publish his recent book *Gay Ideas: Outing and Other Controversies.* The anthology *How Do I Look? Queer Film and Video,* published by Seattle's Bay Press, could not find a domestic printer. In both cases, presses and printers were concerned primarily with images discussed and reproduced in the texts.

9. Litvak's paper, incidentally, was presented at a 1992 MLA panel sponsored by the Gay and Lesbian Caucus whose call for papers was entitled "Classrooms from Hell." By the time of the meeting, the program was retitled "Mourning, Shaming, Trashing, and Pogroms in and around the Queer Studies Classroom." The other presenters were Michele Aina Barale, Sean Holland, and Eve Kosofsky Sedgwick.

10. And yet, it needs to be noted, Litvak joins Sue-Ellen Case in pointing out the vexed position of the lesbian or gay teacher in the classroom.

11. Consider for example two completely different and simultaneous occasions for lesbian and gay studies. In 1992, the Center for Lesbian and Gay Studies under the direction of Martin Duberman at the Graduate School of the City University of New York received a $250,000 Rockefeller grant. That

same year the Auburn Gay and Lesbian Association (AGLA), a queer student
group at Auburn University in Alabama, was denied access to university funds
since AGLA supposedly advocated the violation of state sodomy laws. The
Alabama state senate unanimously approved this censure.

12. Once again, I cite Sedgwick's "White Glasses" for an excellent discussion of the tenuous nature of speaking subjects and (our) health, in particular
as it relates to our positions around HIV and AIDS.

13. See, for instance and for starters, Andrew Sullivan, "Gay Life, Gay
Death." Moreover, to test positive for human immunodeficiency virus (HIV)
is not the same as to be diagnosed with AIDS. In other words, HIV and AIDS
are not coterminous and/or interchangeable terms.

Works Cited

Abraham, Julie. "I Know What Boys Like: Tales from the Dyke Side." *Village
    Voice Literary Supplement,* June 1992, 20–23.
"Age of AIDS: A Death in the Family." *Village Voice,* Mar. 23, 1993, 13.
Butler, Judith. "The Force of Fantasy: Feminism, Mapplethorpe, and Discur-
    sive Excess." *differences* 2 (1990): 105–25.
———. Letter to the Editor. *NYQ,* Apr. 12, 1992.
Case, Sue-Ellen. "The Student and the Strap: Authority and Seduction in the
    Class/Room." Forthcoming in *Professions of Desire,* ed. Haggerty and Zimerman.
Crimp, Douglas, with Adam Rolston. *AIDS Demographics.* Seattle, Wash.: Bay
    Press, 1990.
———. "Right On, Girlfriend!" *Social Text* 33 (1992): 2–19.
D'Emilio, John. *Making Trouble: Essays on Gay History, Politics, and the University.*
    New York: Routledge, 1992.
Duberman, Martin. Interview by M. L. Cooper. *Lambda Book Report* 3, no. 8
    (1993): 10–11.
Easton, Richard. "Canonical Criminalizations: Homosexuality, Art History,
    Surrealism, and Abjection." *differences* 4 (1993): 133–75.
Epps, Brad. "Sense and Sensibility: Eros, Pedagogy, and (In)discretion in Ana
    María Moix, Esther Tusquets, and Carme Riera." Paper presented at "Gen-
    der, Sexuality, and the State: A Latino/Hispanic Context Conference," Uni-
    versity of California–Berkeley, 1993.
Escoffier, Jeffrey. "Inside the Ivory Closet: The Challenges Facing Lesbian and
    Gay Studies." *Outlook,* Fall 1990, 40–48.
Greenblatt, Stephen. *Shakespearean Negotiations: The Circulation of Social Energy
    in Renaissance England.* Berkeley: University of California Press, 1988.
Haggerty, George, and Bonnie Zimerman, eds. *Professions of Desire: Gay and Les-
    bian Studies in Literature.* New York: MLA Publications, forthcoming.
Harper, Phillip Brian. "Eloquence and Epitaph: Black Nationalism and the
    Homophobic Impulse in Responses to the Death of Max Robinson." Pp.
    117–39 in *Writing AIDS: Gay Literature, Language, and Analysis,* ed. Timothy
    F. Murphy and Suzanne Poirier. New York: Columbia University Press,
    1993.

Kimball, Roger. "'Heterosexuality' and Other Literary Matters." *Wall Street Journal*, Dec. 31, 1992.

Kushner, Tony. *Angels in America, Part 1: Millennium Approaches.* New York: Theatre Communications Group, 1993.

Litvak, Joseph. "Teaching and Melancholia." Paper presented at the Modern Language Association conference, New York, 1992.

Nussbaum, Martha. "A Classical Case for Gay Studies." *New Republic,* July 13 and 20 (double issue), 1992, 26–35.

Patton, Cindy. *Inventing AIDS.* New York: Routledge, 1990.

Riggs, Marlon. "Unleash the Queen." Pp. 99–105 in *Black Popular Culture,* ed. Gina Dent. Seattle, Wash.: Bay Press, 1993.

Román, David. "Teaching Differences: Theory and Practice in a Lesbian and Gay Studies Seminar." Forthcoming in *Professions of Desire,* ed. Haggerty and Zimerman.

Sedgwick, Eve Kosofsky. "White Glasses." *Yale Journal of Criticism* 5 (1992): 193–208.

Sullivan, Andrew. "Gay Life, Gay Death." *New Republic,* Dec. 17, 1990, 19–25.

Turner, Victor. *The Ritual Process: Structure and Anti-Structure.* New York: Aldine, 1969.

Warner, Michael. "From Queer to Eternity: An Army of Theorists Cannot Fail." *Village Voice Literary Supplement,* June 1992, 18–19.

Watney, Simon. "Lesbian and Gay Studies in the Age of AIDS." *NYQ,* Mar. 22, 1992, 42.

Yarbro-Bejarano, Yvonne. "Expanding the Categories of Race and Sexuality in Lesbian and Gay Studies." Forthcoming in *Professions of Desire,* ed. Haggerty and Zimerman.

10

Buckling Down or Knuckling Under: Discipline or Punish in Lesbian and Gay Studies

The rubric "gay and lesbian studies," or any of its several equally distributive, more or less synonymous epithets (lesbian and gay studies; lesbian, gay, and bisexual studies; gay, lesbian, and bisexual studies), has come to stand for a distinct, if interdisciplinary, academic focus. A conscious alliance, lesbian and gay studies represents a kind of corporate merger—a wedding even—between somewhat disparate interests whose common element often seems to be only an analogous sexuality defined in relation to heterosexuality.[1] Gay and lesbian studies "has become important in postmodern discourses by analogy to other 'species' of difference like race, class, and gender," as Thomas Yingling points out in "Fetishism, Identity, Politics" (in this volume). Presumably a category of difference referring, as Elizabeth Grosz notes (in this volume), to those who "do" certain sexual acts, gay and lesbian appears to embody the "sexual" difference that in the 1990s completes the set of socially oppressible differences. Moreover, it is very important that the category of gay and lesbian look just like one of these other categories, so that it can perform, almost surreptitiously, a quite different function.

The category of gay and lesbian, seemingly so analogous to other "differences," is in fact not an analogous category at all, nor even a single category, but a somewhat unstable amalgamation produced by the complex confluence of institutional politics, consumer culture, and gender and sexual anxieties. The joinder of lesbian and gay has been as much a matter of disciplinary space and the operation of ideologies limiting the scope of diversity as it has been a product of either coalition politics or intellectual commonality.[2] Not really an academic discipline in the traditional meaning of the word or even a discrete field, gay and lesbian studies is a discipline in the Foucauldian sense, functioning ambivalently to display, empower, control, limit, and repress sexuality. This is not to say that such a discipline does not have its uses; both Yingling and Grosz point out the positive value of visibility and the political possibilities of open-endedness, while reminding us what is necessarily lost or repressed in the categorical gesture. Rather, it is to suggest that the combinatory quality of that unwieldy couple gay and lesbian is a symptom of the ways its disciplinarity works, the repressions it enacts, the kinds of authority it endows, and the very specific, strategic ways it deploys that authority in academia.

Docile Bodies[3]

As its appellation would indicate, "lesbian and gay" bespeaks a judicious binary, sometimes tertiary, distribution, an inclusive equity whose performative inventory seems to identify candidly its subject matter.[4] Its listing seems to connote an intersection, some conjunction of interests in the world of all possible interests, while its plastic ordering seems to defy rank and hierarchy. Its superficial distribution, however, masks and posits another relation: between individuals and the sexual multiplicity organized, tabulated, and contained within the expansive appearance of the enumeration. The rubric's dual role is to fix individuals within a sexual category and to locate that sexual category within a larger disciplinary scheme. On its face democratic, gay and lesbian studies is, like all categories of "multiplicity," relegated to the margins where it can sustain and track on behalf of a very singular heterologos the multifarious adherents of scandalous variety.

The necessity of the category "lesbian and gay" and its particular form arises in part as the solution to a set of new disciplinary difficulties that beset the academy (and American culture) in the early to mid-eighties. Having in the early 1970s successfully incorporated the emerging perspectives of African Americans and women by simply giving them their own aptly named, uncertainly situated, and generally underfunded (or just funded enough) slots in the systematic index of identifiable erudition, the inevitable recognition of diversity even within these emblematically diverse loci confounds again the tidy interrelations of academic parts, freeing multiplicity and requiring new modes of categorization. This revivified diversity is accompanied (not coincidentally) by a "crisis" in the academy in the form of a nostalgic ruing of the disciplines of yore, an attempt to return to the homey, familiar categories of the good old days, and the proclamation of a rise in universal ignorance à la E. D. Hirsch and Allan Bloom.[5] The mutual influence of diversity and decadence conjoins with the increasing commercialization of the academy (again, à la Hirsch and Bloom), both cause and effect of shrinking state funding, shifting class structures, and the mass introjection of digital information systems into higher education. While modes of daily surveillance become much easier via computer systems, computers also force a kind of individuality never before possible, reflected in the affirmative action tracking of ethnicity, but having its effect in the final institutionalization of formerly "fringe" disciplines and the consolidation of interdisciplinarity within traditional departments rather than as new categories.[6]

The emergence of the trackable individual forces a new organization of disciplines that welds individuals more definitely with appropriate categories. These categories are both organized in relation to and premised upon the newly expanded terms of diversity. The key word of this new discipline is "identity," which conveniently aligns individuals marked with "multiplicity" to the same discrete categories by which multiplicity is organized and understood. Instead of being an intellectual choice (or the appearance of one), academic endeavor becomes a matter of identity, of an essentialized position that is culturally defined, creating and based upon certain epistemological positions, and reflecting the progressive organization of differences *from* the perspective of white bourgeois patriarchy. The link between identity, epistemology, and discipline appears to open the academy, while in practice it restricts thought, limits and consolidates authority under the guise of distributing it, and sequesters individuals within manageable consumer groups with discrete market interests.

The distribution of diverse groups in diverse "disciplines" appears to be a pragmatic institutional reorganization; minor as it may seem, it represents not some kind of institutional economy but a shift to an economy of commercially useful categories. The surfacing of the link between knowledge and capital occurs at the very moment such a link seems to fail as a supposed victim of economic recession and beset state budgets, but perhaps more a symptom of education's systematic shift from public to private, from civil right to purchased privilege, from process and experience to definable, consumable product characterized by consumer rather than pedagogical dynamics.[7] Identity, as the premise for discipline, becomes the discipline's object of study; an individual establishes and consumes herself as a self defined within a disciplinary range in the paradoxical register of multiculturalism. Education for those marked as nondominant threatens to become the quest to explain self *in relation to dominant culture,* locally liberating but still limited by the culture that has defined the individual as different in the first place.

The emergence of the consumer discipline represents the illusory alliance of identity, subject matter, and institutional position that in turn creates the consumable academic object. The institutional re- structuring of disciplines is itself linked to a cultural shift from mi- metic representation to simulation.[8] The disciplines of the modern American academy had been mimetic, that is, had represented some convergence of industry need and tradition in "majors" where edu- cation was defined in a one-on-one correlation of proficiency to trade within the vestiges of liberality. This mimeticism circumscribed areas of expertise and defined expertise in terms of depth rather than breadth. Simulation (image referring to image) promotes and is pro- duced by the appearance of disciplinary expertise (students still ma- jor in something) but marks the dispensation of substance and depth in exchange for a general concept of education defined in highly util- itarian terms. This gloss of innovative pragmatism, this appearance of the concrete and marketable in a place previously occupied by "ar- cane" and impractical theory, enables and promotes a consumer model as the salvation of higher education and the progress of hu- man knowledge, installing with it concepts of agency, debt, warran- ty, contract, and product as the determining structure of education and supporting and encouraging the realignment of disciplines into consumable entities.[9]

In this shift from mimeticism to simulation several major institu- tional changes occur that appear to force, foster, found, and/or con- found the emergence of a lesbian and gay studies. First, the seemingly conscientious institutionalization of feminism, accompanied (in the world of identity = discipline) by an assumed identity between female academics and women's studies provokes a reaction that takes three forms: (1) some male academics become feminists, (2) some males fabricate a new area, "men's" studies, based on the feminist model, and (3) male homosexuality becomes visible as an epistemological category and object of study. Following the model of women's stud- ies, male homosexuality defines its own long tradition, rediscovers its lost writers, deciphers encoded literature, demarcates an écriture ho- mosexuelle, and so on.[10]

Second, the recognition of racial, sexual, ethnic, and generational diversities within feminist studies and African American studies pro- vokes what seems to be a necessary redistribution of multiplicity that does not break up either women's or African American studies, which are already ensconced as institutions. Instead, this recognition produces a displaced splitting reflected in the proliferation of other "studies" areas. Fomenting or fortifying such cognate or analogous fields as ethnic studies, American studies, or Latin American studies (whose existence seems all the more natural for the emergence of such multiplicity within the now traditional institutional sites of multiplicity), this displacement also creates the model and space for studies of sexuality that, under the program of distributing multiplicity, emerges as the seemingly discrete category "gay and lesbian studies." At the same time, these "newer" cognate areas representing race, multiculturalism, ethnicity, religion, and sexuality are "mainstreamed"—asked to relocate their scattered disciplinarity within traditional academic departments so that each discipline has its regimented and surveillable representatives of diversity (but only one of each).

Third, an ideological overemphasis on the First Amendment, rather than owing its resurrection to what appears to be the desperate need of suddenly centrifugalized white males for a defense mechanism against "political correctness," actually precedes and invents political correctness as a means of organizing another relation between white male heterosexual individuals and all of this other stuff, making political correctness a category of oppression. The narrative of oppression presumably caused by political correctness has to do with white males (more often than not) feeling suddenly aggressively prevented from saying whatever they want, which all at once has become an urgent need to insult women, African Americans, and other minorities in a public forum. This is really the obverse of the fact that considerations about speech come from the visibility of previously unacknowledged or underrated interests. In this sense, First Amendment complaints are a secondary defense to the fact that white males have been decentered before they even speak. Emerging as the locus for the displaced fears of white males during organizational transformation, "free" speech becomes the supposed battleground for the maintenance of sacred tradition, individuality, and democracy. Nonetheless, within the category of the politically correct, the diverse, who provide the angst against which the First Amendment performs, strive openly against one another within a consumer logic of the attractive forbidden, while paradoxically, the iconization of such reactionary personae as Dinesh daSouza and Camille Paglia reinforces and actually contributes to the development of the "diversity" that white males rail against.

Finally, academic book publishing becomes big business as commercial publishers compete in the traditional low-volume arena and as there are more "cross-over" volumes.[11] This is partly due to the shift to a simulation mode of representation that enables a more generic marketing, but it is also dependent upon the sustenance of identity categories that provide the market for identity books. While traditional academic books still languish in commercial doldrums, identity-based studies and studies of popular culture become more saleable and are more aggressively marketed to their identity-defined audiences.[12]

At the nexus of all of this in the mid-1980s, gay and lesbian studies emerges without an academic home, without a discrete institutional unit, but with serious, if squeamish, institutional play. This may in part be due to the number of gays and lesbians in academe, but it also traces the performance of another institutional distancing act by which the body academic organizes its relation to diversity. While there is no doubt that work done within the rubric of lesbian and gay studies is interesting, challenging, worthwhile, necessary, significant, and long overdue, the place occupied by gay and lesbian studies only simulates a traditional academic discipline. Its function as a holding ground becomes quite evident if we examine what occupies its space.

Panopticism

Unlike women's studies or African American studies whose models it emulates, gay and lesbian studies is neither as candid nor unified as its designation connotes or as its gender or ethnic/racially based prototypes sometimes have presented themselves. In fact, the name lesbian and gay studies betrays the disciplinary difficulties of a designation masquerading as a discipline. Haunted by conjunctions, asymmetries, and unassimilable diversities, gay and lesbian studies is still a makeshift moniker, standing for the default organization of what is not yet and may never be a coherent field, reflecting the tensions, hostilities, lack of correlation, differences in interests, cultural positions, and issues, and the absence of any systematizing, unifying set of questions, methodologies, or even subject matters that incorporate or ally its various constituent parts.

The "and" in gay and lesbian seems to portend a symmetry between two complementary and presumably parallel cultural categories, superficially determined by whether one's sexual object is of the same or a different gender, but distinguished from one another by gender. This common pattern of desiring someone of the same gender and its associated broadly defined social oppressions (e.g., job discrimination) may be all these two terms really have in common. In fact, their forced parallelism is the result of a binary gender logic that both assumes the complementarity and symmetry of sexual difference and accepts a very facile understanding of any homosexuality as simply a matter of reduplicating gender, of like loving like. "Gay and lesbian" is like "men and women" or any other such set of trite ideological correlates.

What "and" both obscures and exposes is a lack of correlation and commonality, a relation more like "apples and oranges": both are fruits, but that is where the similarity ends. Lesbian and gay as a disciplinary combo denotes two very different, conflicting possibilities: either a lesbian and gay studies with common methodology, principles, and issues, akin to women's studies whose internal divisions and diversity enrich methodology and enlarge its scope and issues, or two primarily different areas of study—gay and lesbian—allied on the basis of a paradigmatic similarity. Is there such a thing as a lesbian *and* gay studies? Does anyone consider both equally and at the same time? What kinds of work are considered as obvious parts of this endeavor and what do such works have in common? Or another, more Foucauldian way to pose the question: how does the combo "gay and lesbian" define "in relation to multiplicities" a "tactics of power" that increases "both the docility and the utility of all the elements of the system" (Foucault 218)—in this case the conjunction of sexual discourses, capitalism, and institutions of education and culture?

Looking, for example, at volume 20, number 2 (July 1993) of the *Lesbian and Gay Studies Newsletter,* we can get an idea of what Margaret Morrison and the *Newsletter*'s various subeditors conceive of as a "lesbian and gay studies." The book review section, edited by Jonathan Goldberg, perhaps most directly conveys the scope of an academic discipline. In this issue twelve books are reviewed: five focus on gay males, one on lesbians, one on feminist/maybe lesbian, one on AIDS, and four include some gay and lesbian work in larger collections on culture, sexuality, and/or erotics. While the disparity in the distribution of subject matter might be explained by its relation to real numbers, the more telling problem has to do with the various principles by which these studies are defined as gay and lesbian. The five books on gay males, for example, are widely diverse in what makes the books gay: one is about literature depicting gayness (gay as overt subject matter), one is on the figure of sodomy (a metaphorical "gay" structure working through history, but a curiously narcissistic inclusion as it is the editor's own book), two are about gay male authors (gay as identity), and one is on opera (gay as cultural phenomenon). The other works, particularly those about a more general sexuality or erotics, suggest that "gay and lesbian" functions as a cover term for "the sexual" as freed from the exigencies of reproductive bourgeois patriarchal culture. Anything that refers to free-floating sexuality (subject matter, identity, sexual representations in general, AIDS) belongs in the discipline of gay and lesbian studies. These twelve books represent no coherent shared methodology, no sustained question except, perhaps, the iteration of a sexually based, culturally deployed identity.

The combination of sexuality and identity, represented under the rubric of its two gendered "brands" (one of which is already clearly underrepresented), organizes the excess free-floating sexuality gay and lesbian studies apparently represents, binding it to "respectable," locatable, controllable identity categories—to a discipline through which it is defused and managed. The *Newsletter* happily provides a clue to the anxiety about free-floating sexuality and power in the institution, as gay and lesbian performs for its readers a disciplinary containment appearing under the guise of a failure of containment, such as would perpetuate a gay and lesbian studies' topic.

The letters to the editor include four letters and an editor's note. The first letter, from Jane Gallop, objects to the *Newsletter*'s irresponsible announcement that students had lodged complaints that Gallop was sexually harassing lesbians. Pointing out that allegations are often mistaken for juridical condemnations and that the announcement of the allegation was made in a gossip column and was thus both trivialized and unlikely to be followed responsibly, Gallop attempts to contain what she recognizes is most certainly uncontainable—the combination of pedagogy and eroticism made visible in the last ten years by feminist scholarship, feminist psychoanalytic work, and Marxist power analyses. The *Newsletter*'s disclosure of student complaints against Gallop is not simply the fickle exercise of academic rumor or the responsible monitoring of alleged sexually based abuses of power; it is a deliberate inclusion by the gossip columnist who is one of the students making the complaint. The student's choice of a disciplinary vehicle as a public forum for the communication of allegations is itself an exercise of power in the name of the discipline. On the surface an attempt to control this dangerous excess, the publication of the news was itself an excess, proliferated through the discipline instead of contained by it.

Gallop's letter, in attempting to staunch this flow of sexual innuendo, appeals to ethics but also to the discipline (in the persona of its adherents) as responsible for containment: "lesbian and gay people ought to be more than usually sensitive to the way sexual gossip can destroy someone's professional reputation" (2). The editor's note following Gallop's letter rather weakly acknowledges her point, identifies the columnist as one of complainants (something Gallop does not do), and apologizes for "a lapse in good judgment" (2). While announcing that the gossip editor had resigned, the editor, like Gallop, displaces the operation of discipline to the readers: "We also trust that *LGSN* readers know the difference between charges brought against a person and a judgment made, after due process, of that person's innocence or guilt" (2). Discipline is shifted from ethics to individual discrimination and reason as that which will finally contain sexual excess. In a sense the discipline as discipline in the *LGSN* serves only as a means of distributing various individual responsibilities, apparently organizing the relation of individuals to multiplicities and power through the guise of individual savvy at the very moment it fails to regulate those relations. As such it becomes the repository for the circulation of sexuality and power, the locus for the exposure of those issues in relation to the larger institution which can relocate them in gay and lesbians studies' convenient "sexual" department.

This is the fear expressed by the second letter published in the *Newsletter*, sent by Joseph Litvak who worries about the connection between the "eroticization of the classroom" and gay and lesbian studies as the issue emerged publicly in the guerilla publicity around the Center for Twentieth-Century Studies' Conference on Pedagogy (the conference was organized by Gallop). While Litvak believes that pedagogical erotics damage the reputation of lesbian and gay studies, he also recognizes their necessary connection: "The numerous student and faculty sources who worry about '"eroticization" of the classroom' would no doubt find their anxieties diminished if lesbian and gay studies would just disappear" (3). For Litvak, control is also a matter of good judgment and proper use of discipline: "Not all readers of *LGSN* want to endorse the potential violence of such a self-mystifying act of disciplinary enforcement" (3).

The interchange around Gallop and *Lingua Franca*'s later more thoughtful essay about her by Margaret Talbot expose the internal working of discipline in its surveillance function (keeping track of sexuality and power), its distributive function that regulates the relation of individuals to multiplicity and keeps them docile through the highly economic appeal to a discipline that has become coterminous with identity. Associating an eroticized classroom with gay and lesbian studies is the discipline's function; the discipline exists to contain any erotic connection, to regulate and theorize sexual excess as a means of controlling it, codifying it, and allowing its continued play. The problem Litvak identifies—that the eroticized classroom is associated with gay and lesbian studies—constitutes gay and lesbian studies' disciplinary function in the larger institutional scheme. While allegations of heterosexual harassment are bruited briefly and die in the dust of cynicism and covert congratulations, the allegations against Gallop are already overdetermined, representing the uneasy relation between erotic power and the academy via almost larger-than-life, allegorical personae: teacher/student, powerful theorist of sexuality and representation/gossip columnist lesbian.

Even as protections against sexual harassment threaten to be eroded by conservative overemphasis on the First Amendment, gay and lesbian studies as a discipline stands to absorb the anxieties of sexualized power that can no longer be recognized as playing out among heterosexuals.[13] That this issue of harassment erupts in the middle of lesbian and gay studies is symptomatic of the disruption the faux discipline is constructed to maintain and express.

Complete and Austere Institutions

The location of gay and lesbian studies at the nexus of power and eroticism does not invalidate any of the work done in its name, which, among other things, performs the function of naming and analyzing the relations between power and sexualities. Its location also does not account for the field's binary nomenclature. Homosexual studies would serve just as well for these disciplinary purposes (as it does for the purposes of some of the discipline's journals—for example, the *Journal of Homosexuality*). The duality itself must represent some excess, anxiety, or disciplinary rift. Since the word "homosexuality" does not in itself convey lesbian, the inclusion of lesbian might be some ploy of affirmative action visibility, a recognition of a presence that, as the books reviewed by the *Newsletter* might indicate, is not too much of a presence at all.

But in light of the *LGSN* letter exchange, the overt naming of the lesbian might signal another function: that of the locus for disturbances in the field of homosexual studies. Largely outnumbered, with more openly mixed allegiances in their overt connection to feminist studies, lesbians in gay studies occupy the metaphorical locus of "theory": that which interrupts gay praxis and activism, limits and polices the potentially infinite play of gay male eroticism, and whose language is taken as incomprehensible (hence not populist), identification-breaking jargon.[14] The very openness and insistence of lesbian dilemmas such as that posed by the emergence of lesbian s/m bespeak, among other things, the very embattled configuration of discipline, or disciplined configuration of embattlement, that characterizes the dynamic of lesbian and gay studies as a unified discipline.[15] Appearing to reiterate the same old sexism, the position of the lesbian in gay and lesbian studies actually operates as the locus of disciplinary complexity, self-contradiction, lack of cohesion, and site of educational erotics.

Lesbian and gay studies as a somewhat disarticulated but fully functioning discipline can, however, evade the connection Litvak rightly worries about. Because this connection is partially enabled by an unwillingness to recognize the political and ideological importance of gender, by acknowledging the value of gender differences as the ideological but very operative categories for disparate treatment, gay and lesbian studies might recognize and make use of the meaning of the absence of symmetry, analogy, and identity among gay men and lesbians. Recognizing gender as a separate dynamic has the effect of confusing the sexual gloss of the gay and lesbian locus. While this does not require the destruction of the valuable coalition between gay men and lesbians, it does disenable the lesbian's containment function. Moreover, recognizing gender difference would certainly dispel some of the issues of authority that arise when any individual tries to speak in the name of gay and lesbian studies.

If the differences between gay male and lesbian studies are recognized, then so might their similarities in method, philosophy, and issues. If that happens, lesbian studies and gay studies as two distinct and separate branches might together form a discipline whose common denominator—sexuality—openly named and already anatomized, might deflect the academy's use of the discipline as its eroticism-anxiety dumping ground. At the same time, the identification of method and theories of sexualities might influence and become an essential part of any analysis of power in much the same way feminist theories have become entrenched in some critical methodologies. In this way, too, lesbian and gay studies might cease to be a field of containment, the site of punishment knuckled under for the duration, and become instead a systematized mode of inquiry, a buckled-down discipline that influences the never complete and hopefully not-so-austere institution.

Judith Roof

Notes

1. Because of the complicated relation of lesbian studies to feminism and women's studies, and because of the phenomena of lesbian separatism, occasional gay male misogyny, and the very different cultural space assigned to

gay males and lesbians, academic alliances between gay male and lesbian studies came long after their sociopolitical alliances. Some gay scholars, such as Jonathan Katz, still maintain a distinction between political activism and the academy.

2. Following an identity politics practice that has recently dominated the logic for establishing disciplines, gay and lesbian studies' somewhat awkward combination refers ambiguously to identity. The general assumption is an identity between scholar and work except in the case of heterosexual women working on gay men. Heterosexual men working on lesbians or claiming a lesbian position are viewed suspiciously. This asymmetry in itself exposes the crucial role played by gender.

3. The concept of discipline and the section titles are from Michel Foucault's *Discipline and Punish*.

4. Curiously, while gay might refer to someone of either gender, in this epithet it only refers to males. The equation between gay and male elides women altogether.

5. Books by these two authors made a reformist splash in the late 1980s. For an idea of what kind of splash, note the title of Bloom's book: *The Closing of the American Mind: How Higher Education Has Failed Democracy and Impoverished the Souls of Today's Students*.

6. Those categories that cannot be discerned from affirmative action lists might therefore be determined by interest area.

7. Evidence of this lies in the establishment of for-profit universities, the idea of the course syllabus as a contract, and administrators' constant use of a consumer metaphor to understand student/teacher/university relations. This encourages certain modes of interaction: students demanding their rights, taking advantage of loopholes, and treating teachers like employees.

8. The term "simulation" is from Jean Baudrillard, *Simulations*.

9. Though this has always been the case in technical disciplines such as engineering, the introduction of vocational "majors" in disciplines such as English betrays a consumer orientation that will justify the study of literature *instead of* literature justifying the acquisition of vocational skills.

10. Though its relation to feminism seems somewhat tortured and ambivalent. For an example, see Joseph Boone and Michael Cadden, *Engendering Men*.

11. Academic publishers have begun lobbying for academic books without academic language so that they can gain a larger market. A good example of such a book is Lillian Faderman's *Lost Girls and Twilight Lovers*.

12. Witness the number of special promotions based on identity categories while traditional academic books are hidden in the "literature" section.

13. Suggestions that the Fourteenth Amendment–based federal protections against sexual harassment contained in Title VII might fall under the First Amendment logic used by the Supreme Court in adjudicating "hate speech" cases conveniently "forget" the Fourteenth Amendment (and the diversity it represents).

14. The evocation of Judith Butler has served as both the emblem of the-

ory and the emblem of "jargon." Male ambivalence about Butler is manifestly evident in the number of times her name is mentioned at any gay studies conference.

15. This is not to imply that lesbian s/m has anything to do with battling; rather, the emergence of s/m as an issue in lesbian studies occurs at the same time homosexuality becomes the venue for problems of eroticism and power in the academy.

Works Cited

Baudrillard, Jean. *Simulations*. Trans. Paul Foss, Paul Patton, and Philip Beitchman. New York: Semiotext(e), 1983.

Bloom, Allan. *The Closing of the American Mind: How Higher Education Has Failed Democracy and Impoverished the Souls of Today's Students*. New York: Simon and Schuster, 1987.

Boone, Joseph, and Michael Cadden, eds. *Engendering Men*. New York: Routledge, 1990.

Faderman, Lillian. *Lost Girls and Twilight Lovers*. New York: Columbia University Press, 1991.

Foucault, Michel. *Discipline and Punish: The Birth of the Prison*. Trans. Alan Sheridan. New York: Vintage, 1979.

Talbot, Margaret. "A Most Dangerous Method." *Lingua Franca*, Feb. 1994, 1, 24–40.

Part Four

Figures of Speech

Body Talk

The ideological connection between the body and identity endows a certain authority to speak about that body, but even as we assume authority about our own bodies and identities, in critical discourse some bodies offer more authority than others. For example, if we understand a particular kind of body to be the signifier of social or discursive oppression, then we expect the subject with such a body to have had instructive experience about its oppression. Only oppressed bodies are supposed to understand the power relations in which they are caught; they become the "subjects supposed to know." There is, however, no such thing as a "subject supposed to know," except in our imaginations, in our desperate appeals for authority.

The knowledge the subject is supposed to know is the product of a particular way of thinking about the body. Having an inside and an outside—a surface and an essence—this body reduces the complex intersection of the social and the psyche to the same thing. In this scenario, the imaginary inside a body represents what is expected from its outside—the psyche is defined by the social. Its outside is imagined as a site of material effects that bears the specific marks and symptoms of privilege and oppression. Its inside cannot exceed its outside: it cannot know more than its body's cultural position would dictate and its outside cannot escape social dicta.

The outside confers authority to the inside to speak of (and only of) the outside, the already culturally determined matrix by which that body is read. Reading bodies that we imagine as identities actually bestows a significance to bodies that have already been interpreted, whose manner of reading has already been set according to the rules—the dualistic overdetermination—by which the body came to signify in the first place. What we read is, in short, what has already been read.

This does not mean, however, that reading the body and the already interpreted body are identical. The difference between the process and the product is a catachresis whose revelation is an occasional source of embarrassment for the reader "caught out." To assume, for instance, a critic's specialty by reading the culturally determined significations of her body is to mistake one body for another. Being caught out challenges, not authority, but the system by which reading and body are aligned in the first place.

Embarrassment comes from the sudden disorientation of a body eclipsing its cultural signification—of its inside clearly exceeding its outside or, more crucially, of the revelation that the binary inside/outside is itself an ideological construction upon which the body's power is premised and by which the subject's authority is limited. Recovery from embarrassment comes through a number of possible mechanisms: (1) a defensive overcompensatory reassertion of the original system by which bodies signify and authorize—"What would you know about my experience of oppression as a white heterosexual middle-class male?," (2) a sheepish adjustment in the system whose small correction serves to bolster the original—"Okay, some African Americans can be wealthy and highly educated, but they can still speak authoritatively about oppression," or (3) the replacement of one set of terms by another whose shards of humility reauthorize an obsequious but very insidious speech and whose simple exchange maintains the system—"You don't look like a lesbian."

These possibilities, these ways of returning to a specious logic suggest a closed system wherein change is unlikely if not impossible. In the contemporary academy, such a return to the same often seems to be the case. What is necessary is another system (if we can call it that)—a radically different relation among bodies, power, and discourse as well as a different way to read them.

11

The Vicar and Virago: Feminism and the Problem of Identity

In Britain in 1988, the British Broadcasting Corporation (BBC) expressed interest in the work of a new writer, Rahila Khan, a feminist from the Indian subcontinent whose work purported to describe the life and experiences of young Asian women in Margaret Thatcher's Britain. Khan's first success, the story "Pictures," was broadcast twice on BBC radio. Then, Virago, the prominent feminist publishing house, agreed to publish Rahila Khan's collection of short stories, which addressed issues of gender, ethnicity, and class, for their *Upstarts* series featuring new young writers. This seemed to fulfill one of Virago's laudable objectives, that of publishing the work of a diverse group of contemporary feminist authors. Another feminist publishing house, the Women's Press, also accepted a story by Khan about Asian girls for an anthology but requested that the author rewrite it in the first person. An editor at Virago likewise queried the fact that the stories about third world adolescent girls were always in the third person: "I wondered whether this represented your feelings about the place of Asian women particularly in Britain, that the *sense* of *"otherness"* is still so great that it feels still an impossibility to write in first person as opposed to third" (Forward 21, emphasis added).

The editor's incisive phrasing not only demonstrates the pressure from first world publishers to have the experience of the third world delivered in the unmediated authenticity of first person but also unwittingly foreshadows what were to become the key terms in the subsequent public debate. The controversy was ignited when Khan's agent, who was negotiating a contract for the writer's second novel, arranged several publicity events for the writer, including interviews with the BBC and the *Guardian*. At this point, Rahila Khan was compelled to reveal himself as a male, middle-class, white vicar from Brighton named Toby Forward.

In the ensuing furor, which became known in England as the Vicar and Virago Affair, Forward claimed that experience should not be required to validate utterance: "The unspoken assumption behind most of this was that all imaginative literature, all fiction, is autobiographical. Later I was to be accused of pretending to occupy a position I didn't hold, to speak with a voice that wasn't mine. I had thought that was the purpose of art" (22). Forward's position comports with the long-held liberal humanist assumption used to buttress the white male canon that the author's race and gender are irrelevant. The crucial contradiction of the liberal humanist aesthetic is that individual identity and personal experience are paramount aspects of art so long as they provide evidence of a universal human nature on the model of the privileged white male; but they become specious once they mark specificities (gender, race, etc.) that are diametrically opposed to this hegemonic model of identity. It was neither their whiteness nor maleness that secured canonical authors a place in literary history, as the argument goes, but objective standards of literary merit which, by historical accident, largely accrued to those both white and male.

In an endeavor to unravel recent problems of authorial identity, one of America's most eminent African American critics, Henry Louis Gates, Jr., advances a position in a *New York Times Book Review* article whose ideological destination seems to betray a disturbing similarity to Forward's self-defense: "Death-of-the-author types cannot come to grips with the fact that a book is a cultural event; authorial identity, mystified or not, can be part of that event. What the idealogues of authenticity cannot quite deal with is that fact and fiction have always exerted a reciprocal effect on each other. . . . The distasteful truth will out: like it or not, all writers are 'cultural impersonators'" (29). The plea for authenticity, Gates argues, ignores the literariness of writing and its generic and historical situatedness. This is not to discount the importance of social positioning, he contends, but to resist the notion that race has a transparent relation to language. According to Gates, the case for authenticity amounts to an argument for segregation, an endeavor to make impenetrable the boundaries of ethnicity, race, and gender.[1] While it is certainly true that even in the face of the most egregious appropriations of identity we cannot assume a perfect correspondence between author and text, the contention that the imagination knows no boundary will not suffice either.

A sample of recent instances of authorial impersonation indicates the telling way in which this phenomenon constellates around race:

ex-Klan leader David Duke's *African Atto* (1973) appeared under the nom de plume Mohammed X (Reed 341); the Klan member Asa Earl Carter, alias Forrest Carter, penned *The Education of Little Tree*, the "true story" of a child's return to his American Indian roots; and "Latino" author Danny Santiago's award-winning prose was actually authored by a WASP from Yale University (Gates 26). The appropriation of subordinate identities by privileged whites demonstrates that endeavors to compensate for the exclusion of racial "minorities" from the means of literary production can become the very means for continuing this exclusion. Indeed, the above incursions on racially marked ethnic identities involve deliberate attempts to obscure the author's white identity and to present the work as an authentic transcription of "minority" experience. Such writing demonstrates not only a bid to control and define the culture of racial others but also to invent an ethnicity that will color the blandness of white (non)identity, which has become so normalized as to be entirely devoid of racial marking. White racial transparency is at once the perfect "neutral" base from which to assume and appropriate all other identities and a condition of perpetual lack that in turn provides the rationale for all colonizing gestures (see also hooks 21–39).

The mechanism whereby identities are colonized is the process of commodification. This phenomenon makes the debate about authenticity, at least in Gates's presentation of it, something of a historically belated shibboleth. For the business of authorial identity can no longer present itself as being about the expansive capacities of human imagination. In a symbolic economy dominated by the commodity, identity becomes, as Terry Eagleton explains, "the ephemeral function of this or that act of consumption, media experience, sexual relationship, trend or fashion" (145). Thus, the self-sovereign agent of an earlier phase of capitalist development, while it remains (residually) powerful in certain contexts and arenas, is in fact no longer the *only* subjectivity required by the endless proliferations of late capitalism. Humanism as an ideology, held so long as unsullied by politics and commercial transactions, has itself been disarticulated from liberalism by contemporary market conditions. In the process, some of its hitherto invisible ideological operations have become blatantly apparent— so apparent in fact that humanism's allegedly ameliorative imperatives (such as the "civilizing" mandate of imperialism) are unveiled in stark economic terms. As Forward observes: "We had found a gap in the market and we set about filling it" (22).

Notably, attempts to foreground difference have not immunized feminism from the brutal colonizing gestures of the marketplace. Indeed, what is distinctive about the Forward case is that *feminist* readers and institutions were particularly susceptible to his ploys. While it is beside the point to rebuke feminist readers at Virago and the Women's Press for failing to distinguish an authentic Indian woman from a vicar masquerading as one, it remains the case that the debacle was in part the result of feminism's participation in the commodification of ethnic identity, a signal of white feminism's still troubled encounter with racial difference.

But the Vicar and Virago Affair, like other instances of the phenomena of racial impersonation is not the only manifestation of the "problem" of identity. Feminist theory, for instance, often manifests this problem through strategies of displacement that occlude the conspicuously *white* identity crisis that underlies its contemporary theoretical obsessions. Lacking the reassurance of absolute hegemonic subjective and social identities (which, by definition, can never be secure enough), significant feminist theoretical texts can be understood as playing out a white identity crisis that, despite all assertions to the contrary, reinstates white hegemony via a complicity with what Gayatri Chakravorty Spivak has called "the persistent constitution of the Other as the Self's shadow" (280). It is this crisis and its constitutive othering that concern me, for the white subject's tendency to constitute the other as marginal is *not* a general problem but a specifically *white* problem (see Spivak 293). This chapter will move, by a necessarily circuitous route, from a critique of current efforts to problematize identity in the theoretical underpinnings of white feminism's identity crisis to the question of how various white theorists construct themselves as unraced and the other as their shadows.

Identity

Defenses of humanist conceptions of identity have reemerged within feminism as critiques of what are regarded by some feminists as the politically disabling tenets of postmodernism. In certain respects this is not surprising since there is a long tradition of Anglo-American feminism that posits the liberatory conception of the self as one in which the self-identical, rational subject is both the origin of agency and the guarantee of authenticity. Indeed, rationality is the basis and guarantee of the individual's democratic rights. As Daryl McGowan Tress notes: "The denial of depth to the self, the refusal of firm and legitimate grounding to claims of any kind, the contempt for reason, and the preoccupation with appearances—themes that have become the hallmark of the postmodern attitude—should serve as ready evidence that, ultimately, this philosophical orientation will not produce the deep understanding that women and society as a whole want and need" (197). The core self is posited here as the basis for socially functional consciousness, and reason is placed not as the epitome of oppressive Enlightenment epistemology, but as that which keeps psychosis at bay. Similarly, the analyst Jane Flax, who works with the "painful and disabling fragments" of self in her patients and who acknowledges that dominant notions of the self have also been congruent with definitions of masculinity, nonetheless argues for the psychic necessity of the "core self": "Those who celebrate or call for a 'decentered' self strike me as self-deceptively naive and unaware of the basic cohesion within themselves which makes the fragments of experience something other than a terrifying slide into psychosis" (92–93).

Biddy Martin and Chandra Mohanty are also hesitant about embracing anti-Enlightenment conceptions of identity; their interest is not so much in psychic interiority (as for Flax) but in the social privilege that underlies feminist objections to humanism: "The claim to a lack of identity or positionality is itself based on privilege, on a refusal to accept responsibility for one's implication in actual historical or social relations, or a denial that positionalities exist or that they matter, the denial of one's own personal history and the claim to a total separation from it" (Martin and Mohanty 208). Martin and Mohanty arrive at a state of affairs where the humanist subject, which has Western white man as its prototype, is finally *more political* than the postmodern one.

To be fair, these authors are trying to confront the disturbing prospect of "feminism without women." This is Tania Modleski's phrase, which she uses to highlight the way that an antiessentialist feminism may inadvertently erase women from its politics, especially in a post-feminist moment where women and feminism, and the challenge they present to dominant culture and social practices, are no longer objects of concern. For Modleski and others, the postmodern topography of the human subject as a complex map of disturbing determinants is one in which political identity is so fractured and dispersed that it seems to preclude anything so naive as a locus of resistance. But it is precisely in such circumstances that being "overly theoretical" (208), as Martin and Mohanty put it, necessarily involves being *overtly* theoretical—confronting the challenge of postmodernity. While postmodern conceptions of human identity are hardly causes for unreserved celebration, there can be no going back to the liberal humanist notion of the self. As Michele Barrett urges, "post-modernism is not something that you can be for or against: the reiteration of old knowledges will not make it vanish. For it is a cultural climate as well as an intellectu-al position, a political reality as well as an academic fashion" (xxxiv).

While it may seem to have become increasingly difficult to distin-guish the politically radical from the flagrantly reactionary, there is nothing *inherently* progressive or reactionary about any theory of subjective or social identity.[2] This does not mean that theories about identity are neutral but that identities are always embedded in spe-cific discursive, historical, cultural, and social contexts. The political force of the construction of the debate itself necessitates that femi-nist politics refuse to frame the problem of identity in terms of an absolute choice between humanism and postmodernism, politics and theory. Martin and Mohanty are wrong, it seems to me, to suggest that there is something inherently apolitical about theory and some-thing inherently pragmatic, political, and activist about humanism. Rather, I would argue that we are simultaneously interpellated *as both humanist individuals and postmodern subjects.* In other words, we cannot continue to accept the conceptual limits of the issue of iden-tity as given—as a debate about the relative merits of humanism and postmodernism, in which the only possible alternatives are to come down on the side of one or the other, or to be caught hovering pre-cariously in between.[3]

Most importantly, when staged in this way (as a stark antithesis be-tween experience/humanism and theory/postmodernism), the problem of identity cannot articulate the complexities of race. Indeed, white su-premacy and racism thrive in both humanist and postmodern regimes of identity. What is occluded in the current formulation of identity is its relationship to the development of capitalism in which commodifica-tion includes not only overtly economic mechanisms but also the ideo-logical mapping of a multicultural face that bears the appearance of white and first world hegemonies. This recidivist remapping is very much apparent in the recent work of white academic feminists who have retreated from oppositional, historically situated identity into de-racialized, personal, experiential narrative. Moreover, it is precisely this kind of narrative that they, in complete self-contradiction, characterize as a specifically theoretical progression.

The Race for Identity

As we saw in the Vicar and Virago Affair, the problem of identity is exacerbated to the point of hypervisibilty in the relation between the cultural inscription of race as color and the erasure of race in the dom-inant construction of white identity. Whites are feverishly clutching at their/our ethnicities—and at everyone else's— and are threatened by the knowledge that the racially hegemonic invisibility so long cultivated may now spell disappearance. In its worst manifestations, this becomes neo-Nazism, but even at its best, this attempt to register and mark whiteness *as* a racial identity risks reproducing the notion of race as an objective (rather than socially constructed) spectrum of human identity. "Equalizing" racial categories will only succeed in suspending the history of racism and making whiteness, *as opposed to white privilege*, visible.

The white feminist recovery of identity has been in the sphere of experience, and its generic form is personal narrative. White feminists, never before asked to establish their authentic specificity, are now doing so with a vengeance. The effect is a recourse to concrete experience and a micropolitics of the self that Spivak argues is a contemporary version of the positivism that serves as the ideological foundation for neocolonialism (275). It is precisely this ideologically occluded connection between feminist experience and white hegemony that I want to mark in white women's personal narratives. Importantly, whiteness is presented in these texts *as* personal experience, which reinforces the invisibility on which its dominance relies. Note that my argument is not that white women's experiential narratives simply have the negative effect of omitting race (all personal narratives, like all identities, are raced, whether or not they admit it). Instead, I am arguing that such recourse to personal narrative produces feminist understandings of identity in a way that perpetually marginalizes racial difference.

Jane Tompkins's essay, "Me and My Shadow," is exemplary in the degree to which race appears to be extraneous to its subject matter. For Tompkins, theory and academic writing generally suppress the authentic private self. Therefore, she attacks not only theory of the poststructuralist variety with its impersonal technical vocabulary but also epistemology on the grounds that it too is "a *theory* about the origins and nature of knowledge" (171). For her, there can be no theory or framework for explaining our beliefs and actions. Instead, her project is to "express something you yourself have felt or will help you to find a part of yourself that you would like to express" (173). The revolt against theory, however, paints Tompkins into something of a tight corner, as she reluctantly acknowledges, "I am, on the one hand, demanding a connection between literary theory and my own life, and asserting, on the other, that there is no connection" (176). The connection she offers proves to be a personal one—a person, in fact—none other than her husband, Stanley Fish, who has, as she says, taught her everything she knows about epistemology. Explanatory frameworks thus dissolve into personal narrative.

The reinscription of bourgeois individualism here is flagrant and unapologetic, as Tompkins goes on to posit heterosexuality as the grounds of women's knowledge: "The disdain for popular psychology and for words like *love* and *giving* is part of the police action that academic intellectuals wage ceaselessly against feeling, against women, against what is personal" (178). Knowledge, for Tompkins, is founded on the repudiation of emotion:

> Intellectual debate, if it were in the right spirit, would be wonderful. But I don't know how to be in the right spirit, exactly, can't make points without sounding rather superior and smug. Most of all, I don't know how to enter the debate without leaving everything else behind—the birds outside my window, my grief over Janice, just myself as a person sitting here in stockinged feet, a little bit chilly because the windows are open, and thinking about going to the bathroom. But not going yet. (173)

Tompkins's halfhearted desire to urinate while writing is ostensibly justified on the grounds that records of somatic phenomena, body reports, constitute a critique of the mind/body dualism that has structured Western thought and erased the specificity of the female body. Yet, recovering the body by reversing the binarism simply leaves us confined within the limits of the same problematic. Woman is still equated with the body, even if that equation is now presented as positive. While that body is self-consciously gendered, it remains unconsciously and disturbingly unraced—that is, its whiteness is transparent, without explanation. While concerned with the personal, with the private(s), race remains for Tompkins an impersonal category beyond the reach of personal revelation. Such obliviousness to racial otherness, as well as to her own raced identity is somewhat astonishing given the essay's title. There can hardly be a word in the English language with more specifically racialized connotations than "shadow." The shadow that haunts Tompkins, however, is the private, married to Stanley Fish, urinating, "authentic" self. As such it is a displacement and further suppression of the racial other, the repression of the social at the expense of the psychic.

Nancy Miller also attempts to recover the personal not by renouncing theory, as Tompkins does, but by renovating it *as theory.* Roland Barthes's valorization of the body provides authorization for this maneuver: "The only effective marginalization is individualism. . . . The mere fact, for instance, of thinking my body until I reach the point at which I know that I can think *only* my body is an attitude that comes up against science, fashion, morality, all collectivities" (Miller xiii). Yet even when using Barthes as the theoretical ballast for her personalism, Miller's argument takes an antitheoretical turn by claiming "the resistance particularity offers" to abstraction (i.e., theory) (xiii). The result is a rationalization for the substitution of the political with the personal. Miller argues that the personal can be viewed as a recognition of boundaries whose political goal is "a vividly renegotiated sociality" (xiv). She asserts that this is not "personal territorialism . . . but rather the very condition of exchange with another limited other" (xiv). It is impossible to discern what makes this any different from liberal humanist claims that we must reach out to one another as individuals. The primary difference between Miller and Tompkins is that Miller embraces the poststructuralist lexicon and thereby expands the boundaries between the theoretical and the personal so that, in chiasmatic fashion, they encompass one another.

Miller, aware of the impasse in Tompkins's renunciation of theory, is also conscious of its omission of race and promptly adds these missing ingredients to her analysis. Recording her experience of teaching Tompkins's essay at the Dartmouth School of Criticism and Theory, she writes, "many of the third-world women—several of whom were not, according to their own declarations, feminists—were made quite angry by the essay's assertions about women and their feelings. . . . I know I was not successful in countering their objections. I know because I'm not sure I can answer them now" (6-7). In fact, Miller never tries to do so. Third world women remain marked here by their nonidentity with Miller and Tompkins. While other essays used in Miller's classes (including articles by Gloria Anzaldúa and Barbara Christian) were problematic because of their essentialism, there was, Miller tells us, "something about 'Me and My Shadow' that wouldn't go away" (7). But the objections of the third world women do "go away," and we never learn why they found it difficult, in the context of Miller's enthusiasm for Tompkins's essay, to identify as feminists.

What is especially egregious about Miller's *Getting Personal* is that Tompkins's essay, clearly the most valorized of all the texts she references, is placed alongside a hasty reference to the explicitly oppositional autobiographical writing *about oppression* by third world women (7). The brief juxtaposition suggests equivalence with Tompkins's micturitions. The justification for this move is a skewed conception that the private experience of privileged women is in and of itself marginal and profoundly theoretical:

> If one of the original premises of seventies feminism (emerging out of sixties slogans) was that "the personal is political," eighties feminism has made it possible to see that the personal is also the theoretical: the personal is part of theory's material. Put another way, what may distinguish contemporary feminism from other postmodern thought is the expansion in the definition of cultural material. . . . Somewhere in the self-fiction of the personal voice is a belief that the writing is worth the risk. In this sense, by turning its authorial voice into spectacle, personal writing theorizes the stakes of its own performance: a personal materialism. (Miller 21, 24)

Miller exhibits here a distorted understanding of the feminist slogan "the personal is political," which was coined to demand public recognition for those aspects of women's oppression that were relegated to the realms of the private and hence the irrelevant. The slogan argued for a connection between the personal and the political, not for their conflation or for the substitution of the one for the other. As Teresa de Lauretis remarks, "'the personal is political' all too often translates into 'the personal instead of the political'" (167).

Miller's book and Tompkins's essay are symptomatic of the feminist return to essence, experience, identity, and personal narrative either as a humanist riposte to postmodern theories of authorial identity or as a postmodern renovation of humanist identity. Notably, the political effects of these approaches are alarmingly similar. In both cases, self-referentiality is offered as a substitute for the politically urgent engagement with racial difference. Tompkins's dark other is only her shadow, her repressed self. Similarly, Miller, who can sweep away the objections of angry third world women in her Dartmouth seminar, conveniently finds that the shadow raised by her white colleague "won't go away" (7).

While it remains important to denaturalize identity, this cannot be achieved by attending to the micropractices of the female body alone, a practice that serves only to reinstantiate "private experience" as authentic and authentically deracialized and, finally, as white. This critical mode leaves us in the realm of the shadow, the fictive projection of the privileged white subject. The displacements of racial difference with white feminist self-referentiality is conceptually connected to the dynamics of the Vicar and Virago Affair with which this chapter began. For it is self-referentiality that simultaneously erases race in relation to whiteness and produces racial difference in relation to color as an "always already" appropriated sign of difference. Whiteness thus becomes a nonidentity while the articulation of raced identity is something on the order of product differentiation, as in, for instance, the "United Colors of Benetton," where raced identity is so thoroughly commodified that it can be constructed as analogous to the color of a sweater. The Benetton advertising campaign offers a utopian fantasy that race is just an/other "color"—blue, green, or purple. In the words of Michael Jackson's song, "It makes no difference if you're black or white." In these various contexts, racial difference is presented not in terms of asymmetrical power relations but in terms of a heterogeneity of equivalence that flattens out power differentials, such as the rigid hierarchy between the first and third worlds. Thus, "difference" becomes variety and pluralism, which Ellen Rooney calls the seductive logic of late capitalism (1–2).[4]

But all identities are not the same: oppositional, collective identities have a very different political destination from the personal identities of a revamped individualism. Donna Haraway, for example, has argued that "woman of color" is a preeminently postmodern, oppositional identity that marks the fragmentation of Western man as well as its own otherness, difference, and specificity, and is, therefore, "fully political, whatever might be said of other possible postmodernisms" (197). Such oppositional positioning does not work to "fix" identity, either at the subjective or social level. Rather, it insists on the fixity of certain feminist political goals, such as the end of patriarchy and the class system.

Identity is always socially produced—in both its subjective and political dimensions. We cannot help, then, but bear raced, gendered identities as both social situations and psychic interiorities; we are both constrained and enabled by them; our subjectivity is constituted through them. The "dilemma" of identity is crucially structured through and around the issue of "race" and inescapably inflected by it, marking a discursive space where questions of the subject remain to be negotiated but upon which the viability of feminist politics depends. However, the epistemological status of these categories is not, finally, as important as the degree to which they can be mobilized for explicitly oppositional ends. It is vital, in fact, to understand identities in ways that are neither naturalized nor essentialized without at the same time dispatching the political resonance or necessity of the category of identity itself. The goal of emancipatory politics should not be the dissolution of difference but the dismantling of hierarchies. Identities, after all, are not metaphysical but socially produced.

Dympna Callaghan

Notes

1. Gates offers the compelling example of slave narratives, which, even when inauthentic, could be used for the abolitionist cause, and when genuine nonetheless participated in the same literary conventions as fictional narratives (26–29).

2. Terry Eagleton's pithy description of the contradictions around subjectivity and identity in postmodernism is instructive, a "choice, so to speak, between feminism and fascism" (144).

3. Crucially, too, the articulation of identity as conceptual conundrum obscures the fact that the humanist ideology of identity, even in its heyday, was never seamless or devoid of contradiction.

4. The mechanisms of pluralist inclusivity are complex because they repeatedly disavow universalism while still operating within its structures. As Denise Riley points out, the "move to replace the tacit universal with the qualified 'some women's experience' is both necessary yet in the end inadequate. Below the newly pluralized surfaces, the old problems still linger" (99). Registering the fact that some Western white women's experience is not representative of the experience of all women produces a largely cosmetic effect of equality, as do white feminist attempts at ever expansive inclusivity because the "voices" of Chicana women, American Indian women, African American women, ethnically diverse lesbian women, and so on are included on the basis of their identity with the hegemonic, white female subject.

Works Cited

Barrett, Michelle. *Women's Oppression Today: The Marxist/Feminist Encounter.* 1980. Rev. ed. London: Verso, 1988.

de Lauretis, Teresa. "Aesthetics and Feminist Theory: Rethinking Women's Cinema." *New German Critique* 34 (winter 1985): 154–75.

Eagleton, Terry. *Against the Grain: Essays, 1975–1985.* London: Verso, 1986.

Flax, Jane. "Remembering the Selves: Is the Repressed Gendered?" *Michigan Quarterly Review* 26, no. 1 (1987): 92–110.

Forward, Toby. "Diary." *London Review of Books,* Feb. 4, 1988, 21–22.

Gates, Henry Louis, Jr. "'Authenticity,' or the Lesson of Little Tree." *New York Times Book Review,* Nov. 24, 1991, 1, 26–29.

Haraway, Donna. "A Manifesto for Cyborgs: Science, Technology, and Socialist Feminism in the 1980s." Pp. 190–233 in *Feminism and Postmodernism,* ed. Linda J. Nicholson. New York: Routledge, 1990.

hooks, bell. *Black Looks: Race and Representation.* Boston: South End Press, 1992.

Martin, Biddy, and Chandra Talpade Mohanty. "Feminist Politics: What's Home Got to Do with It?" Pp. 191–212 in *Feminist Studies/Critical Studies,* ed. Teresa de Lauretis. Bloomington: Indiana University Press, 1986.

Miller, Nancy. *Getting Personal: Feminist Occasions and Other Autobiographical Acts.* New York: Routledge, 1991.

Modleski, Tania. *Feminism without Women: Culture and Criticism in a "Postfeminist" Age*. New York: Routledge, 1991.

Reed, Julia. "Hate with a Pretty Face." *Vogue,* Nov. 1991, 280–83, 340–41.

Riley, Denise. *"Am I That Name?" Feminism and the Category of Woman in History.* Minneapolis: University of Minnesota Press, 1988.

Rooney, Ellen. *Seductive Reasoning: Pluralism as the Problematic of Contemporary Literary Theory.* Ithaca, N.Y.: Cornell University Press, 1989.

Spivak, Gayatri Chakravorty. "Can the Subaltern Speak?" Pp. 271–313 in *Marxism and the Interpretation of Culture,* ed. Cary Nelson and Lawrence Grossberg. Urbana: University of Illinois Press, 1988.

Tompkins, Jane. "Me and My Shadow." *New Literary History* 19, no. 1 (1987): 169–178.

Tress, Daryl McGowan. "Commentary on Flax's 'Postmodernism and Gender Relations in Feminist Theory.'" *Signs: Journal of Women in Culture and Society* 14 (1988): 196–200.

12

The Joke and the Hoax:
(Not) Speaking as the Other

The Joke

> I talk a lot, right? And when I get very excited I interrupt peo-
> ple; and I am making a joke, but in fact it is never perceived as a
> joke unless I tell them. I will quite often say, "You know, in my
> culture it shows interest and respect if someone interrupts"; and
> immediately there are these very pious faces, and people allow
> me to interrupt.
>
> —Gayatri Chakravorty Spivak,
>   "Questions of Multi-culturalism"

Gayatri Chakravorty Spivak recounted this anecdote to Sneja
Gunew during a discussion about the desire of dominant groups to
apprehend an "authentic" identity of subordinate groups. Her creation
of a spurious cultural tradition is a response to a number of pressures,
both internal and external. On the one hand, the example of Spivak's
humor-in-action seems a cheap shot at the ignorance of her audience
and their gullibility regarding the values or traditions prevalent in
cultures other than their own. On the other hand, this anecdote provides a salutary example of an unspoken but nonetheless pernicious
coercion toward the members of subordinate groups to enact their
differences in the broadest possible gestures. In other words, the members of subordinate groups are constantly buffeted by the desire of the
"well-meaning" members of the dominant group to stage their "exoticism" such that their peculiarities may be easily understood and the
dominant members may be granted an opportunity to make a ritual-
ized gesture of piety toward cultural differences.

Without wishing to deny that Spivak's motivations may in part be
simply to get out of a sticky situation (after all, who wants to be labeled

ill-mannered if she has recourse to an easy getaway?), I think it is worthwhile to consider her anecdote in some detail. The locution is somewhat confusing in that we are not quite certain whether the "joke" refers to the interruption or to the explanation for the interruption.[1] My argument, however, concentrates on the joke itself—the misleading explanation of the interruption. The practical joke that Spivak plays on her audience, and which she rather gleefully recounts, mocks the susceptibility of her listeners, especially when they are confronted with a person from a different, "exotic" cultural tradition.

The contextual discussion that prompted the narration of this joke examines the construction of "authenticity" as it is articulated within consciously multicultural societies existing, for instance, in the United States or Australia. Both Spivak and Gunew place particular emphasis on the ways in which certain token members of minority groups are adopted by the majority, not only to provide an alibi against discrimination but also to camouflage the ignorance of the majority.

According to Spivak, "When the cardcarrying listeners, the hegemonic people, the dominant people, talk about listening to someone 'speaking as' something or the other, I think *there* one encounters a problem. . . . They cover over the fact of the ignorance that they are allowed to possess, into a kind of homogenization" (Harasym 60). Gunew responds, "Yes, and they choose what parts they want to hear, and they choose what they then do with this material, and what seems to happen in very crude ways, within the context of multiculturalism, is that certain people are elevated very quickly to those who speak for all immigrants: in terms of funding, and in terms of the dissemination of their work, etc. As a result you don't hear about the rest, because 'we have covered that,' and those few token figures function as a very secure alibi" (Harasym 60). Given this context, where complete and utter ignorance seems to present no obstacle to condescension, and where a partial truth or even an untruth can provide a pretext for an air of cosmopolitan knowledge, Spivak's jest becomes particularly significant. The practical joke that she disingenuously plays on her audience, which excuses her rudeness via a reference to her ethnic origins, replaces their blank ignorance with disinformation. At a certain level of interpretation the joke is revealed as a form of resistance: resistance to a tokenism that is couched in blandly patronizing terms. This (perhaps) unwittingly repeats the benevolent imperialism of the colonial masters.

The context that prompts Spivak to indulge in a bit of leg-pulling is one in which members of the subordinate group are urged to collude in providing a set of representations that deny their own specificity and heterogeneity and are solicited to act as "native informants." The impulse underlying such urging may not be directly related to an assertion of economic or territorial control. Rather, it is motivated by a desire to inscribe the other in a subject position that reinforces the implicit centrality of the dominant group. In other words, the "otherness" of the other that must be negotiated in any encounter between two people—even within the same group (howsoever we may define a group)—is, in this case, overlooked in favor of constituting the member of the subordinate group as a site for gathering information. Thus, the subjectivity of the other is erased in order to countenance its construction as an object, as an *effect* of knowledge for the subject.

We must recognize, however, that in a majority of these situations the other participates in this project, and cheerfully relegates him/herself to a position of frame for the dominant subject(s). There is no use of force or strong-arm tactics, nothing but an implicit understanding between the two. In return for being adopted as a token member and for gaining entry into the privileged group, the representative of the subordinate group must comply with the demands placed on him/her. For it is, after all, the exhibition of differences, an admirable performance of otherness, that had initially vouchsafed the subordinate member's access to the dominant group. In order to solidify that access, the performance must continue to fulfill the bargain. Spivak's joke, of course, collapses the agreement. While pretending to comply with the demands, she overturns the power hierarchy by refusing to occupy the position of a trustworthy "native informant." The easy access to information that would justify patronage is now planted with hidden mines that may explode at any moment, revealing the rather embarrassing ignorance of the patronizers.

The Hoax

> I'd failed to pull out of the deal with Virago and now it got more and more uncomfortable. At last a contract arrived and I thought there was a humorous providence at work as I signed and dated it April the First. But who was the fool? Them for not checking me, or me for hiding myself in a self-destroying disguise?
>
> —Toby Forward, "Diary"

Dympna Callaghan's essay, "The Vicar and the Virago" (in this volume), provides us with the delightfully funny account of the hoax perpetrated by Toby Forward, a vicar from Brighton. Pretending to be a South Asian woman, Rahila Khan, Forward's work was accepted by, among others, Virago, the Women's Press, and the British Broadcasting Corporation (BBC). His collection of short stories, *Down the Road, Worlds Away,* published by Virago in 1987, delineates the experiences of young South Asian girls and adolescent white boys in Margaret Thatcher's Britain. The two different groups may live just down the road from each other in the same neighborhood, but their familial and personal experiences are worlds apart. Both sets of stories, though largely unimpressive, are fairly well-written; the emotional traumas and conflicts of adolescence are sensitively portrayed. Aside from the small, infrequent lapses, such as "Her evenings were not spent in the quiet, enclosed *Urdu* world of other girls" (34, emphasis added), that betray an ignorance of the correct nomenclature, Toby Forward does a fairly convincing job as Rahila Khan.

In her assessment of the Vicar and Virago Affair as a symptom of "white feminism's still troubled encounter with racial difference," Callaghan maintains a parallel between the "self-referentiality" of white feminists and the attempt by "privileged whites" to appropriate "subordinate identities." The numerous instances of white men rushing to make a killing in the "ethnic bazaar" and the narcissism of white feminists are predicated on a coincidence of whiteness with blankness, such that "color" functions merely as another item—easily discounted or blithely appropriated.

What interests me particularly about the Forward/Khan episode is the fact that this incident provides us with another example, albeit slightly skewed, of the type of unspoken bargain that exists between the dominant and subordinate groups that I sketched earlier. As Forward relates the inception and development of Rahila Khan, he refers to his correspondence with the BBC: "The producer had asked her to send something else and had said that they wanted things 'with a genuine "ethnic" background'" ("Diary" 21). Given this wondrously vague demand, is it any surprise that Rahila Khan produced work specifically tailored to meet the requirements of the market? "We had found a gap in the market and we set about filling it." According to Forward, the ease with which Rahila Khan was accepted and the gentleness with which she was treated by the producers, publishers, and editors made her his preferred doppelgänger. Despite Forward's occasional qualms at the perpetuation of the deception (he "suggested to the agent that there was some 'tokenism' going on"), the hoax continued until he was finally forced to reveal himself ("Diary" 21).

The enthusiastic adoption of Toby Forward as Rahila Khan and the extraordinary demand for her work reveal the pitfalls inherent in any multicultural interaction, where dominant and subordinate groups have uneven access to power and authority.[2] In fact, Toby Forward's expertise in masquerade lays bare another truth: the episode presents a concrete example of the exacerbating effects of patronage and tokenism that so aggravate Spivak and Gunew. On the one hand, Rahila Khan assumes the ideal persona to assuage white-liberal guilt and, on the other, she placidly inhabits the margin, presumably providing a colorful border for the dominant white subjects. The encouragement she received to provide "genuine ethnic" material (whatever that means!) in the first person, transforms Rahila Khan into an anthropological case study, an artifact who, as Callaghan points out, is presumed to have an unmediated relation with her ethnicity and whose information can then be appropriated for the benefit, improvement, and entertainment of the members of the dominant culture.[3]

Callaghan's point that identities are colonized through commodification, that the vicar and Virago "debacle was in part the result of feminism's participation in the commodification of ethnic identity," is especially compelling. Implicit in this argument is a reading of the terms of agreement that exist between the dominant and subordinate groups in which ethnic identity becomes just another object demanded by market forces. Understanding this function of the market, however, obliges me to qualify Callaghan's praise for Virago's "laudable" objective of publishing works that meet the guidelines of "multicultural diversity." In other words, Virago's attempt to carve a niche for themselves in an expanding market makes perfect commercial sense; there is no need to credit the publishing house with a quixotic idealism.[4] I believe it would be more productive to investigate the recent economic and social interests undergirding the commodification of ethnicity.

Meanwhile, we can certainly sympathize with Callaghan's outrage at the hoaxes which demonstrate "that endeavors to compensate for the exclusion of racial 'minorities' from the means of literary production can become the very means for continuing this exclusion." However, while a Toby Forward or an Asa Carter may induce a certain discomfort or unease, it is the enterprise of "compensation" that should be the focus of our suspicions.[5] That is to say, I am slightly troubled by Callaghan's endorsement of compensation as a valid rationale for the inclusion of racial minorities in the fields of literary and cultural productions. The concept of making amends inevitably leads to problems, both systemic and strategic.

If frauds worry us because they exploit the "compensation principle," then the disguised Rahila Khans are not the only ones of whom we should be leery. Given the increased visibility of "ethnic" writings on syllabi and book review lists, it may be prudent to be skeptical of claims that portfolios have been diversified in order to redress old wrongs. Should we then engage in a witchhunt to distinguish the motives of those genuinely committed to reparations from smart opportunists? Should we demand testimonials of identity along with statements of motive? The problem here is not only the practical impossibility of carrying out such exercises but the absurdity of the whole enterprise.

In certain parts of Europe and North America, the desire to publish and study works from hitherto marginalized cultures does not stem from some fuzzy moral precept. If we persist in believing that, there are a couple of problems that immediately come to mind. First, despite the glow of self-righteous approval that comes with faith in our nobility, we shall be doing a major disservice to precisely those texts that we are interested in studying. By tying them irrevocably to an essentialized identity of the presumed author, we insist that the texts merely bear witness to a particular identity—based on race, gender, and ethnicity. Second, accepting the gloss of benevolence relieves us of the need to question and investigate the sudden popularity of such texts in the contemporary marketplace. The next section deals with both of these issues at greater length.

(Not) Speaking as the Other

At this point, it is important to recognize that just as the members of a subordinate group do not form a homogeneous, undifferentiated mass, such that any one may be substituted for any other, neither do the members of the dominant group form a cohesive whole, acting in concert with each other. The liberal demand for a staging of exoticism is countered by the conservative insistence on an eradication of differences.[6] Notwithstanding the disparity between the two injunctions, it is clear that both groups are in a position to exert their claims to power by urging a compliance with their demands. For members of the subordinate group to gain access to positions of privilege, occupied so "naturally" by the members of the dominant group, they have to enact a deliberate lie. They can either hide all differences or exaggerate and flaunt them. Most of us can attest to the immense effort expended in trying to maintain an uneasy compromise: to avoid presenting our differences in too radical and hence threatening a form and to explain our practices and habits as cute, little, interesting variations from the norm.

The response to these conflicting demands must not be an irritated

"Get your act together, for Heaven's sake! At least be consistent in what you demand from us" or a repeated assertion of identity that will ultimately lead to an impoverishing ghettoization of knowledge. Rather, the response should be an intervention in the configuration of authority involved in the maintenance of center and margin: we must interrogate the means through which a center/margin dichotomy is created and maintained. According to this line of interpretation, the significance of the two examples with which I have dealt—the Spivak joke and the Forward hoax—lies not so much in the fact that a lie was perpetrated, as in the conditions surrounding the emergence of the lie.

These examples reveal a great deal about the configurations of cultural authority and the type of demands placed on the members of subordinate groups. Gratitude at being noticed after having been ignored or derided must not be allowed to blind us to the motivations underlying such condescension. While most of this chapter deals with some of the problems arising from (white) liberal guilt, the nexus of power/knowledge must not be ignored. We must question the tactical advantages that accrue through an imbrication of techniques of knowledge with strategies of power.[7] In *The History of Sexuality,* Michel Foucault warns us:

> Between techniques of knowledge and strategies of power there is no exteriority, even if they have specific roles and are linked together on the basis of their difference. . . . We must seek rather for the pattern of the modifications which the relationships of force imply by the very nature of their process. The "distribution of power" and the "appropriations of knowledge" never represent only instantaneous slices. . . . Relations of power-knowledge are not static forms of distribution, they are "matrices of transformations." (98–99)

These "matrices of transformation" do not only possess pentagonal significance but also maintain their screened function in our everyday lives. In other words, the academic or social interactions in which most of us engage provide a model of signification that contains the disruption that might arise from an encounter with the other. While difference between subordinate and dominant groups is recognized, this difference is allowed to operate only within the limits set by the members of the dominant group. The project of demarcating "safe" areas, where difference is not only tolerated but actively encouraged and appreciated, places everybody involved in these interactions in a false position. These situations lead to a reification of differences; the habitual mores or personality quirks belonging to members of subordinate groups are treated as curios, bits of unrelated whatnots, collected in order to enhance the self-esteem of the collector. The reification of differences leads to a reification of identity, such that the substantive weight of difference constitutes the only ground of identity for the other.[8]

This participation in the production of identity through differences, this proffering of information as if it constituted, in some sense, a metonymic relation to the totality of cross-cultural understanding and knowledge, is, even without any deliberate mischievousness, a sham. For the sake of argument, let us imagine that in the culture that Spivak is postulating as her own, interruption is really seen as a sign of respect and that a Rahila Khan really exists who wrote the works attributed to her. What does the imparting of their knowledges—Khan's and Spivak's—really accomplish, in this context? First, their generalized references to cultural phenomena conceal more than they reveal. In Spivak's case, for instance, we do not know whether this example applies only within certain contexts or whether class, gender, clan, caste, or religious boundaries and affiliations serve to delimit its operation. Without such specific particularities, which at certain levels of interpretation might contradict the initial assertion of cultural explanation, a facile and falsely homogeneous perspective is engendered.

More significantly, however, the dispensing of this fact as a gift of knowledge comes wrapped in false papers. It pretends to proffer an explanation of identity by a reference to origins and cultural authority precisely by alienating cultural authority from itself. That is to say, the complex cultural construction that we conveniently label "identity" is reduced to a graspable concept, to an image of identity that may be easily removed from its context and repeated elsewhere. The desire to connect, to provide a commensurability between the two cultures leads to an avoidance of the predicaments that necessarily accompany such interactions.[9]

But this analysis is based on a refusal to question the explanations of either Spivak or Khan regarding their stories of origins or ethnicities. What happens when we know that the explanation in one case and the identity in the other are deliberate subterfuges? There are two issues that we must consider. First, the "joke" intervenes radically in the existing power relations and subtly shifts the balance of power. By mocking the ignorance of her interlocutors, Spivak is enacting a deliberate refusal to occupy the position of the "native informant." But the joke goes beyond determining who has the upper hand in this game of one-upmanship. While Spivak rebuffs the desire of her companions to gain an understanding of differences through an easy, short conversation, Forward attempts to pander to such demands. His book promises to grant an illusory, superficial understanding through an effortlessly quick skimming of an unchallenging collection of short stories, which will then presumably allow the members of the dominant group to veil their ignorance. Both episodes highlight the manner in which the other is adopted merely to provide an opportunity for the adopters to masquerade as saviors of marginality. Spivak, with a roguish foreknowledge, and Forward, unwittingly and unknowingly, participate in this puncturing of the balloon of liberal benevolence.

The second issue that confronts us, as Spivak enacts a lie and Forward impersonates Rahila Khan, is the *staging* of a cultural/ethnic identity. The fact that Spivak had to explain her joke and that Forward could not be detected behind the persona of Khan, underscores the extent to which any cultural identity is part of a performance, a staging of the self. The notion of an essential self—a self presumed to have its origins in a specific culture, ethnicity, or nation—is debunked by the performative and discursive configurations that participate in the production of these selves. These instances direct us to look beyond the stubborn linkage of "origin" and "essence," forcing us to confront the political, historical, and discursive origin of identity. In other words, the performances of Spivak and Forward denaturalize the concept of an authentic, natural identity and dramatize the mechanisms of its staging.[10]

By displacing the "originals," these deceptions or imitations enable us to re-view cultural identity through its various expressions. Impersonation in any manifestation of cultural articulation demonstrates the manner in which such articulation is constructed, thus subverting the notion of a homogeneous or transparent identity. The disclosure of the mechanisms through which a specific identity is inscribed and then institutionalized critiques the politics of identity that essentializes and binds subjects as unified and unitary selves. Constituted as we are, through a multiplicity of subject positions—some of which may be contradictory—any attempt to fix identity relies on a denial of these contradictions and self-differences. The diversity of discourses through which our various selves are inscribed and staged forecloses any shortcuts toward gaining an understanding of the other. Of course, if all we seek is a balm to assuage our guilt, then we must not be annoyed if the jokes and hoaxes continue.

Sabina Sawhney

Notes

1. This confusion can lead to different interpretations. For instance, Spivak could quite easily be saying that when she is excited, she interrupts people

and makes a joke, but nobody gets the joke, and realizing that her joke (meant for public consumption) is unintelligible, she proceeds to make a private joke, referring to her cultural traditions. This explanation then grants her carte blanche to interrupt, except that by now she is caught in an endless spiral of verbiage: nobody understands her interruptions or her explanations about the interruptions, but she is compelled to interrupt since her "traditions" demand that she do so.

2. The scandal surrounding Indrani Aikath-Gyaltsen's fiction provides us with another instance of the booby traps laid for the unwary and indiscriminate. Her first novel, *Daughters of the House* (New York: Ballantine Books, 1991) was an exquisite story, beautifully written and widely praised by critics and reviewers. Her second novel, *Cranes' Morning* (New York: Ballantine Books, 1993) was seriously flawed: the story seemed thin and weak, the descriptions wildly improbable, and the resolution hurried and patchy. Nevertheless, this novel too garnered feverish praise from the reviewers, surprising most of the readers (I reread it, thinking I must have missed something significant). The scandal erupted when a number of well-informed readers pointed out that *Cranes' Morning* was plagiarized from *The Rosemary Tree,* by Elizabeth Goudge. When *The Rosemary Tree* first appeared in 1956, the *New York Times Book Review* had criticized its "slight plot" and "sentimentally ecstatic" approach. But as Molly Moore points out, after Goudge's work reappeared as Aikath-Gyaltsen's (the setting was recast to an Indian village—but the story was the same, almost word-for-word), the *Times* called it "magic" and "full of humor and insight." Moore also quotes Paul Kafka, the reviewer for the *Washington Post,* who characterized *Cranes' Morning* as "at once achingly familiar and breathtakingly new."

Well, the mistakes of the reviewers are not particularly scandalous—tastes change—and we certainly cannot hold them to account for every review with which we disagree. However, when Paul Kafka was confronted with his glowing review for a novel plagiarized from a dated pop romance, he excused his lapse in judgment by saying that now "there's a phrase 'aesthetic affirmative action.' If something comes from exotic parts, it's read very differently than if it's domestically grown." Then he proceeded to contradict himself further by insisting that *Cranes' Morning* is "pretty delightful. Maybe Elizabeth Goudge is a writer who hasn't gotten her due" (Moore).

So then which is it? Aesthetic affirmative action that praises a bad piece of writing simply because the author comes from a particular racial and ethnic background or delayed recognition for a good piece of work that had suffered from the reviewers' carelessness when it first came out? Determining the logic behind such convoluted reasoning is, fortunately, not my intent, since the exercise demands expertise beyond my abilities. I merely wish to draw attention to the ease with which slipshod and careless reviewing is excused through the bogey of aesthetic affirmative action. What, after all, is the point of focusing attention on nonmale and nonwhite writers? Where before they were all dismissed out of hand, now they are all praised indiscriminately. It is a zero-sum game, and the benefits that would accrue if multiculturalism were taken seriously still elude us.

3. In "Postcoloniality and Value," Spivak remarks that when "a cultural identity is thrust upon one because the centre wants an identifiable margin, claims for marginality assure validation from the centre" (221).

4. My reference to the market forces that influenced Virago's publishing decisions does not imply that there now exists an enormous horde of people breathlessly waiting for texts that meet their demands for diversity. Most of us, especially in academia, are fully aware of the obstacles that not only thwart easy accessibility to the reading lists of our choice but also the inclusion of such texts in syllabi.

5. As my argument demonstrates, I am not interested in castigating members of the dominant group for participating in this new "ethnic commodity market." What, after all, do we say to them? Do we appeal to their sense of justice and fair play: "C'mon, boys, you've had your fun, it's our turn now!"? And what if they respond that they personally never had fun, do we then hierarchize victimhood? In "The Politics of Knowledge," Edward Said writes that we cannot "surround ourselves with the sanctimonious piety of historical and cultural victimhood as a way of making our presence felt" (26).

6. For a particularly pernicious example of the way market forces influence cultural identities, consider the following advertisement: "Indian Accents Erased With This Powerful Audio-Visual Tool!! Of all the books and courses on English, none, up to now, has exclusively attacked the critical problem of how to erase foreign accents from the speech of Indians who already know how to speak English. The dynamite program we are offering and the audio-cassettes that accompany it are a first! How to speak English without a Foreign Accent finally fills the needs of those millions of Indians who desire to polish their communication skills by mastering the color, sounds, and inflections of standard American-English. It Works!!" (*India Abroad*, Oct. 23, 1992, 45).

7. This is not merely a theoretical point made in the rarefied arena of abstract knowledge. In the wake of the World Trade Center bombing (1994), the U.S. Justice Department and the Federal Bureau of Investigation have redoubled their efforts to indict suspected terrorists. On April 1, 1994, four alleged members of the Abu Nidal terrorist organization were charged with running a racketeering enterprise and conspiring to engage in terrorist activities. One of the defendants, Zein Isa, was already convicted for the murder of his sixteen-year-old daughter, Tina Isa. The 1991 murder trial that convicted Zein Isa and his wife Maria relied heavily on taped telephone conversations in which Isa discussed with his other daughters the rebellious, westernized behavior of Tina. According to ABC News, Tina had been killed in accordance with an "ancient Middle-Eastern custom" related to the concept of honor.

Recent investigations, however, seem to suggest that the cause of Tina's death was not her flouting of traditional values but her inadvertent knowledge of her father's terrorist activities. If Tina was killed because she represented a security threat, then she could not have been killed because her behavior cast aspersions on the family honor. However, the convictions of Isa and Maria were based on the latter assumption. My question is very simple: How many of us "Rahila Khans" collaborated to produce fragmentary portrayals of West Asian families (portrayals produced in accordance with the social, personal, and economic demands exerted by the dominant groups) that would support stereotypes to such an extent that these stereotypes would be utilized in a murder trial?

8. I am obviously arguing against the claim that there exists an original or genuine identity for the figures of difference which the subject presumed to know is denying or ignoring deliberately. This analysis is based on the premise that identities are a complex cultural construction, and it is the effect of dominance that some of these identities get inscribed as natural or original. Within this schema, however, radical identity is denied to the other, such that the other is not viewed as a desiring subject but only as an object that fulfills its purpose by confirming the identity of the subject as original and originary. Difference, then, is seen as an interesting variation on the norm. The norm itself gets reaffirmed, authorizing the self-confirmation of the subject's own preeminence.

9. While discussing Richard Rorty's *Philosophy and the Mirror of Nature*, Homi Bhabha notes, "The signifiers of ambivalent, hybrid cultural knowledges—neither 'one' nor 'other'—are ethnocentrically elided in the search for cultural commensurability" in "Articulating the Archaic: Notes on Colonial Nonsense" (207).

10. Judith Butler makes a similar point when she analyzes the manner in which parodic practices such as drag intervene in the construction of a gender identity: "In imitating gender, drag implicitly reveals the imitative structure of gender itself—as well as its contingency. . . . In the place of an original identification which serves as a determining cause, gender identity might be reconceived as a personal/cultural history of received meanings subject to a set of imitative practices which refer laterally to other imitations and which, jointly, construct the illusion of a primary and interior gendered self or parody the mechanism of that construction" (137–38).

Works Cited

Bhabha, Homi. "Articulating the Archaic: Notes on Colonial Nonsense." Pp. 203–18 in *Literary Theory Today*, ed. Peter Collier and Helga Geyer-Ryan. Ithaca, N.Y.: Cornell University Press, 1991.

Butler, Judith. *Gender Trouble: Feminism and the Subversion of Identity*. London: Routledge, 1990.

Forward, Toby. "Diary." *London Review of Books*, Feb. 4, 1988, 21–22.

——— (as Rahila Khan). *Down the Road, Worlds Away*. London: Virago, 1987.

Foucault, Michel. *The History of Sexuality*. Vol. 1. Trans. Robert Hurley. New York: Random House, 1978.

Moore, Molly. "Plagiarism by Indian Writer." *Washington Post Foreign Service*, Apr. 27, 1994.

Spivak, Gayatri Chakravorty. "Postcoloniality and Value." Pp. 219–44 in *Literary Theory Today,* ed. Peter Collier and Helga Geyer-Ryan. Ithaca, N.Y.: Cornell University Press, 1991.

———. "Questions of Multi-culturalism." Pp. 59–66 in *The Post-Colonial Critic,* ed. Sarah Harasym. London: Routledge, 1990.

13

Bodies and Pleasures in Queer Theory

Prologue

This essay was written before I had read Thomas Yingling's "Fetishism, Identity, Politics" (in this volume). I was struck, on my first reading, by some remarkable points of congruence between his essay and my own, as well as by the quite striking differences in source texts and frames of reference. Both chapters articulate a concern about the current moves to institutionalize "minor knowledges," pleasures and practices in the burgeoning of gay and lesbian studies programs in universities throughout the United States and elsewhere, about taking too seriously and too uncritically the demand within elements of gay and lesbian cultures and communities for acceptance and celebration of the political radicality of sexual practices and lifestyles that are themselves never pure or free of the very systems of domination that situate and infuse them through and through. Both are concerned with creating too broad a rift between erotics and politics, even while we are careful to ensure that we do not make our sexuality the center of our being, as Michel Foucault warns. Yingling's and my essays, written continents apart—while nevertheless sharing certain contemporary concerns in academic situations that have little in common, one by a man and the other by a woman, who never met—are both clearly products of the flowering of a new academic enterprise. But this enterprise is fraught with danger signs and worries that could be signposted more or less in advance, insofar as they replay many of the problems entailed by institutionalization and mainstreaming of minority concerns.

Not only do our two essays resonate with similar worries about the kinds of power that lesbian and gay studies may finally achieve, but perhaps just as significantly, they raise these questions from very different frameworks: where Yingling talks of canons, I use the language of ontology; where he relies on the insights of Foucault's analytics of power, my essay is framed by the not incompatible writings of Gilles Deleuze on force; where his concerns are acknowledged as those of a man, mine are explicitly positioned in feminist terms; where he talks of desire in psychoanalytic terms as a lack (linking it to violence and death—a crucial dimension for gay men in the current AIDS crisis, but one that seems to me much less obvious and more tenuous for women and lesbians), I prefer to discuss it in terms of a positivity or an activity. If those anxieties about the institutionalization of queerness as an academic discipline are in some way to be alleviated, these moments of convergence and difference are crucial to explore, ponder, and negotiate—particularly if lesbian and gay studies is to become anything more than an apology and uncritical celebration of personal lifestyles or merely a defiant reaction to the overwhelming heterosexuality of the academy and the broader social world within which it is situated and functions.

Affective Bodies

I want to explore the relevance of the work of Gilles Deleuze in understanding the difference between what a body is and what a body can do, between an ontology and a pragmatics. If a body is what a body does, then lesbian and gay sexualities and lifestyles produce lesbian and gay bodies, bodies distinguished not only by sex, race, and class characteristics but also by sexual desires and practices.

Deleuze reads Friedrich Nietzsche in terms of the distinction between active and reactive forces. Active force is that which stretches itself, takes itself as far as it can go (a limit that cannot be known in advance), without regard for anything other than its own free expansion, mindless of others. It is guileless and open to what befalls it. Reactive forces are cunning, clandestine, restrictive, intervening, obedient. They function ingenuously, living on sentiment (nostalgia, self-justification, and hatred of the other are its primary features). Where active forces affirm, produce, and stretch, reactive forces judge, pontificate, produce ideologies, explanations, devise theories, and compromise. They produce religion, morality, and law, systems constrained to endless reproduction of the same, without affirming the infinite nature of chance, change, and transformation. Reactive forces convert active forces into reaction, separating a force from its effects through the creation of myth, symbolism, fantasy, and falsification. In a certain sense, reactive force can be regarded as seductive, enticing, and luring: it ensnares active force into its own means and procedures, its own falsifications and rationalizations.

Although it is common to see affirmation as the domain of the powerful (those *in* power) and negation or *ressentiment* as attributes of the oppressed and powerless, this simplifies Nietzsche's understanding of these as microforces that function *within* as much as *between* individuals. It can just as readily be claimed that homophobia, heterosexism, and racism are *reactive* forces that function to *prevent* alternatives, to negate and ruminate on how to destroy them, and that gay and lesbian sexualities and lifestyles can be seen as innovative, inventive, productive, and thus active, insofar as they aim at their own pleasures, distributions, and free expansion. The regime of compulsive heterosexuality *can* be understood as a series of reactive forces, separating a body from what it can do, reducing a body to what it is rather than what it can become; while gay and lesbian sexual practices and lifestyles, insofar as they risk a certain stability, a certain social security and ease, *can* be seen as a triumph of active and productive forces.

We are prevented from too ready a generalization of straights as the crippled emotional slaves and gays, lesbians, and other queers as the transgressive sexual radicals. In each of us there are elements and impulses that strive for conformity and elements that seek instability and change. It is a question of degree—of more or less—rather than of type, a matter of varying investments that all of us have, one way or another, in a certain type of complicity with stability and social imperative.[1]

This is not to say that all of us are the same but that it is a matter of degree, location, and will. Heterosexuals can remain heterosexual but still undertake transgressive sexual relations outside the stereotyped norm (but do so only rarely). Lesbians and gays can produce sexual relations that duplicate as closely as they can the structures, habits, and patterns of the straightest and most suburban heterosexuals (but succeed only rarely). Indeed, this is why many queers, who do not readily identify with the mores and community "standards" of heterosexuals or homosexuals, sometimes want to devise a third category beyond the limits of either. Simply *being straight* or *being gay,* in itself, provides no guarantee of an individual's position as sexually radical: it depends on how one lives one's queerness or how one renders one's straightness as queer.

Homosexual or Queer?

Contrary to the current popularity of the term "queer," I believe that it is basically a reactive category that can only define itself as oppositional or other to a straight norm. This norm defines, by way of opposition and expulsion, the others that it cannot tolerate and categorizes them together. These others—"deviant" sexual practices of whatever kind—may find that they share very little in common with each other and indeed may be the site of profound tension and contradiction.

The phrase "lesbian and gay" has a readily assumed constituency, a correlative set of identities, a series of easy presumptions and ready-made political answers. The label "queer" problematizes many of these presumptions, but it also carries serious risks. "Queer" is capable of accommodating and will no doubt provide a political rationale and coverage in the near future for many of the most blatant and extreme forms of heterosexual and patriarchal power games, which are, in a certain sense, queer, persecuted, ostracized. Heterosexual sadists, ped-erasts, fetishists, pornographers, pimps, prostitutes, voyeurs, and so on of course suffer from social sanctions. In a certain sense they too can be regarded as "oppressed." But to claim an oppression of the order of lesbian and gay, women's, or racial oppression is to ignore the very real complicity and phallic rewards of what might be called "deviant sexualities."

Moreover, underlying this distinction (gay/queer) are unspoken ontological and political assumptions. Sexual difference is at the very heart of lesbian and gay theory and politics (the designation of "ho-mosexual" irreducibly designates *specific* types of love objects, male or female), while the proliferation of "queer" sexualities has indetermin-able love objects. A proliferation of sexualities beyond the notion of two (the notion of two has been difficult enough!) seems to underlie the rapidly expanding domain and constituency of queerness ("n-sex-es" or polysexuality). While I do not want to prevent this prolifera-tion, nor to judge its transgressiveness or conservatism, the category of queerness ignores the specificities of sexed bodies. Even if we are all composed of a myriad of sexual possibilities, of fluid, changeable forms of sexuality, nevertheless these still conform to the configura-tions of the two sexes: a male sado-masochist does not function in the same way or with the same effects as a female sado-masochist. It *does* make a difference which kind of sexed body enacts the various modes of performance of sexual roles and positions.

Lesbian Bodies

It is clear, especially in the era of the AIDS crisis, that there is an ever more detailed analysis, observation, and theorization not only about heterosexual couples but also in gay and bisexual men's sexual practices. Lesbianism is still largely unspecified—the rates of transmission of the virus in lesbian practices is relatively low and the modes of transmission remain unknown. It is significant too that while gay men's sexual practices have been under the scrutiny of the law for over a century, in Australia at least, there have never been laws specifically prohibiting lesbianism. It remained unrecognized by the law until recent equal opportunity and antidiscrimination legislation. I do not want to suggest that lesbians are either more or less oppressed than gay men or that it is better or worse to be legally recognized (arguments could be made both ways): my point here is simply that there is no representation of lesbians *as* lesbians in certain key discourses (especially legal and medical) that are deeply invested in power relations.

There is, moreover, a manifest inadequacy of erotic language to represent women's sexual organs, sexual pleasures, and sexual practices in terms other than those provided either for male sexuality or by men in their heterosexual (mis)understanding of the sexualities of their partners. All the terms for orgasm, corporeal encounters, and sexual exchanges of whatever kind are not only derived and modified from heterosexual models but, more alarmingly, from the perspective of the men, not the women, involved in these relations. The very terms for sex, pleasure, desire—"fucking," "screwing," "coming," "orgasm," and so on—are most appropriate for and are derived from men's experiences of sexuality (both their own and that of women).

Perhaps the solution to this problem is not simply the addition of a set of new words to the vocabulary. Such an understanding presumes that female sexuality, and especially lesbian sexuality, is readily enumerable and can be described and referred to in terms of distinct organs. To wish to create a new set of terms implies that we know in advance what we want to designate by those terms—that the sexual pleasures, desire, organs, and activities of women are a known or knowable quantity simply awaiting names.

This does not seem possible nor entirely desirable: for to "know" female sexuality, to "know" what lesbian desire is, is to reduce it to models of subjectivity dependent on the ways these terms are defined and have been understood in a male-dominated culture. I do not want to suggest that new labels cannot be created. The regimes of knowledge and power are certainly capable of providing such resources. Perhaps a more interesting question is, given the enormous investment of knowledges in codifying sexuality, why has lesbianism been so decidedly ignored where heterosexuality and male homosexuality are increasingly and thoroughly investigated? Is this a lapse in the regime of sexuality, a sign of its imperfections and its capacity to create sites of resistance; or is it a mode of further delegitimization, a ruse of power itself? This is not an idle question, for how we read it—as a shortfall of power or as one of its strategies—will dictate whether we seek to retain the indeterminacy of lesbianism and of female sexuality (my present inclination) or whether we seek to articulate lesbianism as loudly and thoroughly as possible, which Marilyn Frye seems to advocate.[2]

It is not clear to me that articulateness and representation are in themselves a virtue: the most intense moments of pleasure and the force of their materiality cannot be reduced to terms that capture their force and intensity, no matter how broadly evocable in discourse they may be. A distinction must be drawn between discourse and experience even on the understanding that language is the prior condition for the intelligibility of experience.[3] To submit one's pleasures and desires to enumeration and definitive articulation is to submit processes and becomings to entities, locations, and boundaries, to become welded to an organizing nucleus of fantasy whose goal is not simply pleasure and expansion but control, the production of endless repetition, endless variations of the same—in short, the forces of reaction.[4]

Bodies, Pleasures, and Subversion

Gay oppression has a form quite different from other oppressions. Other forms of oppression are based primarily on what a person *is* quite independent of what they *do*. Or rather, what they do is inflected and read through who they are. Their racial, religious, sexual, and cultural characteristics, which are in some sense undeniable (although their meanings and significances are contestable), are used against them as a rationalization for their being treated inequitably and for their lived realities being discounted or unvalued.

In the case of homosexuals, I believe that it is less a matter of who they are than what they *do* that is considered offensive.[5] It is this split between what we are and what we do that produces the very possibility of a notion like "the closet," a distinction between private and public that refuses integration. Moreover, it also accounts for the possibility of coming out, which is, after all, a quite ridiculous concept in most other forms of oppression. This is what enables homosexuals to "pass" as straight with an ease that is extraordinarily rare for most oppressed groups. Homophobia is an oppression based on the *activities* of members of a group, not on any definitive group attributes.

This is precisely why the forces of cultural reaction are so intent, in the case of homophobia more than in other forms of oppression, on separating a body from what it can do. Homophobia is an attempt to separate being from doing, existence from action. This reduces homosexuality to a legible category and in a certain way minimizes the threat that the idea of a labile indeterminable sexuality, a sexuality based on the contingency of undertaking certain activities, has on the very self-constitution of the heterosexual norm.

Lesbianism thus attests to the fundamental plasticity of women's desire, its inherent openness not only to changes of sexual object (male to female or vice versa), but also its malleability to the forms and types of practices and pleasures available—in other words, to the more or less infinite possibilities of becoming. It attests to the rigidity, the fearfulness, the boring, indeed endless, repetition of form in stable male/female Western sex roles, the roles to which stable relationships often become accustomed, and to the possibilities of change inherent in them, possibilities that need to be ignored or blotted out in order for them to continue. In separating what a body is from what a body does, an essence of sorts is produced, a consolidated nucleus of habits and expectations that take over from experiments and innovations; bodies are sedimented into fixed and repetitive relations, and it is only beyond modes of repetition that any subversion is considered possible. The threat of homosexuality to heterosexuality is its contingency and open-endedness, its tenuous hold over the multiplicity of sexual impulses and possibilities that characterize all human sexuality—its own unnaturalness, its compromise, and reactive status. Lesbian pleasures show that we do not have to settle for the predictable, formulaic, respected. Sexuality in and for all of us is fundamentally provisional, tenuous, mobile, even volatile, igniting in unforeseen contexts with often unpredictable and unsettling effects.

Homosexual relations and lifestyles, expelled from and often ignored by the norms of heterosexuality, nonetheless, seep into the very self-conceptions of what it is to be straight. The rigid alignments of stimuli and responses, the apparently natural coupling of male and female lovers, are unstuck by the existence of lesbians and gays. The very existence of a mode of lesbianism not dependent on the phallus or relations mediated by male sexuality demonstrates that sexuality as such does not require the phallus, as function or as organ. Beyond this flow-on effect that does produce a certain loosening or contagion of the sphere of sexual "normality," it seems to me that we need— rather than to endlessly theorize, explain, analyze, reflect on, reconstruct, reassess, provide new words and concepts for sexuality—to experiment with it, enjoy its various modalities, and seek its moments of heightened intensity, its moments of self-loss where reflection no longer has a place. This is not, I hope and believe, anti-intellectualism or a naive return to a 1960s style polysexualism, pleasure with no responsibility, that fulfilled only men's fantasies of sexual freedom while subsuming women's fantasies under men's imperatives. It is a refusal to link sexual pleasure with the struggle for freedom, a refusal to validate sexuality in terms of a greater cause or a higher purpose, the desire to enjoy, to experience, to make pleasure for its own sake, for where it takes us, for how it changes and makes us, to see it as one but not the only trajectory in the lives of sexed bodies.

                                                                    Elizabeth Grosz

Notes

A longer version of this essay was published in *Supposing the Subject,* ed. Joan Copjec (London: Verso, 1994).

1. Deleuze's reading of Nietzsche makes it clear that the forces of the body are only ever a matter of more or less, a question of differential quantities, and through the differential relation between two quantities, the production of qualities. Nietzsche says, "The attempt should be made to see whether a scientific order of values could be constructed simply on a numerical and quantitative scale of forces. All other 'values' are prejudices, naiveties and misunderstandings. They are everywhere reducible to this numerical and quantitative scale" (710). Deleuze's gloss is as follows: "Qualities are nothing but the corresponding difference in quantity between two forces whose relationship is presupposed. In short, Nietzsche is never interested in the irreducibility of quantity to quality; or rather, he is only interested in it secondarily and as a symptom. What interests him primarily, from the standpoint of quantity itself, is the fact that differences in quantity cannot be reduced to equality. Quality is distinct from quantity, but only because it is that aspect of quantity that cannot be equalized, that cannot be equalized out in the difference between quantities. . . . Quality is nothing but difference in quantity and corresponds each time forces enter into relations" (43–44).

2. In her essay, "Lesbian Sex," Frye seems to believe that the silence on the details of lesbian sexual relations is the product of the obliteration or subsumption of women under heterosexist sexual norms. In her largely phenomenological reflections on lesbian "sex," Frye seems to yearn for a langauge and a mode of representation for lesbian sexual practices. She implies that with-

out an adequate language, without appropriate terms, women's experiences themselves are less rich, less rewarding, less determinate than they could be: "I once perused a large and extensively illustrated book on sexual activity by and for homosexual men. It was astounding for me for one thing in particular, namely, that its pages constituted a huge lexicon of *words:* words for acts and activities, their sub-acts, preludes and denouements, their stylistic variation, their sequences. Gay male sex, I realized then, is *articulate.* It is articulate to a degree that, in my world, lesbian 'sex' does not remotely approach. Lesbian 'sex' as I have known it, most of the time I have known it, is utterly *in*articulate. Most of my lifetime, most of my experience in the realms commonly designated as 'sexual' has been pre-linguistic, non-cognitive. I have, in effect, no linguistic community, no language, and therefore in one important sense, no knowledge. . . . The meaning one's life and experience might generate cannot come fully into operation if they are not woven into language: they are fleeting, or they hover, vague, not fully coalesced, not connected, and hence, not *useful* for explaining or grounding interpretations, desires, complaints, theories" (115).

3. Moreover, it is ironic that the very features Frye attributes to the failure of representation for lesbian desire—that these relations and experiences are rendered "fleeting," that they "hover," are "vague," not "coalesced," "connected," or "useful"—are precisely in accord with the more positive characterization attributed to these concepts and to female sexuality in the writings of Luce Irigaray, for whom female sexuality is itself nonidentical, nonenumerable, not made of distinct and separate parts, and not one (but indeterminably more than one). See, in particular, Irigaray's *Speculum of the Other Woman* and *This Sex Which Is Not One*. See also in her more recent writing where she says, "She does not set herself up as *one,* as a (single) female unit. She is not closed up or around one single truth or essence. The essence of truth remains foreign to her. She neither has nor is being. . . . The/a woman can sub-sist by already being double in her self: both the one and the other. Not: one plus an other, more than one. More than. She is 'foreign' to the unit. And to the countable, to quantification. There to the more than, as it relates to something already quantifiable, even if it were a case of disrupting the operations. If it were necessary to count her/them in units—which is impossible—each unit would already be more than doubly (her). But that would have to be understood in another way. The (female) one being the other, without ever being either one or the other. Ceaselessly in the exchange between the one and the other. With the result that she is always already othered but with no possible identification of her, or of the other" (*Marine Lover* 86).

4. I think this is borne out most clearly in the fascination that sexology has had in the various debates surrounding female sexuality: a clitoral versus a vaginal location for female orgasm, the existence or nonexistence of the legendary "G-spot," the homology (or lack of it) of female stages of sexual excitation and orgasm with male excitation and orgasm, and so on. I continue to find it astounding that these debates exist at all, that there is such confusion not only among male researchers but also among the female

objects of investigation, that there continues to be such mystery and controversy surrounding the most apparently elementary features of female sexuality. Male sexuality by comparison, *seems* to be completely straightforward, completely unconscientious, knowable, measurable, understandable. The manifest asymmetry must be a consequence in part of the imposition of models of knowing, of identity, distinctness, and measurability, that are in some sense alien to or incapable of adequately explaining female sexuality. Instead of assuming an inherent mystery, an undecipherable enigma, female sexuality must be assumed to be knowable, even if it must wait for other forms of knowledge and different modes of discourse to provide a framework and the broad parameter of its understanding.

5. Indeed, there is always the common reaction, that when someone comes out or is "outed" they won't be believed—a reaction that is pretty well unimaginable in the case of other oppressions. If someone confessed to being Jewish or Islamic, there would be no disbelief.

Works Cited

Allen, Jeffner, ed. *Lesbian Philosophies and Cultures.* Albany: State University of New York Press, 1990.

Deleuze, Gilles. *Nietzsche and Philosophy.* Trans. Hugh Tomlinson. London: Athlone Press, 1983.

Frye, Marilyn. "Lesbian Sex." Pp. 109–19 in *Willful Virgin: Essays in Feminism.* Freedom, Calif.: Crossing Press, 1992.

Irigaray, Luce. *Marine Lover of Friedrich Nietzsche.* Trans. Gillian C. Gill. New York: Columbia University Press, 1991.

———. *Speculum of the Other Woman.* Trans. Gillian C. Gill. Ithaca, N.Y.: Cornell University Press, 1985.

———. *This Sex Which Is Not One.* Trans. Catherine Porter with Carolyn Burke. Ithaca, N.Y.: Cornell University Press, 1985.

Nietzsche, Friedrich. *Will to Power.* Trans. Walter Kaufman and R. J. Hollingdale. New York: Random House, 1968.

14

Speak for Yourself

"Speak for yourself." You don't have to represent anybody but yourself. You don't have responsibility for anyone else's views, positions, or problems. Just speak out . . . about yourself.

"Speak for yourself." Despite what you may think, the generalizations you've just made simply aren't true. You don't really know what you're talking about, so you should shut up before you make matters worse.

"Speak for yourself" signals a certain impossibility of speaking. In the first instance, you are being asked to speak only for yourself, to represent only yourself. The task seems straightforward enough, and yet is it really possible? Can a speaking subject be that autonomous, self-reliant, and completely cut off from others? Can a subject appropriate language so absolutely? In the second instance, the grammatical meaning of the rejoinder contradicts the rhetorical one: in being told to speak, you are really being told *not* to speak. Here "speak for yourself" indicates a response to remarks that are presumably so off the mark, so entirely idiomatic, that the speaker should refrain from speaking about the issue altogether. In this case, "speak for yourself" is tantamount to a faintly polite way of saying "shut up."

Given the doubly problematic nature of speaking for yourself, what would happen if this were turned around and we asked instead: what are the circumstances in which it would be possible *not* to speak for yourself? What would it mean to speak for others? Moreover, what would happen if we were to consider the possibility of an other contained within the subjective self, an other that I would call "the body"? Obviously, these questions do little to simplify the matter, but I think they help to reveal that what is consistently at stake is what it *means* to speak. I want to explore this matter in some detail, by way of addressing the common threads in Linda Alcoff's and Elizabeth Grosz's essays (in this volume).

Before I turn to their essays, it is important to recall that the questions I have raised, as well as their potential answers, are linked to the legacy of individualism that we have inherited from the Enlightenment: a persistent faith in the autonomy of the rational subject. According to the logic of the Enlightenment, subjects act for themselves, speak for themselves, and judge for themselves. At least since Immanuel Kant, the result has been a reliance in the West on the subject as the center of both politics and ethics. Subjects are presumed to be able to speak for themselves and thus to carry out independently their political and ethical duties.

Alcoff is not, however, willing to accept this philosophical inheritance without asking some questions that may render the terms of the entire legacy invalid. She wonders whether the boundary between self and other is more fluid than Enlightenment notions of subjectivity concede. Subjects may not be acting independently after all, either speaking only for themselves or not at all. As Alcoff explains, "there is no neutral place to stand free and clear in which my words do not prescriptively affect or mediate the experience of others, nor is there a way to demarcate decisively a boundary between my location and all others." Turning her attention to the same issue in the context of black female creativity, Michele Wallace has used even stronger terms than Alcoff, arguing that "inevitably, we silence others that we may speak at all" (225).

With this dilemma in view, Alcoff thinks that the problem of speaking for and about others can be generally solved if "anyone who speaks for others should only do so out of a concrete analysis of the particular power relations and discursive effects involved." This raises two immediate problems. In whose language is the "concrete analysis" to be undertaken? Who will determine when the analysis is sufficiently "concrete" (when it has set)? These questions point out that Alcoff's answer in no way resolves the problem it sets itself, although it states the problem in more detail. The interesting thing about Alcoff's solution is the attention it draws to the importance of context. Speaking involves senders, receivers, and contexts in which the message is sent and received. As she reminds us, "we cannot simply look at the location of the speaker or her credentials to speak; nor can we look merely at the propositional context of the speech; we must also look at where the speech goes and what it does there." Here Alcoff is able to bring us a long way in understanding the difficulties that lie behind speaking for yourself, but what she has not understood is that such analysis is both necessary *and endless*. While we may long for concrete analysis that can determine precisely the effects of speech, the positions of both sender and receiver may prove to be less stable than Alcoff imagines.

A statement is uttered by a sender, and a receiver apprehends it in a context. That context will guide the way in which the statement is comprehended or interpreted. Yet neither sender nor receiver can absolutely control that context. Thus, it would not be possible to have an exhaustive analysis of concrete context (such as Alcoff seeks) that would absolve us of the guilt of misunderstanding in speaking for others. Furthermore, the same goes for "speaking for oneself." That "a context is never absolutely determinable" in this way is the point that Jacques Derrida sets out to demonstrate in "Signature Event Context" (310). According to Derrida:

> Every sign, linguistic or nonlinguistic, spoken or written in the usual sense of this opposition, as a small or large unity, can be *cited,* put between quotation marks; thereby it can break with every given context, and engender infinitely new contexts in an absolutely nonsaturable fashion. This does not suppose that the mark is valid outside its context, but on the contrary that there are only contexts without any center of absolute anchoring. This citationality, duplication, or duplicity, this iterability of the mark is not an accident or an anomaly, but is that (normal/abnormal) without which a mark could no longer even have a so-called "normal" functioning. (320–21)

To simplify for a moment, we could say, then, that the possibility of all utterances (including "speaking for . . .") depends on the inexhaustibility of their contexts. All statements are made in context, and their meaning is affected by that context. But the description of that context, in an attempt to "fix" the meaning of a statement, also has a context that remains to be determined. So context is necessary, although it is never absolutely identifiable. Any given utterance is not so much taken out of its context as it is situated in an infinitely expanding context, which consequently includes an infinite number of senders and receivers. Significantly, intention does not disappear according to Derrida's argument; however, "it will no longer be able to govern the entire scene and the entire system of utterances" ("Signature" 326).

In this sense, we speak and are responsible for our words, *even though* we do not have control over their meaning, precisely because we do not control the context(s) of their utterance and reception. Responsibility carries beyond intention. There is a certain responsibility for the "misuse" of remarks to which an individual signs her name because it is not entirely up to the author to determine the correct context and proper use of a statement. Derrida's point, then, is that "being taken out of context" and being "misused" are structural hazards of language use, and it would be naive to think otherwise. There is no proper context or point at which we simply speak for and to ourselves alone.

Thus, there is a sense in which it seems that Alcoff would like to be absolved of the guilt that results from speaking and getting it wrong, as it were. She would like to do the right thing and cannot accept that this may be impossible in absolute terms, that it may be impossible to determine—either in advance or once and for all—"where the speech goes and what it does there." For Alcoff, we have done the right thing in speaking *if* that speech will "enable the empowerment of oppressed peoples." This is a noble enough goal. However, we cannot always determine in advance whether it will indeed happen, whether the act of speaking out will have done justice to the other. No preexisting rule can guide our interventions in actual controversies: there is no exemplary speech situation, no fixed rule from which particular contexts deviate. Rather, the risk of speaking for others is precisely that—always a *risk*, a tricky and tactical situation that requires an ethical awareness, not an epistemological rigor. To put this another way, thinking of the question of language use in terms of a distinction between theory and practice is simply not appropriate. The subject cannot calculate its relation to the other as a matter of knowledge; it must engage with the other in the pragmatic field of ethical action. There is no settling of accounts with the other.

This returns us to the problem of the subject and speaking for yourself. Alcoff holds open the possibility of speaking in such a way that we do not appropriate the other's discourse. But such was always the dream of the autonomous subject, which thought it could be separated from the other. In "Force of Law," Derrida recognizes what is at stake when he argues:

> To address oneself to the other in the language of the other is, it seems, the condition of all possible justice, but apparently, in all rigor, it is not only impossible (since I cannot speak the language of the other except to the extent that I appropriate it and assimilate it according to the law of an implicit third) but even excluded by justice as law (*droit*), inasmuch as justice as right [*droit*] seems to imply an element of universality, the appeal to a third party who suspends the unilaterality or singularity of the idioms. (949)

I would like to call attention to two specific aspects of this passage. First, Derrida concedes that any attempt to do justice to the other, to speak of the condition of the other, necessarily involves appropriation of the other's discourse, involves, that is, a certain injustice. The context of the utterance can never be purely that of self or other. To speak to the other immediately evokes the retort, "speak for yourself," with all the possibilities of multiple connotations. Second, there is no third-party arbitration that can resolve the issue of appropriation. No third party can absolutely judge what is right, whether justice has been done to the other, whether we have not merely spoken for ourselves. This would presume, incorrectly, that the context of justice would have been exhausted, that the third party could speak from a neutral place without context. Moreover, any third party that sought to determine absolutely the question of justice would, in its turn, be guilty of "speaking for others" in making its own judgment concerning appropriation.

In emphasizing the inevitability of appropriation and the problem of doing justice to the other once and for all, I am not trying to excuse inaction or suggest less responsibility. The risk of speaking must still be taken, but it always remains *a risk* of doing injustice. Silence may prove the more just act; it may also be a turning away from responsibility. Ignoring the plight of the other is a blatant form of injustice, but addressing it is no guarantee of justice either. As Drucilla Cornell puts it, "We cannot be excused from our role in history because we could not know so as to be reassured that we were 'right' in advance" (169).

Responsibility to the other is excessive, although it is not simply paralyzing. Trying to do justice to the other, trying not to appropriate the other's discourse, is an unresolvable epistemological bind—which still does not mean that we stop trying to be just. Rather, the significance of this predicament lies in an *ethical* not an epistemological recognition: the recognition that there is no guilt-free speech. Injustice and appropriation are part of the violence of language; language can never be completely just, although we can continue to try to make it more so.

It is this simultaneous impossibility and necessity of doing justice to the other that Elizabeth Grosz implicitly recognizes in "Bodies and Pleasures in Queer Theory." This recognition takes the shape of worrying about representation, or more precisely worrying about what is *not* representable. For what Grosz understands is that representation, insofar as it implies both communication and expression, is an attempt to speak for the other, and this attempt may not always prove to be desirable. To see how this is indeed the case, I want to trace more precisely the contours of her argument.

Grosz's main concern could perhaps be best characterized as a worry about "speaking the body," a concern that ends as a discussion of lesbian sexuality and erotic language. But first she frames her argument in more general terms: the separation of "what a body is" from "what a body does." For Grosz, this separation takes an extreme form under the regime of compulsory heterosexuality. As she puts it, "the regime of compulsory heterosexuality *can* be understood as a series of reactive forces, separating a body from what it can do, reducing a body to what it is rather than what it can become; while gay and lesbian sexual practices and lifestyles, insofar as they risk a certain stability, a certain social security and ease, *can* be seen as a triumph of active and productive forces." In other words, the regime of compulsory heterosexuality is an attempt to fix the context of sexuality and determine once and for all what meanings may be assigned to bodies. By contrast, gay and lesbian sexual practices and lifestyles tend to call attention to the infinitely expanding context for sexuality, and they thus challenge fixed inscriptions of the body. If this distinction seems to rely on a certain fixity of context—a specific division between heterosexuality and gay and lesbian sexuality—Grosz quickly nuances her argument when she writes that "we are prevented from too ready a generalization of straights as the crippled emotional slaves, and gay, lesbians, and other queers as the transgressive sexual radicals." Neither homosexuality nor heterosexuality (or any sexual practice, for that matter) is in itself transgressive. There must be a context for context, as it were.

Given this state of affairs, Grosz argues that we need to look more critically at practices of representation and naming. That is to say, we need to examine how naming attempts to confine and control the body (and the other) by making it understandable within the terms of a dominant culture. In part, this has to do with acknowledging what is unrepresented and unrepresentable within the terms of current linguistic practices or contexts—what can or cannot be named. Grosz's important case is the "manifest inadequacy of erotic language to represent women's sexual organs, sexual pleasures, and sexual practices in terms other than those provided either for male sexuality or by men in their heterosexual (mis)understanding of the sexualities of their partners." Thus, the body has been reduced to what "it is": a body spoken of in male and heterosexual terms.

This problem is not resolved, however, by simply creating a new set of terms, as Alcoff's argument might lead us to conclude. Grosz acknowledges that "to wish to create a new set of terms implies that we know in advance what we want to designate by those terms—that the sexual pleasures, desires, organs, and activities of women are a known or knowable quantity simply awaiting names." To speak of women's pleasures, to "know" female sexuality and lesbian desire is to reduce it to models of subjectivity. While new labels and terms are sometimes empowering, they are not necessarily the answer to respecting the unrepresentable. It is not clear that "articulateness and representation are in themselves a virtue; the most intense moments of pleasure and the force of their materiality cannot be reduced to terms that capture their force and intensity, no matter how broadly evocable in discourse they may be." Something is left over, left out, and for Grosz, unlike Alcoff, this is not necessarily a bad thing. This seems to be what has been forgotten in the inclusionary strategies of liberal pluralism. Thus, when Grosz suggests that lesbianism "attests to the fundamental plasticity of women's desire," she is careful *not* to define precisely what those desires are. In effect, this is a way of acknowledging the other that is part of the self—the potential otherness of the body that is not controlled by the rational subject's mind. The other, then, is not purely an object or subject; hence, the problem of the other is not one of intersubjectivity—no amount of agreement between subjects can make the other go away or shore up the boundaries of the self.

The virtue of Grosz's argument is the way in which its phenomenology of the body allows us another way to think about the politics of speech. Reminding us that we do not even speak for ourselves is an important first moment in escaping the political dead end that lies at the conclusion of the struggle between liberal guilt and imperialist self-confidence, a step beyond the dialectical opposition of self and other. In this sense, we can perhaps say that Grosz shows Alcoff how to get out of the difficulty in which she knows herself to be: by relinquishing epistemology as the privileged mode in which we think about what it is to be an individual. Speak for *and against* yourself.

Diane Elam

Works Cited

Cornell, Drucilla. *The Philosophy of the Limit*. New York: Routledge, 1992.
Derrida, Jacques. "Force of Law: The Mystical Foundation of Authority." Trans. Mary Quaintance. *Cardozo Law Review* 11, no. 5–6 (1990): 919–1045.
———. "Signature Event Context." Pp. 307–30 in *Margins of Philosophy*. Trans. Alan Bass. Chicago: University of Chicago Press, 1982.
Wallace, Michele. "Variations on Negation and the Heresy of Black Feminist Creativity." Pp. 213–40 in *Invisibility Blues: From Pop to Theory*. London: Verso, 1990.

Contributors

LINDA MARTÍN ALCOFF teaches philosophy and women's studies at Syracuse University. She is the coeditor, with Elizabeth Potter, of *Feminist Epistemologies* (1993) and the author of *Real Knowing* (forthcoming). She has published articles in *Signs, Cultural Critique, Hypatia, American Literary History,* and *Philosophical Forum.*

MICHAEL AWKWARD is associate professor of English and Afro-American studies at the University of Michigan, where he is director of the Center for Afro-American and African Studies. He is the author of *Negotiating Difference: Race, Gender, and the Politics of Positionality* (1995) and *Inspiriting Influences: Tradition, Revision, and Afro-American Women's Novels* (1989), and the editor of *New Essays on "Their Eyes Were Watching God"* (1990).

DALE M. BAUER is professor of English and women's studies at the University of Wisconsin–Madison, where she directs the Women's Studies Research Center. Her forthcoming book, *Edith Wharton's Brave New Politics,* examines the social and political critique implicit in Wharton's late career. She has also written on Bakhtin and feminism, feminist theory and pedagogy, and American literature and culture.

LESLIE BOW is assistant professor of English at Brown University. A third-generation Chinese American, she has published in the areas of Asian American literature, Latina literature, and multicultural pedagogy. She is currently completing a manuscript on Asian American women's literature and the intersection of sexuality and cultural nationalism.

DYMPNA CALLAGHAN is associate professor of English and textual studies at Syracuse University. She is author of *Woman and Gender in Re-*

naissance Tragedy (1989) and coauthor of *The Weyward Sisters: Shakespeare and Feminist Politics* (1994). She is currently writing a Marxist analysis of the exclusion of women from the Renaissance stage.

DIANE ELAM teaches in the English department at Indiana University and McGill University. She is the author of *Romancing the Postmodern* (1992) and *Feminism and Deconstruction: Ms. en Abyme* (1994).

ELIZABETH GROSZ is director of the Institute for Critical and Cultural Studies at Monash University. She is the author of *Crossing Boundaries* (1988), *Sexual Subversions: Three French Feminists* (1989), *Jacques Lacan: A Feminist Introduction* (1990), and *Volatile Bodies: Toward a Corporeal Feminism* (1994).

SANDRA HARDING is professor of philosophy at the University of Delaware and at University of California–Los Angeles. She is the author of *The Science Question in Feminism* (1986) and *Whose Science? Whose Knowledge? Thinking from Women's Lives* (1991) and the editor of five collections of essays on issues in the philosophy of science, epistemology, feminism, and postcolonialism, including *The "Racial" Economy of Science: Toward a Democratic Future* (1993).

ROSEMARY HENNESSY teaches in the English department of the University at Albany, State University of New York, where she is also affiliated with the women's studies department. She is the author of *Materialist Feminism and the Politics of Discourse* (1993), as well as numerous essays in lesbian and gay studies and feminist theory. Her current work is on the reconfiguration of sexuality in late capitalism.

ANDREW LAKRITZ is currently serving as scholar-in-residence at the United States Information Agency. "Identification and Difference" is part of a larger project entitled "Uncommon Grounds," which examines bourgeois criticism's use of identifications with the working class, the subaltern, and the other. He also publishes on American modernist poetry and poetics.

DAVID ROMÁN is assistant professor of English at the University of Washington in Seattle and visiting assistant professor of women's studies at Yale University where he teaches courses on gay and lesbian studies. His book, *Acts of Intervention: Gay Men, U.S. Theatre, AIDS* is forthcoming. He serves on the editorial board of *GLQ: A Journal of Gay and Lesbian Studies* and is president of the Gay and Lesbian Caucus of the Modern Language Association.

JUDITH ROOF, associate professor of English at Indiana University, is the author of *Come As You Are: Narrative and Sexuality* (forthcoming), *A Lure of Knowledge: Lesbian Sexuality and Theory* (1991) and essays on feminist theory, film, psychoanalysis, and modern drama.

SABINA SAWHNEY teaches English at Daemen College and has published articles on feminism and postcolonial literature. She is currently working on *The Other Colonialists: Imperial Margins of Victorian Literature*, which deals with the impact of colonialism on the narrative structure of nineteenth-century British novels.

ROBYN WIEGMAN is assistant professor of English and women's studies at Indiana University and author of *American Anatomies: Theorizing Race and Gender* (1995).

THOMAS YINGLING was associate professor of English at Syracuse University until the time of his death in 1992. He is the author of *Hart Crane and the Homosexual Text* (1990).

Index